Also from the Editors of *George* Magazine
The Book of Political Lists

250 WAYS
TO MAKE
AMERICA
BETTER

250 WAYS
TO MAKE
AMERICA
BETTER

FROM THE EDITORS OF

George

MAGAZINE

COMPILED BY

CAROLYN MACKLER

VILLARD · NEW YORK

A portion of this book's proceeds is being donated to the East Harlem Tutorial Program, an award-winning not-for-profit educational program serving children, teenagers, and parents. To volunteer or to support their work, please call (212) 831-0650 or write: EHTP, 2050 Second Avenue, New York, NY 10029.

Library of Congress Cataloging-in-Publication Data

250 ways to make America better / from the editors of *George* magazine; compiled by Carolyn Mackler.

p.   cm.

ISBN 0-375-75012-6

1. United States—Politics and government—1993–   —Miscellanea. 2. United States—Social policy—1993–   —Miscellanea. 3. United States—Social conditions—1980–   —Miscellanea. I. Mackler, Carolyn. II. *George* (New York, N.Y.) III. Title: Two-hundred fifty ways to make America better.

E885.A14   1999

973.929—dc21   99-13883

Random House website address: www.atrandom.com

Introduction

BY JOHN F. KENNEDY, JR.

George is not just politics as usual. So when we gathered around the editorial table, planning an anthology of 250 intriguing Americans' suggestions on improving this country, we didn't map a route up Capitol Hill. We combed our Rolodexes for more fax numbers than there are seats in Congress. From moguls to moviemakers, right-wingers to rabble-rousers, cartoonists to convicts to cookbook authors, we envisioned a convergence of ideas as diverse as the great drama of public life in America.

We garnered suggestions from people as young as thirteen-year-old prodigy artist Alexandra Nechita, as controversial as Mumia Abu-Jamal, an African-American journalist on death row, and as surprising as Lisa Simpson, philosopher extraordinaire and, yes, sister of Bart. Music producer Quincy Jones reveals an inspiringly humanitarian agenda. Filmmaker Michael Moore proposes a merging of the Republicans and the Democrats into the Republicrats. Cartoonist Roz Chast thinks that Choco-Mint Life Savers should be reintroduced, while folk-legend Pete Seeger muses on a frontier community, complete with hot tubs for all. As the notoriously conservative Phyllis Schlafly expounds on vital issues of the day, sexpert Susie Bright delves further into—well, the night.

While we sure wouldn't want to pack all of the contributors into the same four walls without calling out the National Guard, *George* has guided them into the spine of one book, portraying a cross section of opinion as wide as the Grand Canyon while leaving the boxing gloves at home. Not just anthologies as usual, right?

250 WAYS
TO MAKE
AMERICA
BETTER

1

We have reversed President Kennedy's admonition to "ask not what your country can do for you, ask what you can do for your country." One way to begin the process of replacing the demand for entitlements with a sense of responsibility and service would be through a universal service bill that would require all Americans, at age eighteen, to spend a year doing public service work. The model is Franklin Roosevelt's Civilian Conservation Corps. It built roads, bridges, parks, and more; the "CCC boys" lived in barracks and came from around the country. One side benefit is that it would bring the youth of the country together, as the draft used to do. Today teenage boys from Harlem hardly know any whites, and white suburban kids know few if any African Americans. Universal service is working today in most European countries. The youngsters who volunteer for the army are then on active duty for six months and in the reserves thereafter; those who opt for service as a medical technician, teacher, or whatever serve for a full year. The work that gets done is beneficial by itself, but the real payoff is in the experiences gained by the youngsters and the change in their attitudes from demanding to giving, from feeling entitled to recognizing their obligation to serve their country.

—*Stephen E. Ambrose*
HISTORIAN/AUTHOR

2

1. Don't let the Chinese beat us with prison labor. Recently, many enlightened American companies have seen the benefits of cheap and abundant prison labor. Spalding has golf balls packaged in prisons in Hawaii. Microsoft has contracted with a company to package software in Washington state penitentiaries. TWA uses inmates in Ventura County, California, to answer its "1-800" reservation number.

I say, let's throw as many people out of work as possible and turn those jobs over to hardened criminals! By forcing millions into a life of unemployment, home repossession, and bankruptcy, it is a surefire guarantee that a certain percentage of them will turn to crime to fulfill their selfish needs of food, shelter, and clothing.

After their apprehension and conviction, they should be thrown back into the factories where they once worked—factories that have now been converted into prisons. We'll give them their old jobs back and three meals a day.

But—and here's the great part—we'll only have to pay them two dollars an hour! Imagine the return on investment for companies smart enough to take advantage of the world's largest prison population. It'll be good for the country, and the Dow Jones will certainly, finally break 10,000.*

2. Merge the Republican and Democratic Parties into one party. They've already unofficially done this on their own. We've always known that the Republicans were the party of wealth and privilege—and now we know the Democrats represent the same money interests. With Clinton selling the Lincoln Bedroom to the highest bidder and holding 103 "coffees" for his corporate contributors, the Democrats are now beholden to the 1 percent who own 40 percent of all the wealth in this country.

---

*Editor's Note: This contribution was written in 1997.

I'm not saying that the wealthy don't deserve political representation—they are, after all, Americans too. I just question why 1 percent of the country gets two political parties and the rest of us get *none*! Friends of mine say, "Hey, how about supporting one of the third parties?" I say, "Third party? What about a *second* party—we don't even have that!"

So let's merge the Democrats and the Republicans into the "Republicrats" and get busy exploring the Labor Party, the Greens, and other new parties that more closely reflect the desires of the electorate.

—*Michael Moore*
FILMMAKER

3

Teach people how to flirt. Think about it: when you can't flirt, you feel disconnected—lonely in the big, wide world. After that come a few halfhearted, ill-timed flirting misfires riddled with annoying come-ons such as "Do you live around here?" and "Hey, baby, I love your socks. Did you pick them out yourself?" This leads to further rejection, frustration, and, eventually, despair. You withdraw from others. Years go by. No proms for you. No Ms. Popularity. No party invitations. What can you do but hang around with others who don't know how to flirt, others consumed with despair and loneliness? What's left? OK, I'll say it: terrorism. What are terrorists but a bunch of guys who can't flirt so they are prey to maniacal misfits who pretend they are either working for God or they themselves are God? If these loners knew how to flirt, they would be emotionally and sexually satisfied and living in the 'burbs. They would sleep more, stop acting out deranged thoughts, and not be so thin. Being too thin is something else that leads to trouble. How can you flirt when you are hungry all the time? Supermodels don't get nearly as much love as they look like they get, and they are not nearly the flirts that they appear to be. They are too hungry. And so, here is my idea: Teach the terrorists and the supermodels how to flirt and then introduce them to each other. Good flirting would end terrorism and the feral look in a supermodel's eyes. This would make America a better place.

—*Sharyn Wolf*
AUTHOR/MARRIAGE COUNSELOR

4

I'd love to see a blossoming of urban agriculture everywhere: garden projects and fruit orchards on the land surrounding housing projects; community gardens at senior centers and on church grounds; "edible schoolyards"; rooftop gardens where tenants can cultivate food for the people in their building. People of all economic backgrounds and ages would learn about growing, cooking with, and eating fruits and vegetables. And just picture the personal pride they would derive from working the land—even if it's just in a flowerpot! My dream is to see public funding dedicated to supporting these projects, to actually pay people real wages for cultivating city lands. Perhaps more of us will get a clue about how this is connected with personal, physical, psychological—and community—health on the most profound level. The more we understand that "nature is us," and the more we feel that there is meaningful, shared work in the production of our food, the more we can live in a state of mutual caring and respect for one another and for our common home, the earth.

—*Mollie Katzen*
COOKBOOK AUTHOR

5

HOW TO IMPROVE AMERICA: THREE SUGGESTIONS

Blow up three-fourths of the shopping malls

KA-BLAM

Send Ralph Reed on a fact-finding trip to Pluto

Bye, everybody!

Re-introduce "Choco-Mint" Lifesavers.

MMMMMMMMM

—*Roz Chast*
CARTOONIST

6

Nuke it. Not a big explosion. Just a minor detonation in an airport or a television production facility. In the short run, things would be worse for lots of people. But not that much worse. The headaches caused by traffic tie-ups and hospital admissions would be far outweighed by the high ratings the networks would enjoy covering the fiasco. In fact, the immense damage and waste would end up giving the economy a *boost* because people would be buying more stuff to replace the old stuff that got destroyed. Not to mention building bomb shelters and buying Geiger counters, gas masks, home first-aid kits, etc. Wall Street would suffer for a month or so, but then the biggest bull run of all time would begin.

Why? Because ultimately the country would pull its collective head out of its collective butt and get constructive. (Sort of a Marshall Plan redux.) After a period of martial law, which would only serve to piss people off, a backlash against the military would begin. Everyone would realize that if there were no bombs in the first place, there wouldn't be any explosions. So the vast spending on armaments would begin to slow down. The freed-up money would be spent on constructive things such as homes and education, feeding needy children. This in turn would make America, instead of a depressed and dying empire, more productive and fun again.

There would be a renewed interest in the environment as people surveyed the devastation. Americans would realize that they have a beautiful country and need to preserve it. A spirituality would ensue because so many people would be thinking about being dead. A revival of empathy would swell up as Americans pulled together and took care of their sick and dying.

In other words, America would have a near-death experience, triggering a new attitude, one based on life instead of greed, sloth, and fear.

Of course, it may not work out this way. I'm not clairvoyant. If it doesn't, I suggest a larger set of detonations, perhaps exterminating all human life on the planet. Downside: everyone dies. Upside: we get to start all over.

—*Eric Bogosian*
ACTOR/AUTHOR

7

As Jackie Kennedy Onassis liked to say, "If you bungle raising your children, I don't think whatever else you do will matter very much." If we want to make America a better place, we need to start by making it an easier place for parents to raise happy and healthy kids.

In the last few years, scientists have proved what parents and grandparents have long suspected: that the first few years of life are a critical time for intellectual, emotional, and social development. Government can't do everything, but we can and should give parents the tools they need to make the most of those critical first three years of life.

We should make it easier for parents to spend quality time with their kids during these early years. The United States is currently the only industrialized country that does not provide paid maternity leave. We should at the very least expand the Family and Medical Leave Act, so that millions more moms and dads can take time off from work when they have a new baby.

In this modern economy, both parents are often forced to work outside the home just to make ends meet. Therefore, we need to ensure that high-quality child care is accessible and affordable for all of America's parents. One way we could do this would be to increase funding for the Early Start program—the part of Head Start that services children in their first three years.

These simple changes in the law could help ensure that America's children are given the care they need in their first years of life to prepare them to grow up to be healthy, productive, and responsible members of society.

—*Rosa L. DeLauro*
POLITICIAN

8

How can we help improve America? I'll tell you how: by trading places. Have Newt Gingrich and all the ultraconservative politicians who are so strongly opposed to social spending exchange lives—for *one* month—with the poor people they regard with such disdain.

Within that period, send the hard-liners through a series of challenges that require them to perform absolute magic with money. That's right, take them through a battery of survival tests that demonstrate just how costly it is to be poor: force them to rise at 5 A.M. every day to catch several buses from city to suburbs to a job that pays minimum wage; make them pay one fourth of that income to live in run-down, crime-ridden public housing; compel them to provide another large portion of their salaries for day care costs (in this case, for 2.5 children); require them to shop for food and clothing only at neighborhood stores, where prices are dramatically higher than anywhere else; finally, throw in another glitch: medical costs. Then have Newt and the gang catch the bus to a public health center—to sit and wait for hours—to get their rising blood pressures checked.*

After thirty days, return the crew of conservatives to their ivory towers on Capitol Hill and ask *them* to tell us, "How can we help improve America?"

—*Nathan McCall*
JOURNALIST/AUTHOR/PROFESSOR

9

The loser of a lawsuit should pay the legal fees. These days, as soon as a person feels slighted or injured (physically or emotionally), they look for someone to sue. In this era of extremely diminished responsibility, people are desperately looking for scapegoats. Freedom does not mean that everyone is free to do anything they want. The hope is not to win, but for the quick $50,000—because it's cheaper to settle than to fight. Since people and companies have to settle, insurance costs go up, prohibitive rules increase, and freedom is diminished. Freedom used to mean that one is free to achieve, to dream, to aspire, to think—free to do what is right. By assigning blame elsewhere, people are taking our freedom away. I believe that if the loser had to pay for the lawyers and court costs, people would think a lot longer before automatically blaming someone else for their own mistakes.

—*Martina Navratilova*
PROFESSIONAL TENNIS PLAYER

Editor's Note: At the time this contribution was written, Newt Gingrich was speaker of the U.S. House of Representatives.

10

1. Give utmost attention to at-risk youth.

2. Pay teachers higher wages.

3. Establish an Urban Peace and Renewal Corps.

4. Appoint an American minister of culture. (Don't worry—I am NOT rallying for the job. I *have* a job. I have *several* jobs!)

5. Do every job as if it's the first time.

6. Live every day as if it's the last one.

7. Have thirst, hunger, and passion for what you do.

8. Each day, do something for yourself, then do something for someone else.

—Quincy Jones
MUSIC PRODUCER

11

President Bill Clinton says that 40 percent of third-graders cannot read. Every week, I meet nice-looking adults who whisper, "I can't read big words." National surveys show that nearly half of our population is, at best, only semiliterate, so it's obvious that the schools have failed in their number one task.

Can our marvelous system of self-government endure if the majority of our people can't, or won't, read books and articles with big words? If you reread the Declaration of Independence, the U.S. Constitution, and the Federalist Papers and compare them to the speeches of our public officials today, it will be obvious that America has suffered a drastic dumbing down in political discourse.

The schools are not going to change. They and the publishers have too much invested in stupid but expensive four-color books that teach children to guess at words by looking at pictures. It's a scandal when six-year-olds can read "hamburger" only if they see a picture of a hamburger on the page. The teachers' unions are more eager to expand job opportunities for the remedial reading bureaucracy, and to service the social problems caused by illiteracy, than they are to teach the basics.

I believe that the most important way to make America better is for parents to teach their own children to read *before* they enter school. That's what I did. I taught my six children to read before they entered school, and I believe every American parent can do this, too. It's the only way to make sure that your child can succeed in school and in life.

It's so important to teach your child to read the right way—by sounding out syllables and putting them together to make words (phonics)—*before* the schools teach your child the bad habit of guessing by looking at the pictures. Don't lose that window of opportunity when your child is so eager to learn to read at age four, five, or six. You will find that teaching your child to read is the most fulfilling thing you will ever do. It was for me.

—*Phyllis Schlafly*
AUTHOR/ATTORNEY

12

I used to have a button I wore to any and all functions that said, in homemade script, SEX IS NOT A CRIME. "Well, I never said it *was*" seemed to be the unanimous response from everyone who screwed up their face to read my message.

I agree that most people don't think consciously of screwing as a felony—no, we're just complacent about letting anachronistic sodomy laws sit on our books; we're callous about "sex criminals" like your friendly neighborhood hooker and inventive about making new crimes out of situations that used to be entirely acceptable: witness the new felons made out of teenagers who make love to each other and then are both found guilty of statutory assaults.

Our present idea of sex education is that it's for postpubescent "children" who need to be given a bogeyman speech about disease and pregnancy. We say nothing to them (nor to our adult selves) about the scope and shape of sexual desire, how creative and imperative it is in our lives.

We thrive on titillation, a nation of blindsided bikini watchers, but we offer nothing frank, honest, or rewarding to people who occasionally have the nerve to be truthful about sex. Our government and its institutions are pathetic in their approach to sexual honesty and leadership. Popular culture, while not as hypocritical, is almost completely out of the loop when it comes to an intellectual and critical approach to eroticism. It's a wonder to me that the human race is still alive with all the sexual prohibition and disgust that we heap on one another.

Give me a presidential veto, and here's what I'd do:

- Encourage an erotic democracy where real people can

say what they think about sex without censorship and disdain. "Bozo meets bimbo" erotic entertainment will never change as long as sexual expression is treated like a con and a guilty pleasure.

- Get victimless sex "crimes" off the books and civil rights extended to all, regardless of sexual orientation, preference, or point of view. Stop punishing people for consensual sexual experiences and end the persecution of erotic expression.

- Stop lying about sex to the American public—get superstition and religion out of sex education. (Note: I'd ask Joycelyn Elders to head up "Masturbation Month," and get Macy's to throw the parade.)

—Susie Bright
SEXPERT

13

Telling stories.

Think of the power stories wield. Upton Sinclair's *The Jungle* turned stomachs. James Agee and Walker Evans's *Let Us Now Praise Famous Men* broke hearts. The television sitcom *All in the Family* pricked our biases and intolerances. Bob Dylan's songs gave voice to a generation—as did Spike Lee's movies thirty years later. The musical *Falsettos* helped us talk honestly about AIDS.

A few years back, Chicago's Hyde Park Bank held a contest, asking children on the city's South Side to submit essays and drawings on their neighborhood. What they received jarred them. Almost to a child, the pictures and accounts depicted the dangers of their communities. In one sketch of a playground bereft of children, seven-year-old Lakina Lollar scrawled, "We can't play. Please stop the shooting." The bank officials were so moved by these written and visual stories, they collected the submissions into a small self-published book called *My Neighborhood*. Reading it angers. As it should.

Telling stories affirms our experiences. It gives them credence. It lets us know we're not alone. It also makes us better listeners. In my first few encounters with nine-year-old Pharoah Rivers, a boy living in a Chicago public housing complex, I wanted to hear of the shootings and stabbings he'd witnessed. I wanted to hear of the broken elevators and of the roach-infested kitchens. One day over a pizza, Pharoah suddenly changed the subject and with gusto recounted for me his efforts to win the school's spelling bee. He laughed at the recollection of dousing himself in cologne the morning of the contest and puffed his slight chest out with pride as he told me how he conquered his stutter. And so I realized I had not been a particularly good listener. Pharoah had a lot more to share with me than just the brutality of his neighborhood.

Telling stories will not, of course, make politicians act rationally. Nor will it build new housing or provide jobs. But it will inform. It will build connections. It will nurture tolerance. It will, in the end, strengthen community.

So, while pushing the political, I would look to the personal and find ways to further storytelling. Give to our children not only a love for reading but also the necessary tools. Return to our schools classes in writing, in music, in painting, in drama. (Yes, many public schools no longer offer these activities or have cut back significantly.) In the cultural marketplace, let us not lose sight of the country's spiritual and cultural vastness.

We can find the language for conversation on the issues of the day—like race, poverty and community—in the fierce power of narrative.

—*Alex Kotlowitz*
AUTHOR

14

AMERICA, HOW WOULD I CHANGE THEE?

Gail Sheehy, American journalist and writer, said, "If we don't change, we don't grow. If we don't grow, we are not really living." I want America to grow! I want America to live! I want to see an America that has every elementary school provide a vegetarian alternative to sloppy joes. I want America to increase educational spending to fund Mississippi blues appreciation curriculums for the second grade. I want America to use the promise of solar energy to forever banish the specter of nuclear power, while still retaining jobs for dangerously unqualified, well-meaning men like my father. I want America to bring about a new golden age for our entire world, where men and women work together as equals, striving toward a more just society, respectful of each individual and of the planet itself, dedicated to peace, honor, liberty, and love. Most of all, I want to live in an America that supplies each neighborhood with a pony as stress therapy for hopelessly misunderstood, highly sensitive overachievers who like historical novels by Gore Vidal, Malibu Stacy dolls, and playing the baritone saxophone. Thank you.

—*Lisa Simpson*
BART'S BRAINY SISTER

15

One of the easiest things the United States could do is lift the unfair embargo on Cuba. The embargo penalizes the people of that beautiful country (where my family has some of its roots), not the political system it was originally meant to subvert. This antiquated Cold War relic of an idea has been a total failure in all respects and is morally unacceptable. It makes us look like fools when in the United Nations 143 countries voted to castigate us for such behavior and only 2 supported our position.

Guns should be made illegal; there is no good reason for them to be legal as they are in this country and almost nowhere else in the civilized world. Nearly 40,000 Americans die each year, all because of the NRA's huge political influence and gun owners' greed. Some of the numbers of murders with handguns during the year 1990 were: Australia 10, Sweden 13, Great Britain 22, Canada 68, Japan 87, and here in the United States 10,567. For *no* good reason.

Most important, we must once and for all discontinue our government's public funding of the military-industrial complex and redirect much of those funds into our public education system—more money for teachers, school buildings, equipment, and the learning environment in general. Contemporary education in the United States has become a privilege of the rich; no longer is this or has it really ever been the land of equal opportunity, particularly when it comes to education. This needs to change now.

—*Brett Ratner*
FILM PRODUCER

16

I think America could become a greater nation if we elected a woman president. I'm not asking for this immediately. We could work up to it by first having a bisexual president. Also, we need to become a friendlier nation. I see us extending our hands to tourists. I see Democrats embracing Republicans. I see Geraldo and O.J. doing the fox-trot.

—*Joan Rivers*
COMEDIAN

17

Imagine a tax code so simple you could file your tax return on a postcard. You write down your total income, subtract a generous family allowance ($33,800 for a family of four), and take 17 percent of the balance. That's your tax bill. There's no death tax, capital gains tax, marriage penalty, or Social Security benefit tax. You make out a check, drop it in the mail, and you're done with the IRS until next year.

That's the flat tax.

Instead of taking eleven hours to prepare your taxes, you do it in eleven minutes. And every American pays the same rate. If your neighbor earns ten times more than you, he pays ten times more in taxes. That's fair.

Businesses, from the mom-and-pop grocery to the Fortune 500 company, will subtract expenses from revenues and pay 17 percent on the remainder.

Gone will be the current 480 IRS tax forms and the 280 sets of instructions that explain how to fill out the 480 forms.

Gone will be the hordes of lobbyists who roam the halls of the U.S. Capitol in search of special favors, deductions, and loopholes.

Gone will be the armies of IRS employees, along with the aggravation and humiliation they visit upon Americans today. Instead of harassing the weak and powerless, tax collectors will once again be servants of the people.

Gone will be the resentment every taxpayer feels about their brother-in-law, who you're sure knows about a tax break he's taking but won't tell you about.

The flat tax will end for Americans the anguish over a tax system that treats them like second-class citizens. It will create a simple and civil tax code that promotes compliance and restores the people's trust in government. And by cutting taxes and ending double taxation, the flat tax will lead to an investment boom and higher living standards.

That will be good for America.

—*Dick Armey*
POLITICIAN

18

I believe America would be a much better place if we could institute a course of study in all American schools that would focus on self-development. This course, which would run for all twelve years of one's schooling, would expand one's self-awareness; nurture and maintain one's self-esteem; teach personal and social responsibility; enhance communication skills; teach nonviolent conflict resolution methods; provide practice with problem-solving methods; provide relaxation and centering skills; foster the discovery of an alignment with one's life purpose; teach the fundamentals of goal setting, achievement motivation, and time management; provide instruction in character, ethics, and values; teach emotional literacy and encourage the expression of one's feelings; provide instruction in accessing one's creativity; and promote the value of service to others.

The course would focus on the skills and insights one needs to live a happy and fulfilling life—those skills that determine the quality of one's life and that are rarely taught in school.

It is my observation that marriages rarely end in divorce because one of the partners failed to learn the five major exports of Brazil or the five causes of the Civil War. We get educated on everything except how to be a happy human being.

We need a curriculum that teaches us how to love, how to forgive, how to speak comfortably in front of a group, how to listen, how to assert ourselves, how to express our feelings in nondestructive ways, how to become aware of our strengths and our weaknesses, how to express our needs, how to deal with verbal and physical abuse, how to relax without drugs, how to motivate ourselves and others, and a host of other life-affirming and life-enhancing skills.

People in America need to be taught how to control their minds, live with their emotions, care for their bodies, use their imaginations, trust their intuition, understand their dreams, and turn their visions into reality. We need to teach students the practical skills of creating a balanced, fulfilling life and not just the skills of making a living.

The curriculum guides, program materials, and educational models currently exist. They just need to be made a priority and put into practice.

—Jack Canfield
AUTHOR

19

1. America needs to make a commitment toward redistribution of wealth by concentrating on the creation of a fuller-employment economy. This would require major corporations (particularly in municipal or urban areas) that receive federal or state tax breaks or any type of support system to commit to mass training and employment.

2. There must be a real drive toward raising the ambitions of young people. America is experiencing a spiritual malady where far too many young people have no goals in life and are absolutely absent of ambition. We must establish in young people (very early on in life) a goal-oriented lifestyle.

3. We need to redefine the American hero/heroine. A hero/heroine should be someone who comes from dire circumstances, works their way through school, and takes care of their family, or an inventor, or a creator. It shouldn't be someone who jumps through a wall and shoots forty cops in a movie.

—Reverend Al Sharpton
COMMUNITY ACTIVIST

20

A very unpleasant step toward enlightenment awaits us if we're really going to save America: we need to throw out our TVs.

My old roommate gave me the gift of a lifetime: no television. Not even a "no cable, only one channel works—and that's PBS!—VCR vehicle" television. He refused. I know, without your TV you think you'll start feeling alone and scared and neurotic, but neurotic is good. Neurosis shows us that our neurons are functioning, right?

I'm the kind of person who can bum a cigarette and not become a smoker. Perhaps you're that way about TV; I'm certainly not. And I believe that for everyone, TV gets hypnotic sooner than we think. Commercials sell us our fears (clotted mascara, dirty ovens, and little wrinkles around your eyes), TV shows create our fantasies (fun, flaky friends and guns that fit in our purses). When we commune with the great glowing screen, we start to forget that *we* dictate the mass media and not vice versa (I think of all the building of radical, alternative media that preceded the advent of gay characters, strong women, and people of color in white-collar jobs on television).

Part of me feels guilty advocating a thinning out, if not a disappearance, of television. Many of my friends are TV actors, and shows/miniseries such as *Roots, thirtysomething,* and *Star Trek: The Next Generation* changed my life (I'm going for honesty here, not glamour). Some would argue that TVs can help us commune around progressive values. I know I did. But now I question that in light of the fact that most stations are owned by corporations with military, antienvironment, and consumer-motivating agendas to uphold.

And besides, our landscape awaits us! The wonders, big and small, of our human, artistic, and natural terrain are disappearing in service of standardized experiences. Right now what we're "buying" is an addiction to generic shopping malls with chain stores, megastores, and suburban sprawl built on spec, with "wildness" as a commodity that we access with large, greenhouse nightmare vehicles, also sold to us (heavily) on television.

We need to find out which parts of our lives are unmediated (un-media-ted). We need to get out there and discover our passions, find out who loves us, what we're proud of, and what we're living for, without convenient media intervention.

And if there's some show that you've just *got* to see, that doesn't mean you need your own television. You need to know someone who owns one, and—let's be real—you do. So throw yours out!

—*Dar Williams*
SINGER/SONGWRITER

21

Politically, don't change a thing. If you carefully examine the members of Congress and the executive branch, you will discover that precious few of them have ever run a business, made a payroll, grown corn, or engaged in any activity where profit was paramount.

This means that our country has found a way to keep the less-than-able occupied. Who is to say that these ungifted people might not have fallen by the wayside—or worse, descended into a life of crime?

I believe our treatment of our president, congresspeople, and senators is proof positive that this is a compassionate and Christian nation.

—*Rita Mae Brown*
AUTHOR

22

ADOPTION: There are today almost 500,000 children in foster care in America. There are also hundreds of thousands of prospective mothers and fathers, unable to have children, who want them. It should be easy to reconcile these two facts; it isn't. There are powerful obstacles: bureaucracies, myths about family, and organized opponents.

America would be a better place if thousands of kids escaped foster care—and in far too many instances an abusive environment—and were placed with a loving family. The Clinton administration has set an admirable goal of doubling the number of adoptions by 2002; that ought to be a minimal target.

Despite a few well-publicized cases of adoptions that haven't panned out, every serious study shows that the vast majority of adopted kids are as well adjusted, as happy, and as successful as biological sons and daughters. As the father of an adopted daughter—as well as two biological sons—I know that the many joys, and occasional tribulations, of parenthood are the same whether a child is adopted or biological.

Yet of the more than 100,000 kids in foster care waiting to be adopted last year, only 20,000 were adopted. These children are disproportionately minorities or kids with disabilities. Further, most have been abused. Every day five kids are killed by one of their parents. That's unacceptable in America in 1997.

Over the past couple years, there has been an effort to improve these conditions and increase adoptions. Bill and Hillary Clinton have played an important role, as have other Democrats such as former Ohio Senator Howard Metzenbaum and Congresswoman Barbara Kennelly of Connecticut, and Republican House members Dave Camp of Michigan, Susan Molinari of New York, Clay Shaw of Florida, and Gerry Solomon of New York (himself an adoptee).*

But more can be done. The private sector as well as government needs to devote more resources so that no desiring family is precluded from adopting a child because of finances. The effort begun by Howard Metzenbaum to break down the barriers to transracial adoptions must continue.

Ideologues from the Left and Right should be stopped from making matters worse. There should be reform of liberal-spawned laws that, however well intended, have had the effect of keeping dysfunctional families together. Federal legislation directing states to make "reasonable efforts" to keep and reunite children with their biological parents seemed eminently reasonable. Yet over almost two decades many young children have suffered when forced back to abusive or negligent parents; these kids would be much better off with an adoptive family. Similarly, the political Right's push for "parental rights" legislation on the state and federal level sounds laudable. Yet, top family law specialists warn, these initiatives would make it considerably harder to take action against abusive parents and would set back efforts to increase adoptions out of the foster care system.

Finally, there are few issues more divisive in America than abortion. Yet both sides in this emotionally charged issue should find common ground on the desirability of adoption as an alternative to abortion.

—Al Hunt

JOURNALIST

Editor's Note: Some of these members have left Congress since this piece was written.

23

I suggest that every man wear lipstick for a week: bright red, bluey pink, even tangerine. No neutral or translucent shades, please.

I thought about this as I walked to the gym one morning. I imagined my doorman, crimson lips upturned in a bright smile of greeting. The raggedy man lying on the street looked less scary, less alien, and more approachable—more like a girl who has partied all night and gone to sleep in her makeup. The butchers and fish sellers dressed in white coats in the market looked up from their work, all sexy and red-lipped, almost ready to burst into song. The businessmen hustling to their jobs seemed alert and excited and turned on to the day.

Lipstick makes men gay, as in happy. It throws them off-kilter. They do not know what to expect, and we would not know what to expect from them, nor they from themselves. They would feel a little foolish, and that would be very liberating. Lipstick adds color to life. It would free men from the dark bondage of their male egos. That bloodred mouth exposes their vulnerabilities, the yellow bellies they so desperately hide. Of course, it also lays open their vanities and accentuates their hunger, and believe me I am in a position to know. We can deal with that.

If every man were required to wear lipstick for a week, there would be a lot less fighting and a lot more kissing. Theater would happen in the streets. Life could be more like a Broadway musical. And the lessons of that week would be remembered, for the lipstick would leave an indelible mark. Men have been taught to use their fists. They reach for a gun. Women have always been the shrewder sex. Our weapons are more subtle. With a tiny lipstick tube, we get ready, take aim, and fire, and with it we can change the world.

—*Veronica Vera*
SEXUAL EVOLUTIONARY

24

The presence of God in the lives of more Americans.

—*Sean "Puffy" Combs*
MUSIC PRODUCER

25

—*Kevin "Kal" Kallagher*
CARTOONIST

26

I graduated from Yale Law School in 1955, then moved to New York. I soon found myself serving as chairman of the Adlai Stevenson for President Committee in the New York City borough of Staten Island. As I look back four decades ago, I remember an America where families stayed together and divorce was the exception rather than the rule. I remember an America where the use of narcotics was infrequent and confined primarily to the entertainment community. I remem-

HOW TO MAKE AMERICA BETTER in 6 EASY STEPS!!!
STEP 1. CAREFULLY CUT OUT IMAGE BELOW
2. FOLD IMAGE IN HALF
3 PRESS & FOLD
SCISSORS ENCLOSED
CUTALONG DOTTED LINE
4. FOLD
FOLD
5 PINCH
6. TOSS
KERR PLUNK!
NO TV!
NOW WHAT?
GRAB A BOOK!
KERR PLUNK!
HERE'S ONE..
"250 WAYS TO MAKE AMERICA BETTER"
KAL 99

ber an America where the streets were safe and where there was a sense of neighborhood and community. I remember an America where the life of the unborn and the elderly was considered precious, where children were taught respect for their parents, where the schools were the best in the world, and where the purpose of education was the transmission of honor, morality, values, and patriotism. More than anything, I remember an America that was one nation under God.

The America of those days had its flaws. There was racial injustice, and women were not accorded their rightful role in society. To our credit, we have righted many of the wrongs caused by racism and sexism. We have created a world of extraordinary prosperity. In the midst of our prosperity we have homeless people sleeping in the streets, broken families, an epidemic of crime, and a startling increase in teenage pregnancy, delinquency, and drug abuse.

A wise king named Solomon wrote almost three thousand years ago, "Without a vision of God, the people run amuck." Regrettably, with all of the extraordinary technology and material advances of the latter part of the twentieth century, we have lost something very precious: the collective sense that this is indeed one nation under God.

Surely no one wants to return to the days of Jim Crow and sweatshops, but would not this be a more wonderful country if husbands and wives observed the biblical standards regarding marriage, if children were brought up in the "nurture and admonition of the Lord," and if we as people affirmed the basic truths that our liberties are derived from a gracious Creator who taught us to love Him and to love our neighbor as ourselves?

—Pat Robertson
RELIGIOUS LEADER

27

I hope that in my lifetime, I'm able to see a woman as the president of the United States. Think about it. Is there anyone in your life who is more powerful, inspiring, or influential than your mother? Imagine, the mother of our country. It's unfortunate that only over the past few years have we seen women come into their own. Sylvia Rhone was named the first woman president of a major record company, Elektra, a few years back. Oprah is the highest-grossing female entertainer, in the top three!

I just feel that with a woman as president, we'd see women fully participating in every aspect of society. First and foremost, more women would be moved to vote. I think with a woman president we'd see important and immediate attention paid to finding cures for AIDS and cancer, a strong action to end homelessness, global restrictions on pollution, a more aggressive program to restructure the public school system, equality and acceptance of every human, and an end to weapons. The hope is that no good mother of our country would allow these things to go on in her household. Isn't it possible that she would bring some much-needed compassion, humanity, and integrity to the political arena? I'd do it. But our country would go broke and the deficit would be permanently irreparable! At least there would be some improvements.

Besides, wouldn't it be great to have a First Man?

—*Dineh Mohajer*
BUSINESS EXECUTIVE

28

Ultimately, when you distill everything down, there are essentially only two requirements for a healthy society: a healthy planet and healthy people to inhabit it.

Let's look at the first. Without a healthy, sustainable planet, we can forget the second, so the necessity of protecting our environment seems obvious. But equally obvious is the complexity of the task. Otherwise, we wouldn't have too many cities with poor air quality, too many (one is too many) unsafe beaches, unfishable lakes and rivers, and, most important, a vastly unacceptable quantity of fossil fuel emissions creating the potentially planet-threatening greenhouse effect called global warming.

If we can find a way to slow down the growth of our population, the technology exists to clean up our environment. We know how to do it. Clearly, the ultimate goal is to do it in a way that doesn't compromise economic growth. Although past efforts show that this is clearly achievable, there are strong forces working very hard to curb environmental regulation.

For the sake of argument, let's stipulate that in order to protect the earth from becoming uninhabitable, we must destroy our economy. In other words, we must make a choice: no Earth or no economy. There is no indication that this is a choice we have to make, but, if we did, there is little question what our choice would be. Clearly, if there were no Earth, we wouldn't really need an economy or much of anything else. So in our avid quest to balance Earth's preservation and a growing economy, if we have to come down slightly on one side or the other, there can't be much of an argument on which side we should fall.

Now, assuming we are taking the right steps to protect Earth, we come to the challenge of fostering healthy people who will inhabit our hopefully life-sustaining planet. The quality of life depends on healthy inhabitants—not just physically healthy but emotionally and intellectually as well. How can we achieve this? This seems as daunting as cleaning up the environment. The problems are certainly as, if not more, complex. When one is facing a climb up an enormous mountain, the task can seem almost impossible. But as we know, if instead of trying to climb the mountain in one giant step, we simply put one foot in front of the other, eventually we will reach the top.

Fortunately, science is now providing us with a new tool to help make that climb successful. New research in brain development tells us in no uncertain terms that, because the human brain grows to 90 percent of its adult size in its first three years, the emotional, intellectual, and physical environment a child is exposed to through the interaction with his or her primary caregivers (mothers, fathers, child care providers) in the first three years of life has a profound impact on how that child will function later on as an adult. Whether he or she will become a healthy, productive member of society or a toxic burden is in very large part determined by the parental and caregiving experiences he or she has from the prenatal period through the first three years.

Studies show that there is a direct nexus between positive emotional, physical, and intellectual nurturing in the early years and success in school and later in life. Positive nurturing likewise has a profound effect on reductions in crime, teen pregnancy, drug abuse, child abuse, welfare dependency, and homelessness. If we expect to achieve the second goal, a healthier populace, we must make an investment in early childhood development. And this investment must be done in a comprehensive, integrated way. We must provide the families of our youngest children with access to health care, quality child care, parent education, and counseling through intervention programs (voluntary at-home visits) for families at risk.

These services should be integrated on a community-by-community basis at family resource centers that, depending on the hub of a particular community, could be a school, a church, a hospital, or a child care center. And they should be funded through a partnership among the federal government, state governments, the corporate community, and individual citizens.

Only through a concerted effort to give each child a healthy foundation can we foster the development of the healthy people we need to make up our healthy world.

—*Rob Reiner*
FILMMAKER

29

I fly a lot. I've found that when the luggage comes off the plane, all the passengers jam up to the carousel so they can see when their bags come off. This makes for some jostling and ill will. My suggestion is to put a mirrored ceiling directly over every airport carousel in America. That way people could stand back and look up to see when their bags arrive. I think this could be mandated by Congress, although there might be some court fights over states' rights.

—*Al Franken*
HUMORIST/ACTOR

30

By and large, we Americans are blindingly ignorant of the effects and ramifications of our most mundane actions. What exactly happens to the ozone when we turn on our air conditioners? How does our drive to the corner store affect our drinking water? How many Post-it notes does it take to fell one tree? What exactly are the conditions under which the chicken in my chicken satay was raised? Did migrant labor make the glass of grape juice I am drinking possible, and at what cost? When I use my ATM card, how many real live human beings lose their jobs? Sure, the nightly news speaks in general terms about all of this, yet individually we rarely make the connections, conveniently opting instead to believe that the choices we make are somehow unrelated to human suffering, community decay, and planetary destruction.

Most corporate and government institutions are more than happy to oblige our delusion; letting people know the real story behind the products we cherish would not be good for business. Imagine a package of chicken breasts emblazoned with a full disclosure of the various synthetic substances injected into the bird, its tiny pen, its unsanitary production facilities. Wouldn't you bear the heat just a little longer if your air conditioner came complete with a notice informing you of just exactly how much each hour of use contributed to acid rain? Wouldn't you buy fewer books and magazines if you knew exactly how many trees it took to fill one bookshelf, how many rivers are polluted by the waste products of one paper mill? And if you wouldn't consume less or differently, don't you think you at least ought to know what would happen if you did?

Of course, most Americans already feel inundated by too much information, and I would have to agree, and add my extra gripe: it's too much and still not the information we need the most. It's everywhere and still not in the places we need to find it. Spinning out yearly or even monthly specials about how the rain forest is disappearing and bacteria is bleeding into the food supply just doesn't do the trick; packaging on everything from sneakers to soap needs to be more explicit, like the warnings on cigarettes. More time needs to be spent explaining to the public at large just how we are individually gobbling up an obscene portion of the earth's resources. Just as health food stores and organic growers are making the extra effort to educate consumers about the positive effects (economic, physical, spiritual, environmental) of "going green," so should "regular" supermarkets inform about the negative (and possibly positive) effects of doing just the opposite. We Americans need to grapple daily, graphically, with the consequences of our actions.

It seems to me that this is more than a matter of protecting ourselves and the environment; it also cuts to the heart of a notion Americans hold near and dear: choice. For how on earth can we choose if we don't know, really, what we are choosing? When I buy a pair of jeans, for instance, from the Gap instead of Levi's, what does that mean? Who made my pants, and how much were they paid? Where did the dye come from, and where did it go once my pants were bagged and shipped? Most of us blithely make our selections with the assumption that someone else, some benign CEO, is "doing the right thing" and taking care of us and the world. A quick look at RJR Nabisco's insistence upon the minimal hazards of smoking should tell us (hello!), that this simply is not the case. It is we, with our curiosity, our demand to know more, who hold corporations accountable, and we should. If we aren't careful, our blissful ignorance will surely kill us—not only because we will destroy our bodies and our earth but because living in any kind of denial insidiously compromises our ability to be fully conscious and alive in each moment. If we don't even know what we are doing, how can we possibly imagine ways to do it better?

—*Rebecca Walker*
AUTHOR/ACTIVIST

31

Invest in youth today.

> *Pick up a book and read to a child.*
> *Listen to their unanswered questions.*
> *Help with their homework.*
> *Mentor a child.*
>
> *Expand a child's horizon.*
>
> *Take a child to an Astros game—*
> *baseball is one of America's favorite pastimes.*
> *Listen to Jimmy Buffet—*
> *you may not change your latitude, but you can change*
> *   your attitude.*
> *Surf the Net.*
>
> *A good education is the key to providing youth with*
> *   the answers for tomorrow and with the skills to suc-*
> *   ceed in today's society.*
>
> *Teach a skill to youth today.*
> *Offer work alternatives after school.*

Support job training programs in the community.

Push education past the classroom boundaries.

Make a positive change.
Get involved in the community.
Discover an issue meaningful to a child.
Become part of the solution for the community.
Empower them to become involved.

Lay a solid foundation for tomorrow's generation.
—Gene Green

POLITICIAN

32

More than fifteen years have passed since John Hinckley, Jr., fired the shots that severely wounded my husband, Jim, and drastically changed our family's life. Unfortunately, our experience is far from unique. Since that time, the same tragedy has struck hundreds of thousands of American families. What's more, the fear of gun violence has affected the quality of life of every American, even those who have never experienced it firsthand. What we forget is that living in fear does not have to be an inevitable part of life in America.

The good news is that we have already begun to reverse the tide of gun violence sweeping across the country. The Brady Law, named for my husband, requires a background check for the purchase of a handgun. Since the law went into effect, background checks have stopped approximately 173,000 criminals and other high-risk persons from buying handguns; gun-related violent crime has been dropping even faster than the violent crime rate overall; and we have seen a dramatic positive impact on interstate gun trafficking, which is how most guns end up on the illegal market.

Clearly, strong gun laws are working, but much more needs to be done. Only through a comprehensive approach to reforming the gun industry will we finally be able to reclaim our streets and protect our children from gun violence. As with many public health crises, the place to begin the healing is in the home. Many parents lock up prescription drugs and require their children to wear seat belts and bicycle safety helmets, but leave a loaded gun accessible in the home. Parents must recognize that the best way to protect families is to remove guns from the home. For those who choose to keep a gun in the home, however, responsible gun ownership means storing the gun unloaded, with the gun and ammunition locked up separately.

We must also put an end to the booming illegal market in handguns that supplies criminals with the tools of their trade. Because gun traffickers rely on bulk handgun purchases to conduct their deadly business, tough laws limiting handgun sales to one per month per person can run them out of business.

Gun manufacturers can also help reduce the use of their product in unintentional shootings and crime by building safety features into the design of handguns. For years gun manufacturers have had the technology to make guns that can be fired only by authorized users but have simply made a business decision not to implement the technology. At the same time, the gun lobby has continued to obstruct passage of sensible gun laws and encouraged gun owners to store guns loaded and at the ready—an accident waiting to happen.

Like the tobacco industry, the gun industry's goals are

antithetical to a sane and healthy society. It is time for the American public to demand that the gun industry be held responsible for the lethal products it manufactures. This is the only way to end the fear of gun violence in America.

—*Sarah Brady*
ACTIVIST

33

Understand that anything worth doing can't be accomplished in this lifetime. Or, as I. F. Stone put it, "If you expect to see the final results of your work, you have not asked a big enough question." So find a big enough question! For me it goes like this. Since none of the problems facing our planet can be solved without changes in our hearts and habits, they can't be solved without our participation. (Few of us change 'cause we're told to.) It follows that only democratic, inclusive approaches have a prayer of a chance. And that means we all have to learn to *do democracy*—to stop thinking of democracy as a stuffy, rigid structure and start *living* it, making democracy what we do every day of our lives—in our classrooms, workplaces, organizations, governments. That means learning the skills that make democracy fun. Fun? Yes, the happiest people I know aren't the couch potatoes but regular folks discovering their power to change the world for the better. Corny but true.

—*Frances Moore Lappé*
AUTHOR/ACTIVIST

34

America would be a better place if children could attend major-league baseball games for free. Ticket prices today keep many children out of the game. Instead of a normal summer outing for families, a trip to the ballpark has become a one-time event for most. It seems that corporations are the only ones that can afford the high prices these days.

When I was a kid, a trip to the ballpark to see the Dodgers was like a trip to Heaven. I was in the stands the day Jackie Robinson took the field for the first time for the Dodgers. The impact of that moment has stayed with me more than fifty years. Everyone on my block knew the stats of all the players on our team. Baseball was a staple of our conversations back then, a bonding ritual. And guess what, it still is today.

My family was on relief when I was growing up (it's called welfare today), but a ticket to a game was still within my reach. And many times the Police Athletic League (PAL) would take all the kids in my neighborhood for free. It became a community event.

Baseball is America's game. It teaches strategy and develops loyalty. It gives kids something to dream about and aspire to on so many levels. So I challenge our nation: play ball! Let's make sure that all of our children can go to the ballpark and cheer on their favorite team.

—Larry King
TELEVISION HOST

35

Women in the United States face injury and death every day from sexual violence and exploitation. There is a contempt for women's dignity and integrity in this country that is at least partly created by the $8-billion-a-year legal market in pornography. In this pornography, women are dehumanized, objectified, and turned into targets for assault. Pornography produces hostility, bias, and aggression against women; promotes rape, battery, and incest; and keeps the civil status of women second class.

Most pornography is made out of the real bodies of hurt or coerced women—prostituted and marginalized women. These women are overwhelmingly the victims of child sexual abuse, poverty, and homelessness. The United States is blighted by this trafficking in abused women and girls—and by the hatred and violence this trafficking creates and condones.

Currently the pornography industry enjoys absolute First Amendment protection as if women's bodies were words or sentences. The so-called speech of panderers and pimps is protected while the civil rights of women are not. In part this is because sex equality is not a principle of justice included in our Constitution.

I want to see two laws passed: an equal rights amendment to the Constitution that guarantees the end of sex discrimination; and a federal civil statute that recognizes pornography as a violation of the civil rights of women—and anyone else hurt in its production or use.

If women's lives and chances are diminished or destroyed in order to make pornography and if pornography is instrumental in sexual abuse, women's rights are systematically abrogated by the brutality of this sexualized degradation. A sexual traffic in human beings should be abhorrent in a democracy.

—*Andrea Dworkin*
AUTHOR

36

What this country needs is more books like this one and more people coming up with ideas like this—and more people who are willing to commit themselves to exploring the prospects of putting these ideas into effect. And more people who will stand up and defend these prospects against their critics, and more people who are open-minded enough to bring the critics and the defenders together to work out alternative ideas and/or prospects, and more people who are attentive enough to keep track of the entire process and make notes, and more people who will take the time to evaluate these notes so as to come up with ideas of how the entire process went tragically wrong. Or *fewer* people.

—*Roy Blount, Jr.*
AUTHOR

37

We, the people, spend too much time hating ourselves. We do leg lifts in front of the mirror, glancing furiously between our reflection and the airbrushed gams on some magazine model. We're comatose for hours while some president/client/M.D. sews hair to our scalps to cover what a chromosome didn't. If our noses are "too big," we chop 'em off. If our tummies are "too fat," we staple 'em up. The way we tear ourselves apart, you'd think we were by-products of Colonel Sanders. Yeah, I'll take the three-piece dinner—legs, breasts, and, oh, a side of self-hatred.

It's little wonder, though. Dodging subliminal messages is as easy as waltzing through a minefield. *Be all that you can be,* but remember . . . *image is everything. Have it your way,* just don't ask for more than *two all-beef patties, special sauce, lettuce, cheese. Choose or lose* . . . so will that be *original* or *extra crispy?* I'm only halfway ashamed to admit that I could sooner sing the jingles for eight popular breakfast cereals than I could sing the national anthem. My responsibility? (*Show 'em you're a tiger.*) My lack of self-education? (*Show 'em what you can do.*) Maybe so.

When my second-grade teacher asked the class how many of us thought we could be president, we all raised our hands: girls and boys, Black kids, Asian kids, White kids, poor kids . . . all of us. But by seventh grade, we had settled for more "modest" aspirations. I was chunky with braces, couldn't afford designer jeans, and couldn't land the essential teen boyfriend. I had never seen a woman president. And I'd be darned if I thought I was cool enough to be the first.

It was the point where my kid fantasies met reality that my dreams recoiled. That one day where loyalty, cleverness, and empathy dropped 10 million points on the Dow Jones Industrial Average, and materialism, elitism, and backstabbing soared. Nobody was there saying, "Come on, I thought you said you wanted to be the president of the United States of America." Instead, the world waved a mascara wand and tried to divert me with semiformal dresses and kissing tips.

Wow, I think I've discovered the problem with America

today. Call out the National Guard and tell them this: We're losing our young in the battle against bright lights and billboards. And once they're gone, it may be for good.

—*Tali Edut*
MEDIAROLOGIST

38

When I was a kid in a poverty-stricken home deep inside the Appalachian hills of eastern Kentucky, all the politicians could lie to me and get away with it because I didn't know any better. Now that I have met the political quacks, drunk with the big-shot politicians, been dragged through the courts, and slipped money to most of them, I know what a bunch of lying, cheating, scheming bastards they are. And if you will support me, I promise that I will expose them to all the world.

—*Larry Flynt*
MAGAZINE PUBLISHER

(From a 1984 statement announcing his candidacy for president)

39

My remedy for many of the woes besetting contemporary American society is, to borrow a chop from my legion of Republicrat neighbors, to see to it that everybody "obeys the law." As might be expected, however, my agenda in this regard is a bit different from theirs.

To be clear, I'm not in the least interested in beefing up an already bloated police apparatus with yet another 100,000 cops, upgraded armaments, and cybertech capacity, or powers to search, seize and "preventively detain" everyone in sight. I have no desire to see the country's penal/slave labor system, now proportionately the largest in the world, doubled in size over the next few years. Nor do I find virtue in discussing the merits of visiting capital punishment upon fourteen-year-olds or of locking kids up en masse for such "deviant" behaviors as smoking cigarettes.

I may be old-fashioned, but it occurs to me that before a government can claim the moral authority to impose its system of rules and regulations on *anybody*, it must first be in at least some degree of compliance with the laws intended to control its own conduct. And this, the government of the United States most conspicuously is not.

Forget for a moment such weighty issues as whether motorists are "getting away with" driving 78 miles per hour rather than 70 in the great outback of western Kansas or whether the Marlboro Man just lit up in the pristine environment outside the doors of O'Hare International Airport. Consider instead, as just one example of what I'm after, the implications of the fact that the U.S. is in violation of the more than 370 still binding treaties into which it historically entered with American Indian nations.

According to Article VI of the U.S. Constitution, a ratified treaty is "the supreme Law of the Land." According to the final report of the government's own Indian Claims Commission, the complex of treaties with native peoples guarantees permanent indigenous possession of and jurisdiction over about a third of the forty-eight contiguous states. Yet Indians retain even the most nominal control over less than 5 percent of that area.

It follows that every square inch of treaty-reserved territory taken by the United States is illegally occupied, every ounce of minerals removed from it is stolen. We're talking millions of acres and billions of dollars in theft, not to mention the "usurpation of legitimate governments," as George Bush once put it. It's big-time organized crime by any definition.

The United States today has no more "right" to Indian country—or Hawai'i for that matter—than Germany had to Poland in the 1940s, far less than Iraq to Kuwait in the '90s. "Good Americans" who are genuinely committed to the ideals of Law Enforcement, rather than merely using the term as a slogan behind which to mask the preservation of privileges they derive from perpetuating a patently criminal order, will be eager to do whatever it takes to ensure that the U.S. at last obeys the law of its own Indian treaties.

To the extent they are, we can all set out together to forge a whole new matrix of relations among the peoples now resident in North America, one based in honesty, integrity, and mutually accepted standards of comportment. This, in turn, will open up an all-but-limitless panorama of constructive possibilities for the future generations of this continent.

In the alternative, Demopublican America's rhetoric of "law and order" will be exposed once and for all as a putrid, self-serving sham. Things will continue to get a helluva lot worse in this country, and they'll never get better, at least until such time as the status quo is suffocated on the excrement of its own mentality and pronouncements. The choice is ours to make.

—*Ward Churchill*
AUTHOR

40

WHAT THIS COUNTRY NEEDS

Silence

—*Signe Wilkinson*

CARTOONIST

41

1. During a court case, when somebody's suing, the person who loses should pay. This will eliminate further frivolous lawsuits as there would be consequences for suing. Let them pay the money, and they'll leave you alone.

2. Considering how much it costs to put people in prison, the United States should spend less money on law enforcement and more on education and rehabilitation.

3. Getting a college education shouldn't require a trust fund or $150,000 in the bank. Attending a first-rate university should be merit-based, not class-based. If a person keeps up their grade point average and wants to continue on, they should be able to go all the way through.

4. Set up high schools (especially in the inner cities) more like colleges. In the tenth grade, they should start priming kids for what they want to do with their lives. As it is, people hit the twelfth grade and still have no direction.

—Ice T
RAPPER

42

I think one of the ways to make America better as we dance joyfully (or clumsily, as it may be) across the border from the second into the third millennium would be a mass adoption by society of a new mantra—namely, the words, "I hear ya." This would be a gigantic societal change, after all, because at present no one is hearing anyone other than himself or herself. We have so many technological apparatuses clicking at us, beeping, winking and blinking around us that we have neither the time to listen to others nor the serenity to accept any of their ideas.

Let's remove our earplugs. Let's begin to listen—quietly—to one another. Let's give one another the dignity of hearing one another out. Let's stop a minute and concentrate on the human side of things, not the material. Let's say to everyone with whom we come into contact, "I hear ya." A lot of very good things just might happen.

—*Letitia Baldrige*
COLUMNIST

43

Labels . . . Black-American, Middle-Class-American, Disabled-American, American Athlete, Gay-American, and more. It never ends. Is it really that tough to define ourselves as individuals? Shouldn't we all be held accountable to each other to provide all the rights and privileges that this country has to offer regardless of race, lifestyle choice, economic status, and so on? By putting a label on someone, we define them before they have a chance to define themselves. As for me, I'm Charles Linwood Williams. If you want to call me anything, just call me "Buck."

—*Buck Williams*
ATHLETE

44

1. Writers and thinkers of the white, male variety should stop assuming in the "we" and making racial, ethnic, and gender identifications only when the subject is not a white male. "We" are *not* the world. Those who do not adhere to rule 1 will be given the silent treatment at home, at work, and on all the stupid talk shows on which they appear. A few days spent experiencing just a taste of invisibility might be enlightening.

2. We should call an end to all handouts, preferences, special treatment, whatever you want to call them, for white men, i.e., fraternities, hand-me-down education and jobs to friends and relatives, corporate subsidies, etc. An end to affirmative action for white men would be a good kick start into the new millennium.

3. We should institute across-the-board uniformity, equality, and equal access to prenatal care and public schooling, K–12, all of it paid for happily by the federal government, not local districts whose tax bases vary wildly.

The fact that we have a president who is asking for volunteers to help teach children to read is an embarassment to him and to our country. People who say that money can't solve problems in public education are people who can afford to patronize private schools and raise children who will maintain the inequality that now exists.

Treating our children (*all* our children) like cherished human beings is just a start to extending that treatment to all our citizens.

—*Jim McKay*

FILMMAKER

45

1. Make America a healthier place—join a gym, take the stairs.
2. Get a library card. If you already have one, get one for your children.
3. Show up at family birthday parties and weddings.
4. Get to know your neighbors—organize a community watch or hold a yard sale.
5. Attend a minor-league baseball game and show your support for athletes with big dreams who work hard for little pay.
6. Tired of traffic tie-ups? Telecommute from home (in your pajamas).
7. Run for public office at least once in your life, or at least post a yard sign.
8. Adopt a pet; not only will you have a new friend, studies show that people who have pets live longer, healthier lives.
9. Pray when things are going well, too.
10. Support women's pro basketball. These women athletes make better role models for young girls and boys than most male pro athletes do.
11. Ban the use of the designated hitter.
12. Send your mom flowers.
13. Bring civility back: teach your children manners, and encourage them by example.
14. Stop driving in the passing lane.
15. Smile at everyone, everywhere.
16. Volunteer. Mentor. Listen.

17. Vote Republican.

18. Listen.

—Kellyanne Fitzpatrick and the polling company®
POLLSTER

46

Here's one: Take the heat off of lesbian and gay parents.

A lot of people out there seem to be worried about the fact that lesbians and gay men are raising children in greater numbers, as well as insisting on our legitimacy as families. Aside from the right-wing crazies, whose arguments defy logic, most people seem to couch their bias as concern for the good of the children. As in:

1. The kids will grow up to become gay. Well, as a happy, well-adjusted lesbian, I really don't think that's the worst fate. But the fact is that children of lesbians and gay men are no more likely than those of heterosexuals to be gay. They're just more likely to be more tolerant of people who are different from themselves.

2. It's not healthy to grow up with no father (or no mother). Actually, it's not healthy to grow up without guidance from loving, devoted adults. And most sons and daughters of lesbians and gay men have plenty of women and men who are there to nurture them.

3. Lesbians and gay men shouldn't have children because the kids will be exposed to homophobia, and that's not fair. How true—homophobia *is* unfair, and if you're worried about it, great! You can do something to

minimize homophobic attitudes in society by working with organizations such as P-FLAG (Parents and Friends of Lesbians and Gays). And the very best thing you can do to protect my kids from homophobia is to teach your own children that lesbians and gay men are worthy and equal in every way—including as parents.

I'm not going to bother to cite the dozens of studies that say that children of lesbians and gay men are perfectly well adjusted and as happy as anyone else. I don't need studies to tell me what I know from living with my own children and knowing other lesbian and gay families; these kids are just fine, thanks. Often their biggest problem is dealing with the ignorance of people who think there's something wrong with their families.

—*Barbara Findlen*
WRITER/EDITOR

47

Economic inequality has been increasing in the United States for more than two decades. Even in this boom period, the earnings of most Americans have remained stagnant, while corporate profits, along with CEOs' salaries have grown rapidly, as have the numbers of people living below the poverty line.

I think extreme economic inequality is bad in itself. It also has pervasive cultural consequences that threaten our democratic culture. Just think of other societies that have been sharply hierarchical. In nineteenth-century England, for example, not only were the rich much richer, but that meant they were also taller and more upright, and attitudes of superiority and subservience permeated English society. By contrast, the United States has always rightly celebrated a democratic culture in which most people look more or less the same, and, at least among whites, working-class people did not shuffle, hat in hand, before the rich.

Extremes of inequality threaten to destroy that heritage as social differences widen. The affluent fuss over health foods and exercise, while people just getting by, who work ever-longer hours, settle for fast foods or TV dinners and the very poor line up at the food pantry. Residential communities become separate worlds, as the better-off retreat to gated communities or heavily guarded apartment complexes and never even see the neighborhoods or daily life of the poor of the inner cities or of the fading small towns. At the extremes, people even come to speak a different language, as the growing distinctiveness of black English dialect observed by linguists demonstrates. Even the life expectancies of the rich and the poor have come to diverge sharply.

Moreover, the culture we still share, of hedonistic consumerism, ensures that those who are excluded will be resentful. This, together with what remains of a sense of democratic birthright, helps to nourish defiant subcultures of crime and drug use, which then further polarize us.

Economic inequality also destroys the democratic political process, and that is finally our only avenue for restoring a measure of equality and community. Thus extremes of wealth are registered in the pervasive political influence of business, while the extremes of poverty take their toll in political hopelessness and quietude. The campaign finance scandals reflect these dual corruptions, although the press has managed to generate remarkable confusion by talking about politicians who use the wrong phone rather than pointing the finger of blame at the stream of business money that is the source of the corruption of our politics.

The consequences are readily apparent. Political talk is business talk, celebrating privatization and the unregulated market and discrediting government, the only agency powerful enough to regulate the market. In this ideological atmosphere, business-backed campaigns for government action to favor business—and increase inequality—succeed. Public regulation of the workplace and environment is rolled back, government rulings become more hostile to unions, taxes are slashed in ways tilted to favor the best-off and corporations, and inevitably public spending is slashed, especially public spending on services and income protections that reach the middle class and the poor.

To make America better, in sum, we should mobilize to reverse the widening economic inequalities that are at the root of so many of our troubles.

—Frances Fox Piven
PROFESSOR

48

As a young man, I spent countless hours listening to short-wave radio and remember being intrigued at hearing Radio Havana's self-description: "Radio Free America." I learned that Cubans saw themselves as Americans, just as did millions of Latinamericanos.

Yankees, on the other hand, were seen as Norteamericanos—North Americans.

It's in that context that one considers the question before

us: How to make America better? It begs the question: Which America?

It has been more than three decades since the Kerner Commission (1968) noted the existence of "two separate societies" in the nation-state—a White and Black America, forged by centuries of historical conflict.

Despite the synthetic images fed to us by the mercantile media, that reality remains, perhaps exacerbated by the emergence of that which South Africa failed to achieve: a Black, bourgeois middle class that would function as a buffer between the burgeoning Black poor and White capital. It is those who are the treasured targets of politicians, those for whom American public policy has intended the "Gulag Archipelagoes" (to quote Solzhenitsyn) of the prison-industrial complex or the noose.

One wonders: What of *this* America?

How can the lives of people in *this* America be made "better"?

That is the challenge of this era, one that gnaws at the ankle of the American body politic like a junkyard dog.

They are demonized by the corporate media, shifted to schools that demean their speech, ridden to ground by the state's police, spat on by a society that claims their tacit acquiescence, and are "Americans" in name only.

Nigerian writer Wole Soyinka, in questioning the legitimacy of the military regime, asks, "When *is* a Nation?"

Unless means can be found to satisfy the needs of this population, why do we continue to see them as a part of "America"?

Dr. Huey P. Newton, and the Black Panther Party that he founded, called for a "United Nations–sponsored plebiscite" to apprehend the wishes of the Black population, as to whether to accede to U.S. nationality or to secede and form an independent state. If the fate of the Black poor is to be but the military or political cannon fodder of others, why not seriously consider a secession that brings independence and a chance to live in a state of freedom?

A "better" America may require a New America—an Africa-America where a new life may be forged.

—*Mumia Abu-Jamal*
AUTHOR/JOURNALIST

49

Bill Gates takes one half of his net worth—roughly $25 billion—and invests it in low-interest, short-term government bonds. After five years, he gets the capital back and uses the interest to buy every schoolkid in America a spanking new iMac. We become the most prosperous, technologically advanced, and equitable culture in the world.

—*Jon Katz*
MEDIA CRITIC

50

Demolish shopping malls (by not shopping there). Get rid of cars (insist on a public transportation system in your town). Insist by staging a sit-in (great way to meet new folks) or the more conventional (and less fun) tug of the old election lever. Put a sign in your car window that says, "Mr. President, I'd rather be on an excellent, federally financed, nonpolluting transportation system than in this death trap."

Return to that old-fashioned notion "Make love, not war." Since we seem to be making war only on ourselves (hatred of gay Americans; fear of black Americans; enmity toward the poor), we have the distinct historical advantage of being able to end war without even crossing our borders.

"Making love" requires a dismantling of the entertainment, advertising, and capitalist enterprises that define our impoverished notion of what makes this country great. Instead of the fake corporate sex we see on television, in movies, and in advertising, which promulgate absurd answers to the eternal quest for pleasure, we need to turn toward the peculiar and particular sexiness of the people we actually are and have to live with. So you're not a supermodel or a celebrity—who cares? These people never get laid anyway. They're too busy being famous and adored by strangers to get down and dirty in the trenches of real intimacy.

Enough with the fake sex in mainstream music—all that blabbing on and on about faux sexual experiences that somehow always stay within the rigid parameters of both heterosexuality and ridiculous gender stereotypes, therefore rendering their so-called sexiness a flaccid joke. Everyone knows that if you put a "t" in Beethoven's Symphony No. 3, the "Eroica," you have "Erotica." And what about Duke Ellington and Johnny Mercer? If you can't swing to that, you can't swing.

Encourage teenage girls to buy a vibrator for their sweet sixteen instead of some cheesy clichéd "sexy" outfit used to rope in boys. Emphasize pleasure over procreation. This would keep strangers from leaning over three-year-old boys and braying, "Is that little blonde your giiiiirlfriend?" thus enforcing compulsory heterosexuality. Keep the lovely absurdity of the fashion industry in its proper place and emphasize instead how nice it feels to walk to work in shoes that don't destroy your spinal column. Save curse words for the really big moments in life: divorce, death, orgasm, financial ruin, etc. And finally, a prosex, antiwar, pro–public transportation, anti–corporate shopping environment would force people to jump off the Information Superhighway and perambulate on the wild side.

—*Maria Maggenti*
FILMMAKER

51

We begin with a question: Why are hundreds of thousands of American children dangling and dangerous and millions more failing to thrive? The fact is, too many children are being born without a skin, with none of the protective armor that, in the past, was provided by loving parents and supportive communities. At the heart of our children's agony is *a truly frightening erosion of the parental role*—of the ability of moms and dads to come through for their children. This is happening not because moms and dads are less devoted than they used to be. They do not love their children less. The truth is, the whole world is pitted against them. One of the best-kept secrets of the last thirty years is that big business, government, and the wider culture have waged *a silent war against parents,* undercutting and undermining the work that they do. Some of the hostility has been inadvertent, and some of it has been deliberate. But whatever the constellation of forces responsible for the war against parents, one thing is for sure: parents have been left twisting in the wind by a society intent on other agendas.

So how do we turn this thing around? How do we some-how give new and self-conscious value to the enterprise of parenting?

We think we have found the answer. In a manner analo-gous to seniors and the AARP, our solutions center on em-powering moms and dads in the political arena. By crafting a *Parents' Agenda* that unites mothers and fathers across race and class, we intend to send America's 62 million parents to the polls. This will have the magical effect of tilting our entire political culture in a direction that supports and values the work that parents do. We call our Parents' Agenda a *G.I. Bill for the Twenty-first Century,* and it is a document of enormous power and significance. It comprises a pragmatic agenda that delivers on two fronts: it tells us how to relieve the intense economic pressures on parents and solve the parental time famine, and it shows us how to rewrite our cultural script so as to give new status and standing to the parental role. Spe-cific recommendations range from tax and education policies that "privilege" adults raising children, to housing subsidies that target families with children, to measures that encourage the entertainment industry to celebrate the parenting role.

Our project together amounts to nothing less than trans-forming the political culture, and it is important to appreciate the enormous heft and weight of the task at hand. Giving new and self-conscious value to the enterprise of parenting and giving a massive amount of new status and support to mothers and fathers are initiatives that have extraordinary potential be-cause of the ways in which *the parent-child bond is the most fundamental building block of human society.* When this is hollowed out, the wellspring of care and commitment dries up, and this has a huge impact beyond the home: community life shrivels up, and so does our democracy. America's stock of social and human capital becomes dangerously depleted. In other words, if we can produce this magical parent power, we can go to the very heart of our darkness and make the center hold.

—*Sylvia Ann Hewlett and Cornel West**

AUTHORS

---

*A black man and a white woman come together to confront our nation's *war against parents* and our consequent inability to cherish our children. Such a collaboration is rare and precious. Given the sharp segregation that marks late-twentieth-century American life, it is hard to find examples of sustained projects that rest on a black-white partnership.

52

—*Jeff Danziger*

CARTOONIST

53

All radio, television stations, Internet nets, airports, super-markets, elevators, and public address systems in general, as well as skywriters and beach biplane sky advertising, would be required to produce interviews with average, above-average, and less-than-average Americans from diverse geographic locations based on the question: How would you make America a better place to live in?

We might hear a report like "Hi, I'm Mary Watkins from Scranton, Pennsylvania, and I'm an average American who thinks we can better our country in a positive way by driving our cars only every other day. This would force you to find creative ways to get around on your noncar day, like biking, hitch-hiking, or (imagine) even walking. I know my car fouls the air we live in. I use it only when I have to, and even then I sometimes don't. Join me, please, and see how your life can also enter into a place of graceful serendipity. (Oh, please don't be offended by the word 'serendipity.' My son who goes to college now at last taught that one to me. I think it means the delightful encounter of situations by chance. And I just love that.)

"And take it from me, if you drive every other day, you will not only cut down on the general pollution of the air, you will also increase your chances of delightful and whimsical serendipity. A neighbor I never knew for years gave me a ride to the post office on her tandem bike. Get on with it! Cut down on pollution. I love America. Don't you?"

—*Spalding Gray*
MONOLOGIST/AUTHOR

54

Civic leadership in metropolitan areas should plan, encourage, and budget for more urban green space.

—*William P. Stiritz*

BUSINESS EXECUTIVE

55

America would be better, I think, if more women had positions of power and leadership. You've heard that before, yes, but this approach is *new*: I think we have to do it ourselves! Yes, Virginia, there is a glass ceiling, and, yes, Virginia, we've shattered patches of it, but plenty of ceiling is left to be shattered. You think "they" (male bosses and CEOs) are the ones to do the shattering? I don't think so. As Tony Brown, gifted (black) television host of the long-running *Tony Brown's Journal*, told a mostly black audience recently, "All we've got is *us*. . . . Nobody's going to do it for us. . . . *We* have to make it [success] happen." You don't like lumping women and blacks together? We do have things in common. Both groups benefited from plenty of consciousness raising and legal decisions—no longer can one be hired (or *not* hired) or fired on grounds of gender, color, age. We've made it impressively into middle management. Now, to move higher (to CEO, president, chairman, COO, CFO), I think we have to depend not on laws or moral imperatives but on *us* (us females) simply by using massive amounts of energy, dedication, guts, drive, and chutzpah! A few women, not by whining or suing, have already made it to upper echelons. . . . They just got in there and worked their brains out. Linda Wachner, CEO of Warnaco; Cathie Black, president of Hearst Magazines; Christine Whitman, governor of New Jersey; and Sherry Lansing, head of production at Paramount, come to mind. So do Barbara Walters, Diane Sawyer, Rosie O'Donnell. Oprah? Has *anybody* of either sex got more clout than Oprah? In the forties, fifties, and sixties some of us got pretty far along *despite* lack of serious male co-operation. (I had a pushy husband.) Talent (if I may), drive, nerve have always worked. Women need them more than ever for the Big Push. When we *get* to the really top jobs, that will be great for America. We may not do it better than men, but we'll do it *as well*. After all, half the brains are ours. Shouldn't everybody get the good out of them?

—*Helen Gurley Brown*
MAGAZINE EDITOR

56

There are still major factors that continue to keep America rusted at the root. A public consensus remains that actions speak louder than words; however, apologetic words are a lot better than silence. The silence of Uncle Sam has been mistaken, by some, as good old American racism. In other words, silence has been a contribution to the pattern of the past. Bill Clinton at least started the ball rolling by apologizing to Black folks for U.S. slavery.

Okay, cool. But what must then happen is action after the words, of course. To fix America is akin to fixing a car with many problems. You don't just shine it, change the wheels, and call it a done deal. You have to get under the hood.

Control of education, economics, and enforcement is still a fantasy to the descendants of slaves in the United States. Those three factors are key in determining whether an environment is a community or a plantation/ghetto. Reparations will continue to be a touchy issue for non-Blacks who maintain that they weren't there in the beginning without realizing that they've benefited at others' expense.

EDUCATION

America should and could consist of a worldly people who recognize who they are and from where they came. Yet people need the proper preparation to understand and control their own destiny. Americans continue to believe that our 2,000-by-3,000-mile area is the be-all, end-all of the world (save a few jet-set trips to Europe) and slap derogatory labels on other countries like "Third World" (completely skipping over the Second World). Our contributions to the planet are ultimately capsized by our immense ill will. With education, people could gain a broad perspective, unlimited in the knowledge of different lands, cultures, and understanding. But by propagandizing people in the education system, you end up with a processed people, not unlike the processed chickens and cows being injected with hormones. We're shot up with American homogeneity.

The educational process is one-sided. Even though people say supplemental education should come from the home, slavery was such a traumatic experience for so long a time that the paradigm is highly unbreakable without a countertraumatic program. People need to learn what this country did to become the mighty United States of America. It wasn't all so peachy keen.

ECONOMICS

Education should teach people to have and support their own. The whole existence of supercorporations eating up smaller entities takes advantage of the community as it loosens people's sense of togetherness. For example, the Black community has never been tight because it is still suffering the posttraumatic effect. The reliance on the supercorporation is a relationship similar to that of the master to the slave owner for necessity and existence.

And what about supercorporations' investments in prisons? That's legalized slavery for the twenty-first century. If you don't have a system that lays out options and education, the people who are suffering the posttraumatic effects of slavery will be conditioned to go right into jail: from one big institution that doesn't supply you with the goods to another.

SUPERCORPORATIONS

Supercorporations influence the "dumbing down" of Americans. If they foster American's cluelessness by not recognizing the rest of the world, then they can program people into being mindless drones. When people don't have control over their realities in their communities, a fantasy world (perfect for the consumer) can be sold to them. Americans think they are making the choices for themselves, but they're really just handed down in a candy-coated package.

And the emphasis on athletes and entertainers in the Black community is completely out of hand. It's not *sexy* enough for supercorporations to support scientists or teachers, and therefore they're overlooked when it comes to the big bucks. It all boils down to this: a community that is not given the understanding of its reality will therefore be subjugated to be a slave to a fantasy world. And sports and entertainment are fantasy. Of course, people need releases, but when their outlets become their dependencies, then they're not dealing with the cause at hand. People should be taught to pick and choose their fantasy worlds, not have them forced down their throats.

Ultimately, America needs a sense of worldly accomplishment (look at Thomas Edison, Jonas Salk, and Noam Chomsky or their terribly underacknowledged African-American counterparts like chemical engineer Dr. Yvonne Clark, pioneer of blood transfusion science Dr. Charles Drew, astronaut Guilion Beauford, and newspaperwoman Pearl Stuart) to progress human beings forward to a point where we can take care of the world and make it a wonderful place to exist all the way around, not just in different pockets.

—Chuck D
RAPPER

57

I believe America would be a better place if all legislators took one week a year to live in the woods, alone. Their shelter should have no electricity, and their food should be adequate but simple. They might have along a book or two and a pad of paper; if there is an amenity, it ought to be a mirror. My hope is that by taking such an annual retreat, people in positions of power might become, over time, deeper and more interesting. I think it would encourage them to be honest with themselves; I think it might help them renew their connection with need and beauty and nature. I think too it might humble them and change them, though in some cases it may in fact only bore them. Those cases ought to go anyway, if only that they may for once bore themselves as deeply as they bore us.

—*Gish Jen*
AUTHOR

58

Jukeboxes. Bring them back with 45-rpm records (big holes) and five selections for a quarter. Put them inside every lonely saloon along every blue highway . . . and have them available to everybody who's in love and especially those who are not. Jukeboxes are cheaper than therapy. Selection J-3: "Louie, Louie." Because hey, "We gotta go."

—*Pat O'Brien*
SPORTS/ENTERTAINMENT ANCHOR

59

If the perennial genie were to offer to fulfill three wishes to improve America, here's what I would pick:

1. America's rich are too rich and are becoming increasingly richer—while America's poor are too poor and the gap is increasing exponentially. This growing gap is an invitation to instability. Accordingly, the wealthy have as much stake in reducing the gap as do the poor. Investment bankers, lawyers, advertising executives, and others make

far too much money today, while teachers, social workers, nurses, and other caregivers make far too little.
While I recognize the dangers of any massive governmental redistribution of wealth, I think we can do far more to
share the bounties of this great country in a way that is
fairer and more stabilizing.

2. There are more guns in America than there are people.
Although most gun owners are responsible, far too many
legal guns find their way into the hands of those who will
use them irresponsibly. Make no mistake about it: guns
kill, and the more guns there are in a society, the more
people there are who will kill. While the Second Amendment may impose some constraints on total gun confisca-
tion, there is much more that we can do to keep weapons
of death out of the hands of those who will use them to
kill innocent people.

3. Our current war on drugs has been a total failure. On a
scale of "worse, worser, and worsest" we have moved beyond "worsest." We have made virtually no impact on
drug use, and we have devastated our civil liberties in the
process. Some movement toward decriminalization and
medicalization of most drugs is a prerequisite to reducing
our crime problem.

I certainly realize that whenever you tamper with complex
mechanisms, you create the risk of causing even greater harm.
Nonetheless, I wish we would give more serious consideration
to the above three proposals, each of which would make
America an even greater country than it now is.

—*Alan M. Dershowitz*
LAWYER/PROFESSOR

There are 3.5 million unintended pregnancies in America every year, and while I preach about safer sex all day long, many of these are caused not by a lack of effort but by a contraceptive failure: condoms break, diaphragms must be "rejellied" for a second sexual episode, pills may be forgotten. I even have some sympathy for those who fail to use contraception because every one has a drawback of some sort: condoms dull sensitivity, diaphragms ruin spontaneity, and the pill can cause weight gain or loss of libido.

So what is the one thing that I would do to make America better? I would like to see the money spent on contraception research increased a hundredfold so that Americans, and everyone else in the world, could obtain a 100 percent effective, easy-to-use, no-side-effects, inexpensive method of birth control.

When you think of the long-term costs of all those millions of unintended pregnancies, the extra money that would go into research would be very well spent. Ultimately, the costs of this research would be *more* than offset by the billions of dollars that would otherwise be spent on abortions, medical treatment of children whose mothers did not receive adequate prenatal care, foster care for unwanted/abused children, and the remedial attention that many of these children require.

So what on earth are we waiting for?

—*Dr. Ruth Westheimer*
SEX ADVISER

61

Make America better? No problem. How about we act like a real superpower and provide a safe and nurturing start for our kids? And I know how to pay for it, too.

For more than fifteen years, federal spending on human needs in our cities has been slashed. How can we look a hungry child in the face who has just come home from a disintegrating, ill-equipped school down a garbage-strewn street in a neighborhood where gunshots are an everyday occurrence . . . and say that we don't have the money to repair that school or clean up those streets?

It's not like we don't know what to do. Head Start gets raves from the Right and Left because it saves seven dollars for every dollar invested. Kids who go through that program statistically have a better shot at a productive life. Yet there's only a spot for one in every five eligible kids. Better schools make smarter kids. Child care allows dads and moms to enter the workforce. There's no mystery how to grow a prosperous people. It's called investment.

"We'd like to but can't afford it," we're told by our political leaders. It's a lie. The federal treasury has the money, but the politicians choose to spend it elsewhere.

The Cold War's over, the Soviet Union kaput. Yet the U.S. continues to spend $265 billion every year on our military, about 90 percent of the Cold War average. I know as a businessperson that either companies react swiftly to changing market conditions, or they close their doors. Not the federal government. Local human services aren't so lucky: public health clinics shut down, and schools are pared back.

Not the military. The F-22 fighter plane was designed to

best the next generation of Soviet bombers, which we now know will never be built. Yet military planners propose spending $96 billion for a fleet of the gold-plated gadgets that lack a mission.

We spend more than $9 billion defending Japan and Germany, from whom I don't know, freeing them to invest in their own people and economies.

The U.S. spends about $40 billion annually on submarines and aircraft carriers designed to confront Soviet nuclear submarines now rusting at their docks.

These are big numbers. One billion dollars could hire 40,429 health care workers or 35,268 teachers for a year. It's about priorities.

The "Evil Empire" is gone, so the Pentagon went in search of a new enemy to justify maintaining the military budget. Up popped the so-called rogue nations of Libya, North Korea, Syria, Iraq, and Cuba. But their military spending is $15 billion combined, or about *one seventeenth* what we spend.

Rome and Russia crumbled from within, not at the hands of some foreign enemy. Throughout the Cold War, Americans made financial sacrifices to international security. It's now time to benefit from the peace and attend to our domestic security. Volunteerism is important, philanthropy is critical, and the business community has a responsibility to give back much more to the community. But the real dollars available for investment are in the federal treasury.

Take this from an ice-cream salesman? Don't need to. Try respected soldiers like retired Admirals Gene LaRocque and Jack Shanahan, or former Assistant Secretary of Defense Lawrence Korb, who served under President Ronald Reagan. These are not anti-Pentagon crazies but proud defenders of our nation's security. They've concluded that we could easily maintain our military superiority while transferring $40 billion from the bloated Pentagon to domestic human needs.

What could you get for that money? Today only one in five eligible kids gets a spot in Head Start, the childhood development program that even the conservatives admit works and that saves seven dollars for every buck we invest. For $8 billion every eligible American child could get a head start. Welfare recipients should have jobs, but what's supposed to happen to their kids while Mom and Dad are working for minimum wages? For $6 billion, all low-income working American parents could have access to good-quality child care for their kids so that bringing home a paycheck would be a viable option. That's not much to the Pentagon, but a lot of money to fund needed programs in our communities.

Make America better? Let's have a national debate on how the public's money is spent and redirect just some of the Cold War military budget to our people. That's what Business Leaders for Sensible Priorities is committed to doing. We are four hundred corporate leaders who are organizing a national campaign to change our federal budget priorities. That's our idea for making America better.

—*Ben Cohen*
BUSINESS EXECUTIVE

62

Celibates Wanted: All American presidents, vice presidents, and presidential and vice presidential candidates should be required to be celibate (unmarried) and chaste (asexual in behavior). If, for millennia, men and women have been able to commit themselves to their religious faiths by eschewing sex, why can't those who would run our lives from the White House? Preferably, candidates for these two offices would also be orphans, have no siblings, and be saddled with no offspring from previous alliances, marital or otherwise; ideally, in addition, no uncles or aunts or cousins. As the woeful Clinton administration revealed, sex can undermine everything else. As more than one previous presidency has demonstrated, relatives by blood and marriage can be distressingly time-consuming and bothersome. Taking care of business, in the immortal words of Elvis, necessitates single-mindedness. For some people, this means skirt chasing; for others, pursuing the well-being of the people one serves. Popes can do it; why can't presidents?

—David Brudnoy
RADIO PERSONALITY

63

"Freedom of the press": What does it mean? Does it mean freedom to lie, freedom to create stories that will make news, freedom from having to check facts to ensure that truth is being printed? Does "freedom of the press" mean that as long as words like "allegedly" are used when there is a question as to the authenticity of the story, the story can be printed without conscience? Does "freedom of the press" mean that it is all right to chase people like Princess Diana and other famous people until their lives become so miserable they try to run or to hide? Does "freedom of the press" mean that it is all right to instill panic when there is no reason to panic, to fill people's lives with fear by blowing facts out of proportion? My friend is from Germany. She also has a home in Palm Springs, California. We had a small earthquake a few weeks ago. Her family called, nearly out of their minds with fear. The newspapers and TV cameras were showing a bridge that had collapsed and a couple of roads that had been put out of condition due to the small earthquake. They made it sound like the entire state of California had been destroyed. Is *that* what our forefathers meant when they declared "freedom of the press" as part of our constitutional rights?

Does "freedom of the press" mean that people who write the news are above and beyond the law? That they are allowed to do anything it takes to "get the story," even though people may be injured or even killed in the pursuit? Even though lives are destroyed and reputations are forever destroyed because they didn't get the facts "quite right"? I was told by a newspaper reporter that they too want promotions in their job, and good news doesn't bring promotions. Is *that* what our forefathers meant by "freedom of the press"?

I feel that our nation would be a better nation were it not run by the press! If people who reported the news had to *prove* that the facts of the story are correct! If the names of their "sources" had to be printed in the story. If they had to drop words like "allegedly" that save them from lawsuits. They used to call it "yellow journalism." I guess "freedom of the press" means never having to say you're sorry!

—*Tammy Faye Messner*
AUTHOR

This magnificent country of ours could be made a better place for all if the public and private sectors were to work together in a cooperative and collaborative manner to create jobs for those who are eligible and to enhance opportunities for those with the potential for employment.

We should hold as our goal employment for as many Americans as possible so that—within the realistic constraints of the economy—the only Americans without jobs are those who are physically and mentally incapable, those who are too young or too old, and those who have the financial means to support themselves without work.

In addition to spurring productivity and increasing opportunity and wealth, pursuing this goal will also help America reduce the extraordinary social costs of unemployment from welfare to crime to dysfunctional family life.

Many believe that all Americans should have access to the basic human necessities of housing, food, and health care. Without a job, however, many Americans cannot achieve this access, and we must face the hard fact that our sixty-year-old welfare system cannot adequately provide that access either.

Fine-tuning the American economy so it develops more jobs and more job opportunities is America's best hope for creating wealth from poverty.

This fine-tuning will not be achieved by government alone, because government by itself *cannot* create jobs or job opportunities without creating new and unrealistic tax burdens. Business—large, medium, and small employers—*can* accomplish this task with the appropriate encouragement and incentive provided by government and with the cooperation of organized labor.

Together, employers, government, and labor must all be prepared to put away their old assumptions and ideologies and share a common commitment to expanding jobs and job opportunities. Together, they can explore options in such areas as creating jobs, training those entering the workforce, expanding the skills of current employees for the purposes of development and promotion, ensuring that the employment playing field is level and fair for all, creating new child care options, and ensuring that workplace conditions are family friendly.

Such a tripartite partnership can be achieved with a small scope or a large one, with federal, state, or merely local participation. Its only prerequisite is the commitment and spirit of partnership from business, labor, and government.

—*Willie L. Brown, Jr.*
POLITICIAN

65

In the United States we live in the first country on earth with founding documents that formally guarantee the right to life, liberty, and the pursuit of happiness. Yet we are miserable. We may blame our malaise on circumstances—our jobs, our families—or see everything around us as the source of our unhappiness. A good meal leaves us stuffed and uncomfortable. Attachment to a spouse leaves us worrying about being left alone. Pursuit of good health leads us only to the inevitability of dying. We're chasing shadows, but we see them as real, as holding the key to our happiness.

With the opportunity for freedom and happiness, why are we miserable? Because we are living the biggest lie in human consciousness. That lie goes like this: "It's me, it's me, I'm it, I'm the center of the universe. I come first. I hold it all together." This lie of self-involvement puts us in a state of conflict with most others, who think that they, not we, are the center of the universe. When we live this lie we suffer, because we can never be satisfied or truly at peace.

The way to the real happiness guaranteed by the founders of the United States is to become less self-concerned, a gradual process that leads to enlightenment. There have been millions of people who have awakened to their true reality, who have been called "enlightened," in many civilizations. They see an infinitude of universes, a beginningless, boundless sea of life, energy, and delight, full of goodness, aware of itself in its absolute ultimate peace and security, freedom and happiness. In their view, we are all incorporated in this sea of joy, nothing neglected, no one excluded. And we all have the potential to experience the deep, continuous happiness they experience.

Centuries ago, the Buddha attained enlightenment and envisioned a society that would make it possible for many people to become enlightened. Altruistic individualism was necessary for this process, and this could flourish only in a society where self-government, equality, economic surplus, and educational opportunity were guaranteed. In his lifetime and beyond, in civilizations such as Tibet, his vision was borne out: many individuals found great peace and happiness as they worked toward and attained enlightenment.

America's founders put into place a democracy that fosters these same ideals—a government by the people, for the people; the concept that all people are created equal; the availability of education; a capitalist system that for the moment has created economic surplus; the ideals of freedom and happiness. But the reason we have not achieved our potential for happiness or behaved like an enlightened society is because we have not understood that real happiness is attained not in the pursuit of material things but in the quest for enlightenment.

When we understand that it is possible to attain perfect enlightenment ourselves, our sense of the meaning of our lives changes. Enlightenment is an evolutionary goal. It is perfect freedom—a freedom so total it cannot be lost. It is perfect security, certain of its reality, perfection, and eternal bliss—it is the goal in the quest for happiness.

In the United States we have a government built on democratic principles that could support the growth of individual and collective enlightenment. We have access to the teachings of the Buddha and other enlightened beings to guide our evolution. As individuals we must make enlightenment our primary goal, and as a country we must emphasize the development of resources to help the individual attain true happiness. An America built on the principles and practices of enlightenment would be the greatest country in the world.

—*Robert Thurman*
PROFESSOR/AUTHOR

MAKING AMERICA BETTER: A FEW IDEAS

PRESIDENT OPRAH

OK, AMERICA...
GROUP HUG!

ONLINE AROMATHERAPY

SNIFF SNIFF

A NEW 2ND AMENDMENT

"RIGHT TO BARE MIDRIFFS"?

I FEEL SAFER ALREADY.

—Jeff Shesol
CARTOONIST

In America, we give constant lip service to adult education, often as it relates to our abounding prison population. But we don't really do much about it. While we provide inmates with television, exercise machines, and cautious workloads, if they want to educate or reeducate themselves, it is pretty much up to them.

Why not take a leaf from the Japanese? Nobody may leave a Japanese prison without knowing how to read and write. It's part of the "graduation" ceremony. So we could just make this a simple federal law. Somehow I don't see even contentious Democrats and Republicans arguing about it. Then we would have much less recidivism. Barbara Bush was correct when she said that if the U.S. could lick its literacy problem, a lot of other ills afflicting us would simply disappear.

What I have learned in working for adult literacy in the past twenty years is that acquiring these simple but all-important skills changes people's lives dramatically. And don't we, shouldn't we, want to radically alter the lives of those we place in prison? They are a captive audience of learners, to put it mildly. And this imperative would be a major challenge to changing and rehabilitating their lives.

—*Liz Smith*
COLUMNIST

68

America would be a better place if there were more women in leadership positions. Twenty-five years ago, many of us made it a personal goal to ensure that there are as many women as men in the U.S. Congress. Well, here we are twenty-five years later, and we are nowhere near that goal. How can America possibly do its best without the voices of more than half its population, the women of this country? In 1756, Cherokee Chief Atta-Kull-Kulla, upon meeting with the South Carolina Assembly, asked the question "Where are your women?" As we face the new millennium, this former Cherokee chief asks the same question: "Where are your women?"

America has had many periods of greatness, but it also has had its share of dark days. America would be a better place if we held a national conversation about race and the true history of this country. Most American history books make only a passing reference to the people who lived here for thousands of years before Columbus accidentally stumbled onto the shores. Children are not taught that long before Columbus arrived, native governments existed on this land we now call America. Because there is so little accurate information about Native Americans in the popular culture or educational institutions, stereotypes about Native Americans are pervasive.

America would be a better place if we all shared a common vision of what America is and what it could be. There are no great moral leaders today, no one to listen to all of us and then articulate a clear vision for the future. People in leadership positions tend to shy away from taking strong positions on the great issues of our time.

America would be a better place if the corporate community would assume more responsibility for helping solve problems in the community, particularly problems it creates. Short-term profits drive the management decisions of too many businesses. It is unconscionable that we live in a society where we allow industrial polluters to harm the very things that sustain us: water, air, and land. Which naturally brings me to campaign finance reform. Many of America's largest polluters are major contributors to both political parties. Campaign finance reform would help make America better.

Finally, America would be a better place if leaders would do more long-term thinking. Short-term thinking has led us to the point where we now address the problem of crime by building more prisons and address the health care of children by completely ignoring the fact that millions of children do not have access to the health care they need. Are these solutions? In Iroquois society leaders are encouraged to remember seven generations in the past and consider seven generations in the future when making decisions that affect the people. If leaders everywhere would adopt this simple policy, America would be a much better place.

—*Wilma Mankiller*
ACTIVIST

69

At a time when faith in government programs is low and private organizations are constantly scraping for money, where can we turn for solutions to our many social problems? I suggest the corporate sector. Corporations have the financial, human, and technical resources to help make things better. They should be doing more.

Over the years, I've been involved with several companies

that value good citizenship. Hershey Foods, for example, conducts a track-and-field program for youngsters between the ages of nine and fourteen. The company sponsors local competitions, which lead to statewide qualifying events and, every August, a weekend in Hershey, Pennsylvania, for 250 boys and 250 girls. It's much more than a track meet; it's an enriching educational experience. Judging from the letters we've received, the program has changed the lives of many kids.

USA/VISA helps potential Olympians in skiing, gymnastics, figure skating, and my own event, the decathlon. The company provides financial support for promising decathletes, allowing them to devote more time to training. It makes coaches available for extra assistance and several times a year operates a camp where athletes receive state-of-the-art instruction and training. Each year, Reebok gives awards to "individuals who, early in their careers and against great odds, have significantly raised awareness of human rights and exercised freedom of expression." Many of the recipients, who must be under thirty years of age, have put their lives on the line in places like Cambodia and Cuba. The Reebok Human Rights Award helps them financially and brings their work to the attention of the rest of the world.

In years past, I was involved with the Southland Corporation, which awarded men and women who made significant contributions to sports at all levels, from obscure Little League coaches to renowned athletes. I also worked with People to People International, which was funded by the Hallmark Corporation. Thanks to Joyce Hall, the company's founder, thousands of Americans have traveled to foreign countries or hosted citizens of other nations, furthering tolerance and understanding across national boundaries. In my thirty years with California Special Olympics, we've received funds and an army of volunteers from Great Western Bank,

Toyota, Fox Sports West, Vons Supermarkets, and other organizations that cared about our special athletes.

Companies like these understand that social responsibility is not just morally right, it's good business. Corporate America has come to be associated with greed and a profit-at-any-cost mentality. A little generosity and compassion can help reverse that image and enhance a company's bottom line through goodwill and name recognition. The experts who make America richer can also make it better—if they choose to. They'll be richer in every way if they make that choice.

—*Rafer Johnson*
AUTHOR/ATHLETE

70

A four-day workweek. A workday that stops at seven. More time to dream and read. A restoration of Sunday.

When I was growing up, we had Sundays. Stores were closed, and nobody worked. There was a special hush on the streets, and it was possible to dawdle and lapse into that state suggested by the phrase "summer afternoon," which someone once described as the two sweetest words in the English language.

Our family had a Sunday ritual: My father would take my sister and me to Griffith Park, where we would ride ponies and row a boat on the lake, while my mother read the paper and did the crossword puzzle. Then we'd visit our grandparents and have dinner at the Tick Tock restaurant, which smelled of cinnamon rolls and brown gravy. A few years later, when I was a teenager, the ritual changed: I went to the beach on Sundays with my friends, where we'd lie in the sand and read: *Madame*

Bovary or Thackeray's *Vanity Fair.* Our goal was to finish all the books on the classics shelf in the library by the time we graduated from high school.

Today, sadly, Sunday is no different from other days. Often it's more hectic: we race to do chores and errands we couldn't take care of during the week and to plow through the contents of an overstuffed briefcase so we can, huff huff, catch up.

I can't remember the last time I spent a Sunday afternoon reading a novel—I'd feel guilty, knowing the discount outlets and the photocopy store are open. This leads to my modest proposal for making America better: a mandatory reading period for all members of society. Every day, a half-hour time slot, say from two to two-thirty in the afternoon, would be set aside for reading—pleasure reading of one's choice. Whether at school, work, or home, everyone would find a spot to sit and read. Phone service would be turned off, which would mean the faxes and computers would shut down. All business would be suspended for thirty minutes, except of course for health and safety emergencies. There could be reading circles where people would read aloud and special nooks where one could retreat in blessed silence. At two-thirty, we'd put down our books and return to business, but it would be with renewed spirit.

Oh, you say, but that's not practical. People will cheat. You can't have reading police patrolling our homes, and what about trains and planes? They can't stop running. I hear you, and I don't care. What's important is to establish a standard, a goal. It's probably too late for much of the adult population, but if children are required to read for half an hour every day, they'll adopt it as a necessary habit, like brushing one's teeth, and feel uneasy if they skip a day.

It's wise to remember, I think, that God did not just create the universe. God created rest, a day and night set aside for

contemplation and rejuvenation, and we've destroyed this—
we've obliterated the concept—at our peril.

—*Sara Davidson*
AUTHOR

71

Eliminate the 89th wing of the air force. It exists solely to transport top officials around the country. The Cold War is over. The vice president doesn't need an air force jet to go play golf. I don't understand how a chief of staff to the president could even consider using a government jet to take him to the dentist.

—*Ross Perot*
BUSINESS EXECUTIVE

72

Many Americans have a way of placing people in groups and then judging that group as a whole. I've been interested in one solution to this societal ill: not a government program, not a tax incentive, simply a cultural approach to the problem.

People should spend one day a year in the company of somebody different, someone you ordinarily harbor a negative feeling toward. If you're rich, spend it with somebody poor. If you're gay, spend it with somebody straight. If you're conservative, spend it with somebody liberal. If you're black, spend it with somebody white. If you're a Crip, spend it with a Blood.

Perhaps at the end of the day people would be a little less

angry and fearful, and a little more understanding. Perhaps this could lead to more peaceful and reasonable solutions to problems that exist in our society.

I know that people will read this and think, "What a typical Hollywood, social liberal idea," but so what? Perhaps these people should spend a day with a Hollywood social liberal.

On the other hand, maybe we should just destroy the world and start over.

—*Rob Fried*
PRODUCER

73

Make it be that our nation's most talented recent college graduates—those who are now swept up by Rhodes Scholarships, investment banks, medical schools, and law schools—spend two years working to address the country's most critical needs. They would work in the nation's most underresourced urban and rural communities in areas such as education, medicine, housing, public safety, and family support services.

Imagine the tremendous energy and creativity, the sheer human power, compassion, and dedication they would bring to the overwhelming issues that face those who are growing up in and living in these areas. And imagine how the very consciousness—and the realities—of our nation would change if one day a substantial portion of our leaders had firsthand experience in these underresourced communities.

—*Wendy Kopp*
EDUCATION ADVOCATE

America is not so much a place as a desire. A desire for more. There is a fundamental belief among Americans that we are entitled to more, should be spending more, our waking hours working for more, consuming more, amassing more. People come to America from other places because they feel they don't have enough work, enough excitement, enough money. Our lives are ruled by an ongoing sinking feeling that we should amount to more, that we would feel like more if only we had more: more Nikes, more VCRs, more publicity, more TVs, more burgers, more cars, more fame, more Styrofoam, more money.

I've spoken with cab drivers who don't see this country as a place to live but as a place to work, to make more. They plan, once they have made enough, to return to their former countries and live out their days in happiness. But unfortunately, they get addicted to making more.

I've spoken to refugees who say that the first thing they notice about this country is that everyone's working all the time—that's all Americans do, they say, no life but work. Working to make more work.

We export this desire, this hunger. We do it through seductive advertising, the glamour and picture-perfect world of movies. We make citizens all over the world hungry for the idea of America, this more-making machine, hungry for products that make you smile with bright white teeth. But no one is happy in America. They're too busy making more. Everyone is constantly comparing themselves to the rich and famous, who flaunt their more, creating deeper hunger and craving. But the rich and famous are the most miserable of all. Hoarding their more dominates their lives.

It's time to define enough, locate an image, an idea of enough. Time to see what lies under all this crazy movement for more. Enough is a place. It's located. It's intimate there. There's time for gazing into eyes and gardens and staring off at the sea and stars. There's time for long extended touch and good espresso and aimless conversation and chocolate cake and doing nothing. What would enough look like? How would it feel? By defining enough, we'd define what we're really after. Our focus would shift from making to being. We might actually see one another and care about what was going on around us.

We could collectively put our focus on things that mattered: education, child care, art, prevention of violence, prison reform—rather than focusing all our attention on our individual needs.

I challenge us to stop making more for a minute, to survive the anxiety of the present tense, to feel a full, satisfied moment. I have a feeling that this fullness might in fact translate into love.

—*Eve Ensler*
PLAYWRIGHT

75

As I make my living at public expense, I will limit my suggestions to improvements in the political life of the nation.

The strongest impetus for reform of the federal campaign finance system is the fear that the customary American cynicism about government has in recent years shown signs of becoming something worse, something more dangerous to the country's well-being: indifference and alienation.

I am a conservative, and I believe it is a very healthy thing for Americans to be skeptical about the purposes and practices of public officials, and refrain from expecting too much from their government. Self-reliance is the ethic that has made America great, not consigning personal responsibilities to the state.

However, small-government conservatives are not chasing idealized anarchy. Government is intended to support our constitutional purpose to "establish Justice, insure domestic Tranquility, provide for the common defence, promote the general Welfare, and secure the Blessings of Liberty to ourselves and our Posterity." When the people come to believe that government is so dysfunctional that it no longer serves these ends, basic civil consensus may suffer grave harm and fragment our culture further.

This concern should motivate all public officials to repair both the appearance and the reality of government corruption. Whether great numbers of elected office holders are in fact bribed by campaign contributions to cast votes contrary to the national interest is not the single standard for determining the need for reform. If most Americans feel they have cause to doubt our integrity, we must seek all reasonable means to persuade them otherwise. Reform of our campaign finance laws is indispensable to that end.

As long as the wealthiest among us can make six-figure "soft money" contributions to political parties and gain the special access to power that such generosity confers on the donor, most Americans will dismiss even the most virtuous politician's claim of fairness and patriotism. More important, most Americans will have good cause to doubt their constitutional guarantee to equal protection under the laws we write.

Meaningful campaign finance reform will not cure public cynicism about modern politics, nor will it completely free

politics from influence peddling. But, coupled with other reforms, it may prevent cynicism from becoming utter alienation, as Americans see that their elected officials value their
reputations more highly than their incumbency. I hope it
would even encourage more Americans to seek public office,
not for the honorifics bestowed on election winners but for
the honor of serving a great nation and working to make it better.

—*John McCain*
POLITICIAN

76

Read the Declaration of Independence to your children. Do it
as a tradition every Fourth of July, maybe just after they've had
their fill of hot dogs and hamburgers. Discuss it with them;
ask questions. Make sure they understand why the word "pursuit" precedes the word "happiness."

—*Jeff Bezos*
BUSINESS EXECUTIVE

77

Live more, and fear less. America isn't losing its moral fiber
because of television's corrupting impact, the breakup of the
traditional family, shifting values, or any of the other reasons
the nattering national nannies would have us believe. No, we
are in danger of decline because we are afraid. Despite what

some best-selling authors say, fear is an affliction. Living fearlessly is a gift. If more Americans could shuck off their petty fears and learn to live life fully, the benefits to the country would be inestimable.

Watch the television news any night of the week, and what do you see? Stories about risks to our health, cures for our ills, drugs that are supposed to strengthen us but actually weaken us or worse, dangers and perils like sodium and cholesterol and nicotine and chemical compounds we thought might exist on Mars, but not in our blood levels! We are a nation of hypochondriacs, fearful of pain, aging, decline, injury, and other normal conditions of living.

Nor is our fear confined to our health. Injury looms big as a collective peril. So we wear helmets to bicycle and motorcycle, and someday we will wear them to walk down the street. We drive with passive restraints and active restraints, and someday we will demand air bags to cushion us in case we slip in the bathtub. Or perhaps government will require that we install them in our bathrooms—spurred along by the insurance industry and consumer activists, of course. We want no risk, no danger, no negative impact on our health, whether it's firsthand, secondhand, or a case of distant causality thrice removed.

Imagine what our ancestors—whether the country's pioneers trekking thousands of miles in wagon trains or immigrants far from home and family who arrived penniless to seek their destiny—would think of Americans' fearful preoccupations. We are paralyzed, so fearful of consequences, real and imagined, that we do not take action. Instead we wait, monitoring our pulses, checking our lipoprotein levels, strapping on our helmets, and avoiding risks. No wonder we can't solve minor problems, like giving our kids a decent education. We won't take a chance on eating too much fat or trying and failing with a new policy approach.

We have become a nation that plays it safe. We live cloistered, petty lives of self-preservation. But it does not have to be this way. Fear can be banished. We can all start to live as if this were our one life to live, instead of watching those commercials and news reports about the wonder drugs and their nightmare twins. If we start to live this life as if it really were going to come to an end, maybe we would discover that what we do counts. That, in turn, would lead to a renewal of individual vigor, as people came to understand that they could make a difference with their lives, that they could do more than just leaving a dent in the couch as proof of their passing.

Of course, this requires acknowledging our mortality—facing our fears, so to speak, of the day when all the safety helmets and air bags and wonder drugs just won't prolong consciousness anymore. Owning up to mortality is an enlivening experience. It sharpens our appreciation for living. People who appreciate living—really appreciate it on a deep-down cellular and organic basis—these are the people who get out and make a difference in the world. That difference is usually for the better.

—*John McLaughlin*
TELEVISION HOST

78

Having kids is easy. Being a parent is another thing entirely.

To cut hair, you need a license. Ditto for owning a gun, practicing massage, or importing tropical fish. If you want to drive a car, not only do you need a license but you have to wait sixteen years, take classes, suffer the indignity of a learner's permit, and manage to pilot the Explorer, instructor at your side, through city streets without flattening pedestrians. Even getting married requires official state sanction.

In fact, there's not much you can do anymore without some kind of credential, training, or official authorization. And for good reason. Society has an undeniable interest in making sure you have the proper training to operate that four-ton Suburban Assault Vehicle and a reasonable concern that people involved in certain kinds of activities (such as air traffic control or psychotherapy) have the right temperaments and attitudes.

Unless you want to be a parent, like me. I have to admit, I got into it without proper training. You'd think society would have a bit of interest in making sure parents had some idea of what they were doing, especially given how important the early preschool years are in terms of developing personality, but there are no required courses for being a momma or a poppa.

I actually believed I was pretty good at being a parent until I went to nursery school. I mean, my daughter, Eva Dakar, goes there too, but the place is really for the parents. It took me about three months of regular attendance before I realized I lacked important child-rearing skills.

The school is organized as a parent education class offered through City College of San Francisco. It's also a parent-run cooperative, a little socialist society where the workers make all the decisions.

And it works. At Rocky Mountain Nursery School, fathers and mothers learn how to be parents. We are taught how to develop the tools to deal with all the issues of child rearing:

tantrums, refusals to cooperate, toilet training, meals, violent behavior, and all the rest. We learn how to raise healthy, respectful, self-assured youngsters (without losing our sanity in the process). And I don't have to tell anyone that good kids tend to grow up to be good adults.

So my suggestion to make America a better place is for all new parents to get into some kind of parent education program. *Before* somebody makes you get a parenting license.

—*John Anner*
EDITOR/ACTIVIST

79

In my opinion, we as earthlings would benefit by coming to terms with our mixed symbols of compassion. We're taught to be reverent toward other humans and to pet our dogs, yet we're also taught to eat cows and wear fur. We put up these unconscious walls whether we know it or not.

Here I am, a full-fledged vegetarian, wearing suede shoes. I've tried to rationalize these shoes as being a by-product of other people's diets, etc., and I know there are cruelty-free options—but vinyl shoes are known to rot your toenails off!

Or I see my wonderful little nephew love our dogs yet devour a cheeseburger (beautifully packaged in a Happy Meal, with plenty of ketchup and salt), just as I once did. If you don't think about what you're eating, it's a truly yummy experience. But I wonder how this meat consumption affects us as we go through our lives, not just physically but energetically. I think of the horrible conditions in which animals are being raised. I think of the terror an animal feels as it is being slaughtered. Here, enjoy. Have a little sauce, and it could help you forget.

If Americans could take a slightly closer look at our responsibility and respect for all life-forms, we just may prove ourselves to be more integrated into society.

—*Todd Oldham*
FASHION DESIGNER

80

TWENTY-FOUR LOW-COST, HIGH-FIBER SUGGESTIONS FOR A BETTER AMERICA

Label each product with "production facts" (like food products' "nutrition facts") disclosing socially relevant information about the product's manufacture: how much the workers who made the product were paid, what toxic wastes resulted from the production process, what nonrenewable resources were used up, how many animals were tortured, etc.

Design a bicycle helmet that does not make the wearer look like a hydrocephalic woodpecker.

Require all judges, prosecutors, and police officers to spend at least three months in a high-security prison before assuming their official duties.

Restore the progressive income tax.

In line with the Second Amendment, encourage people to own as many guns as they wish, so long as they are the muzzle-loading rifles that constituted "arms" at the time the amendment was drafted.

Outfit public men's rooms with changing tables.

Abandon tracking and let the fast learners hone their skills by helping the slow ones.

Require corporations to include, on their boards of directors, a representative sample of assembly-line workers, clerical personnel, and other low-paid employees.

Encourage more movies and TV dramas involving hot interracial romances, with the interracial aspect being relatively incidental to the plot.

Treat all children as gifted and interesting people who are temporarily trapped in small and incompetent bodies.

Amend the Constitution to give everyone the right to urinate on demand. This means a generous supply of free public restrooms and the right of workers to relieve themselves when nature calls, rather than when the boss permits.

Tax churches on whatever of their income is left over after they have fulfilled the biblical instruction to give all that they have to the poor.

Establish national standards for hot sauce hotness. There is no reason why someone seeking serious tissue damage should have to settle for a vague hint of jalapeño, or vice versa.

Encourage wild undergrowth. Lawn maintenance is poisoning the environment and suppressing suburban IQs.

Acknowledge that the leading cause of divorce is marriage, and make it harder to get married in the first place. Alternatively, have marriages be renewable on a year-to-year basis, with failure to renew constituting dissolution. (The obligation to care for the children would be binding on both parties, of course, for at least eighteen years.)

Market perfumes with genuinely alluring scents—like Pepperoni Pizza, Roasted Garlic, and Fresh-Baked Bread.

Discourage teen pregnancy by requiring that sex ed

classes include positive, enticing messages about masturbation and homosexuality.

Require all airplane seats to recline to a 120-degree angle, including in coach. In addition, airports should contain spacious areas devoted to stretching, running, and aerobics.

Legalize drugs and ban the miserable living conditions that lead people to rely on them.

Start a vigorous war on light pollution. The inability to see the stars at night engenders a dangerous collective myopia.

Let the terminally ill choose the manner of their dying. Options should include skydiving, crack cocaine, and flagrantly unsafe sex.

End sexual harassment in the armed forces by requiring an all-female military. Gay men may also be included, as well as heterosexual men who are willing and able to pass as gay.

Require that the charters of corporations be subject to biannual review to determine whether said corporations are genuinely serving the public (as well as their shareholders).

Raise the minimum wage to a livable level and establish a maximum one.

—*Barbara Ehrenreich*
AUTHOR/ACTIVIST

81

What gives me hope for our future is that people are seeking a deeper spirituality. People are reassessing their lives and what they stand for, and coming to understand that we are all here together. It is this fundamental Indian understanding of the world, that all things are related, and the confidence in the creative spirit of human nature that will move this country and the world to solve its problems.

We can no longer view ourselves as individuals, detached from everything else. We are recognizing that what happens in Bosnia affects us; what happens to our fellow Native Americans affects us. Relationships are becoming an integral part of our understanding.

We are also coming to understand how the relationships and values of our economic system drive our lives. The values of individual and accumulation are directly at odds with other values we hold important: family, community, and quality of life. While everyone espouses their importance, communities are being dismantled through practices of corporate takeovers. We need the courage to redesign our system to protect and preserve communities and family.

There is hope in today's economy of an increasing value on relationships and community: using loan funds, assessing environmental costs, rating municipal bonds based on the long-term health of a community. It is my hope that people will not polarize around issues but will realize their interdependence and come together in dialogue. Indigenous cultures have life-sustaining values to share in this process as long as we are alive and flourishing.

—*Rebecca L. Adamson*
ACTIVIST

82

—*Ted Rall*
CARTOONIST

FORGET GLOBAL WARMING. FORGET T.V. VIOLENCE. THE BIGGEST PROBLEM IN AMERICA IS RICH PEOPLE.

WHAT?! IF IT WEREN'T FOR US THERE WOULDN'T BE ANY ECONOMY!

WEALTH ISN'T NECESSARILY A BAD THING — UNLESS IT'S TORN OUT OF THE POCKETS OF THE POOR.

THERE'S PLENTY OF JOBS IF YOU WANT THEM — IN MY NEW INDONESIAN FACTORY!

help

WHAT KIND OF SOCIETY WOULD THINK OF TAXING LOW-INCOME WORKERS... AND UNEMPLOYMENT BENEFITS?

THE THOUGHT OF THE TAXES I'VE AVOIDED PAYING GOING TO HELP PEOPLE I'VE LAID OFF DRIVES ME BONKERS!

HOW CAN EMPLOYERS LIVE WITH THEMSELVES AS THEY UNDERPAY AND OVERWORK THEIR EMPLOYEES?

TRUST ME: IT'S EASY.

AMERICA NEEDS A NEW BREED OF RICH PEOPLE — NOT PARTICULARLY KIND OR GENEROUS OR ANYTHING UNUSUAL...

GOOD NEWS! THE BOARD JUST VOTED YOU ANOTHER RAISE!

...JUST SANE.

DISTRIBUTE MY SALARY TO THE STAFF... AND FIRE THE BOARD.

83

Consumer prices need to be lowered. Prices continue to increase, and no one knows exactly where the money is going. The discrepancy between the income of the executives of and the workers in major corporations is just too immense. It really puts people out; the situation has got to change.

—*Jermaine Dupri*
MUSIC PRODUCER

84

Our American culture has woven a tight fabric of rules to which women's bodies are subjected every single day. Women and girls—no matter what our size, no matter what our economic station—find ourselves bound by it. Pressure to conform to a svelte body comes at us from television, advertising, health care professionals, even from within the political arena. We feel the pressure as we walk down the street, care for our daughters, consider whether or not to join the 88 percent of American women who will not wear a bathing suit. We feel it when the same culture that ogles the $1,000 gown worn by a ninety-pound supermodel points an accusing finger at a full-bodied woman as though she has somehow captured a disproportionate amount of the communal pie.

Over the past ten years our culture has just begun to address the consequences of the diet industry and its yo-yo message, of designer clothing only for those below a size 12, of the barrage of images showing female beauty as childishly youthful and childishly thin. As diet drugs are recalled because of safety, health watchdogs question their necessity. As eating disorders require the attention of an entire new line of health specialists, our culture at last criticizes some fashion designers for their ads. As women attain positions of greater authority and visibility, they boldly challenge the view that only those who fit the beauty mold deserve to be in the public eye.

The fabric is unraveling.

Where do we go from here? What new world do we weave? Imagine this: What if we stop assessing ourselves based on current media icons and find new role models, women who look like us? What if we stop critiquing our bodies in front of our kids and make a pact to help our daughters know and love their own bodies? What if we radically redefine our conception of beauty and surround ourselves and our children with images of beauty as colorful, plentiful, and diverse as America herself?

It's time we look at one another, and ourselves, as whole and talented people. It's time we help that young woman gagging up calories in the toilet, losing her creative energy to self-hatred. She needs to come out of the bathroom and join her peers. It's time we persuade the woman of size, the one who's afraid to be seen in public, to find her place in the world, to fulfill herself personally, and to make a difference in her community. She needs to come out of the house without fear of ridicule.

Imagine children growing up loving their bodies. Imagine eating disorders declining as size loses its influence on self-esteem. Imagine the demand for quick-fix diet drugs disappearing. Imagine no more diet-related deaths. Imagine beautiful clothing for every shape. Tolerance for those who differ from us. Appreciation for beauty in all sizes.

We could even like the way we look. Imagine that. The fabric of our new vision.

—Catherine Taylor and Lonnie Hull DuPont
RADIANCE: THE MAGAZINE FOR LARGE WOMEN

85

Turn off the TV. Read a book. The Good Book, for example. *Melrose Place* has nothing on the Bible. Whatever your beliefs, the Old and New Testaments are not the same sanitized happy stories about rainbows and doves when read as an adult. God makes mistakes. Noah gets drunk and exposes himself. Incest, polygamy, and patricide abound. And that's just Chapter 1.

No matter how secular our culture becomes, it will remain drenched in the Bible. When we discuss a book or describe a painting, many times we are referring to the Bible without even knowing it. Since we will be haunted by the Bible even if we don't know it, doesn't it make sense to read it? Not only is it the source of three major religions and endless permutations thereon, it is the basis of our moral code, imagination, and psychology. In our increasingly atomized lives, the Bible serves as a fresh reminder of the importance of community and being held accountable by someone, somehow. If you dare, you will see your own life's adventures, mistakes, and fallibility in the Bible.

The Bible brings together Malcolm X and Mother Teresa. Jews, Muslims, and Christians all rely on the Old Testament as scripture. Rich in metaphor, the Bible shows us how much different cultures really share. And since in this country we all live in the same place, it helps to understand where the deepest feelings of the other side come from.

Whether you think it's the word of God or just words created by human storytellers, the Bible makes a small but important point about the power of books and our ability to imagine. Even if you don't believe the Old and New Testaments are sacred, people have made them sacred. To read the Bible is to be reminded, as Bill Moyers says, "that what is in us is worth more."

—*Tabitha Soren*
TELEVISION PERSONALITY

86

Only a Luddite could deny the benefits of the computer revolution. And even the most committed computer hater would have to acknowledge that American competitiveness in the twenty-first century will largely depend on our ability to master the computer and harness its power. Computers are the future.

A proposal for our computer age: Ban the computer in the classroom. Forget about wiring every classroom for the Internet. Unplug the monitors. Sell the keyboards for scrap. The computer ban should extend to all classes through the eighth-grade level. Incorporate computers in the curriculum from ninth grade on, but not before.

The benefits of this computer ban would be many: in the short run, schools will save money; in the long run, we can develop an educational system that will truly equip students to thrive in the computer age.

First things first: money. The rush to computerize the classroom is gobbling up precious education dollars. For the 1997–98 academic year, public elementary and secondary schools spent an estimated $5.2 billion on technology, an increase of more than 20 percent from the previous year (*Education Week,* November 10, 1997). No other category of education spending is increasing more rapidly; many others, such as arts programs, face deep cuts. Computers are becoming a top priority for local school boards, capturing dollars that could be spent hiring better teachers, reducing class size, upgrading libraries, or providing for such basic things as safety.

The cost would be justified if computers were revolutionizing elementary schools the way they are fields such as Hollywood animation and cancer research. But what are our schools getting for the billions?

While the zeal for computers is shared by educators, parents, and politicians alike, there's been little research on the technology's impact in the classroom. One person who has done research in the area is Barbara Means with SRI International in Menlo Park, California. Here's what she says: "I've seen kids spending a whole period illustrating a color cover of a report, pixel by pixel, when they haven't even done the report yet." For fourth-graders, the number one use of computers is to play games, according to a 1996 National Assessment of Educational Progress survey. For eighth-graders, playing games ranks second, behind writing papers (or, perhaps, creating nifty cover sheets).

Even if computers are used in a purely educational way, they may not belong in the classroom until after eighth grade. Every hour spent in front of the flickering screen is an hour not spent interacting with real flesh-and-blood people such as teachers and fellow students. Socialization and values are critical components of early education; it is hard to imagine that the computer enhances either.

The computer ban would free up time and money for an education in the basics. Yale computer scientist David Gelernter knows as well as anyone what it takes to master computers. "Children are not being taught to read, write, know arithmetic and history," he told *The New York Times*. "In those circumstances, to bring a glitzy toy into the classroom seems to me to be a disaster." It doesn't take a computer to teach kids to read, to write, to think—and those are tools they'll need to thrive in the computer age. First learn the basics; then bring on the machines.

—*Jonathan Karl*
JOURNALIST

87

1. Increase the price of cigarettes by two dollars a pack to cut teen smoking.

2. Distribute condoms in high schools to all students whose parents consent. Forty percent of all girls become pregnant by their twentieth birthday. This has to stop.

3. Enforce statutory rape laws in cases of teen pregnancy. Armed with criminal investigative powers, find the father and sentence him to prison, suspended as long as he pays child support.

4. Negotiate a global treaty banning the use of children in armies.

5. Eliminate teacher tenure and promote, hire, fire, and pay

teachers based on merit. Then, once public schools become competitive, go to a public and private voucher system.

6. Install defibrillators in all public buildings and train people in their use. One in five heart attack deaths is really death due to traffic.

7. Require civil—not criminal—drug tests of all high school students whose parents consent. Provide therapy and, where necessary, residential treatment for repeat drug users. It's constitutional if parental consent is involved since the children are minors.

8. Left and Right should unite around the goal of reducing the number of abortions through reform of adoption, prenatal care, counseling, birth control education, and abstinence programs.

9. Reform Social Security to permit investment in equities and mortgages, so the trust fund can expand without new taxes or fewer benefits.

10. Create a system of medical appeals boards for each HMO, appointed by the public sector, to hear appeals from patients and doctors of HMO decisions on treatment. Appeals should be adjudicated within twenty-four hours and should be binding. Doctors should have a duty to bring appeals when they disagree with the HMOs' decisions and must be protected against retaliation.

11. The FCC should require a reduction in the violence of early childhood programming. There is no First Amendment right to show violence to five-year-olds.

12. Affirmative action should be continued but should be based on income and place of residence, not on race or gender.

13. PACs and soft money should be banned.

14. All tuition should be tax-deductible.

15. Federal aid for school construction should be approved as soon as budget revenues permit.

16. Allow tort suits against media that are overly physically intrusive in covering the private lives of public figures. Differentiate between allowable actions for covering public lives of public figures as opposed to their private lives.

—*Dick Morris*
POLITICAL CONSULTANT

88

Education has become one of today's most popular political and social mantras. But education means different things to different people. For much of our society, it seems to be dictated by the need for computers and is surrounded by the constant flow of electronic images and sounds. For me, education is not complete without encompassing all that the Arts have contributed to society in the last four millennia. Civilizations are judged by their artistic legacies.

I believe that the Arts are essential to a complete education for our nation's young—not as an added adornment but as an integrated part of the basic curriculum. For me, music is the most accessible art form because all children instinctively understand pulse and sound, the basis of music, as they feel the beat of their hearts and the sound of their voices. When we teach children to draw, to sing, to play an instrument, or to dance, we are teaching them to see, to listen, to feel, and to learn. The idea is not to create musicians, dancers, and painters but to form the basis of a civilized society through an understanding of beauty and creativity.

It has been shown many times that children exposed regularly to the Arts in the first few years of school, regardless of ethnicity or cultural differences, realize astonishing improvements in logic, memory, mathematics, and even manners. More than any other I know, the qualities of this education give young people a greater sense of self—an opportunity to find a unique voice and persona.

I am not a professional educator, but I have worked with young people all my life, and I know what can be done when you touch them for a moment with affection, respect, and a passion for what you believe is right. We can all recall for ourselves that single illuminating moment when a teacher, no matter what the subject, "turned on the light in our heads."

Our greatest wealth is the enormous potential of young minds in this country. It is the key to our future, and we all share its responsibility—as citizens, as parents, as people who want to see a world that respects its fellow human beings.

When immigrants came to this country, adding to the tradition and culture of the Native Americans, we brought our cultures, our ethics, our languages. But above all, we brought a burning desire to become Americans—to share equally in this wonderfully variegated pot of gold in a democratic society. Today we are riven by cultural and ethnological nationalisms that drive us apart. It is not an overstatement to say that education in the Arts on a daily basis can be part of the first steps toward reunification.

—*Isaac Stern*
VIOLINIST

89

If men simply did half the housework and child care, this country would be better overnight, if not necessarily cleaner. According to many recent studies, domestic equality is much vaunted but little practiced. Too many of our men (even the sensitive, tuned-in ones) offer lip service in place of cleaning service. Yet it still seems to me that if they could just do their half, if single mothers could be given support instead of blame, if child care were freely available, if birth control and abortion could be included as part of a universal health care system (all of which strike me as aspects of basic domestic responsibility), then we might have half a chance at gender equality. And after equality, respect. In due time, perhaps even gender justice.

Meanwhile, given the ruts our society seems stuck in, I'll temporarily settle for domestic equality. So here's the mop, there's a diaper, get out there and do your share!

—*Alix Kates Shulman*
AUTHOR

90

America could be made better if more of us got off our backsides and into the great outdoors. Recreation in the outdoors is good for the body as well as for the soul. It's the key to a healthy lifestyle and for all the family. It's the key to a healthy America.

Americans need more firsthand and hands-on experience

with America by hiking its many and wonderful trails; biking its many scenic back roads and off roads; canoeing and kayaking its beautiful lakes and streams; camping in its many and magnificent state and national parks; breathing its fresh air; and communing with the natural essence of our great country.

The first step to a better America is shutting off the TV sets and getting out there, where life is real and life is worth living.

—*Leon A. Gorman*
BUSINESS EXECUTIVE

91

So let me get this straight. God talks to Benny Hinn and Jimmy Swaggart, He speaks to wide receivers and defensive linemen: Deion Sanders, et al. But I was an altar boy for seven years—I had to memorize the Latin mass—and I've never heard from the guy. No note. No phone call. No distant voice delivering "the calling" to my subconscious. Meanwhile, He apparently speaks to Reggie White every Saturday night before the big game on Sunday because God obviously is a Green Bay fucking Packers fan.

So I am now officially done. I quit. It's over. I'm starting my own church—the Lapsed Catholic Church—and here are the rules:

1. Everybody's a saint. You. Me. Your dog. Saint Regis, Saint Reagan, Saint Andrew Dice Clay. The Catholic Church kicked out Saint Christopher, the patron saint of travel, claiming he never was *officially* declared a saint. Well, then, who the hell minted all those medals and Saint

Christopher figurines with magnetic bottoms that our parents used to stick onto the dashboard before the long drive to asthmatic Aunt Betty's? *Why* was Saint Christopher kicked out? Did he smoke crack in the rectory? Was he giving people the wrong directions? I'd like to know. In the Lapsed Catholic Church, we'll be minting medals of Saint Strawberry, the patron saint of substance abuse.

2. Thou shalt not covet thy neighbor's wife? Bullshit. You covet his wife, his car, his house, his pool—everything. You know why? Because he'll be coveting every inch of your shit, pal.

3. If you're married to someone longer than six minutes, guess what? *You're married.* No annulments. No refunds. No exchanges. You want a divorce? Fine. But you don't get an annulment after two kids and twelve years of marriage just because you have political connections and money. Let's see, I got married in 1989, I have two kids, so I figure I'm about what—four years and $4 million shy?

4. Monogamy. All those right-wing Bible-belting thunderheads who proclaimed the arrival of AIDS as God's way of saying he disapproved of gay and lesbian lifestyles were wrong. AIDS wasn't God's disapproval of homosexuality; it was God's way of saying to all of us: *Stop sleeping around.* Pick somebody and settle the fuck down. If you're over thirty and you're still chasing down one-night stands, you're not even in the game. As a matter of fact, you're not even on the field. You're up in the stands with your shirt off, red, white, and blue greasepaint smeared all over your chest, and a big plastic piece of fake cheddar cheese on your thick single head.

5. No more communion. Instead, Necco wafers. Six different flavors.

6. As long as you don't kill anybody or have sex with children, you can do whatever the fuck you want in my church.

7. But if you so much as look at an altar boy the wrong way, you don't get transferred to some distant parish in Nova Scotia—no, no, no, no, no. You stand naked in the middle of Times Square wearing a giant neon sign that reads, I CARRY A TORCH FOR KIDS WHO CARRY CANDLES.

8. And guess what? No more magic, no more burning bushes. If you screw up, the Virgin Mother doesn't appear on the back of a highway sign in Texas or on a blueberry muffin someplace in the Midwest or in the form of tears running down the face of a statue in the middle of the Emerald Isle. She shows up in your driveway in full 3-D like Ray Liotta in *Goodfellas*. She pistol-whips you, and then She sets your pants on fire.

9. When it comes to healing in the Lapsed Catholic Church, here's how it works. Unlike Benny Hinn, who places his hands on the foreheads of supposedly blind people, pushes them to the ground, and then they miraculously regain their sight, in my church, if you're blind and I put my hands on your forehead and push you to the ground, guess what? *You're still blind.*

10. Everyone's forgiven, by the way. Frank Gifford—Marv Albert—Ted Kennedy—Richard Nixon—Al Sharpton—Bill Buckner—everybody's forgiven. Except for O.J. I hope his kids pull a Menendez on him. And then *they'll* be forgiven. Ten times over.

11. Penance? Here's your penance: Bring two cases of beer

and three hot pizzas to the Lapsed Catholic Church Softball Field, which is directly across the street from the Catholic church. On Sunday morning at nine o'clock. We're gonna sit around, play softball, drink beer, and eat pizza. That's your penance. Because sin is in. And so we begin.

—*Denis Leary*
COMEDIAN

92

I start with a simple reality-based thesis: What's good for women is good for America. Not just because we're a majority of our country's population. Or that women voters demonstrated our political power by providing President Clinton's re-election margin of victory, though some of us would have preferred Hillary. But because a quick trip through history reveals that women thinkers and activists have been a key force in most of the great social reforms that have made America great.

Here's a small sampling of what women helped initiate and achieve: abolition of slavery, free public schools, public and occupational health programs, social services and welfare, pensions, maternity and child care programs, family-planning and reproductive rights, affordable housing, the Equal Pay Act, the GI Bill of Rights, environmental protection, civil rights and affirmative action, the founding of the United Nations, the nuclear test ban, and, most important, women's suffrage.

It took American women a century of struggle just to win the right to vote. I've always thought it was more than a coin-

cidence that I was born in 1920, the year the suffrage amendment was finally put into our Constitution. I was born with a
mission I've followed since I could walk, read, and raise my
voice: women must have an equal role with men in shaping
and carrying out our country's priorities, policies, and programs—in government, in the economy, in civil society, and
the private sector. Fifty-fifty, or as close as we can get.

(I make exceptions for certain realities: I do not advocate
voting for a woman just because she's a woman. She has to be
committed to policies benefiting women and their families to
get my vote. Unisex public toilets for men and women should
not be mandated, pleeez! Women should not share with men
the right to pilot U.S. military planes designed to drop nuclear
bombs on men, women, children, and all other living things.
No one should have that right.)

In 1997, women held only about 11.5 percent of the seats
in Congress, 21 percent of state legislature seats, and 3 of 100
governorships. One way to change that outrageously low representation is for political parties to give priority to encouraging women to run, nominating women candidates for vacant
seats and in other contests until parity is achieved. Parties
should support electoral reforms such as multimember districts in which the electorate can vote for both a man and a
woman. Campaign-funding reform is a must: spending limita-
tions, guaranteed extensive free TV/radio time for candidates,
a low ceiling on paid advertising. Political power should be
transferred from the corporations to the people. Political parties should open community-based centers (not the old-style,
boss-run party clubs) in which ordinary folks, men *and*
women, can help make public policy, from the grass roots up.

It would take hundreds of pages to list all the ideas and
proposals women have offered to make America better. In fact,
they're already in print. In September 1995, seven thousand

U.S. women went to Beijing to participate in the UN's Fourth World Conference on Women, some as delegates or observers, most as advocates for women's agendas. The UN conference, including the U.S. delegation, approved a Platform for Action that covered twelve major areas of concern to women. The following year, the President's Interagency Council on Women solicited the views of women across the country through questionnaires. Hundreds of ideas poured in. The council held a national teleconference in September 1996, hooking up with meetings in every state, soliciting women's views on what they want to see in a Women's National Action Agenda. The result was a seventy-page document spelling out an impressive agenda of policy goals, changes, and commitments needed to make America a better place for women and men, girls and boys. The U.S. women's movement is alive, diverse, and bursting with great ideas.

Our challenge: Are American men ready to speak out, organize against, and shame the minority of males responsible for our culture of violence, sexual abuse, harassment, degradation, and economic exploitation of women?

The crosscutting theme: Men must be willing to work in equal partnership with women for a better America and a better world.

—*Bella Abzug (1920–1998)*
ACTIVIST

93

America would be better if teenage romances (and even casual acquaintances) didn't lead to disease, infections, and even death. The physical pain of sores, intensified periods, and infections that won't go away is exceeded by the emotional pain of feeling unclean and betrayed by a lover or friend.

America would be better if teenage "love" didn't lead to precious newborns who arrive in incomplete families ill prepared to nurture them. Many of those little ones never have the opportunity to fulfill their great potential. Almost weekly, attention in the halls of Washington turns to the broader, catastrophic social consequences caused by the annual arrival of babies in hundreds of thousands of incomplete families.

America would be better if teenagers who can't decide what to wear to school were not faced with deciding about the life of an unborn child. For those who make a tragic mistake, no court decisions or adult rhetoric can keep them from feeling that something terrible has happened and that they will never be the same.

America would be better if the country were not filled with teenagers whose hearts have been broken by the cotton candy of physical intimacy. They have found the aftertaste empty and bitter. There is no latex protection for the heart and soul. Teenagers listen to the rationalizations of "liberated" adults, but in their hearts they know they have violated important values and that their innocence is forever gone.

America would be better if parents, teachers, government leaders, community leaders, sports figures, entertainment stars, and religious leaders spoke with one voice to say to teenagers:

- Sex is one of God's most beautiful and imaginative creations, and likely will be a source of great joy and human warmth in your life.
- God, who designed both human beings and sex, is the only true authority on sexuality. Fortunately, He sent us

an instruction book. He says that sex in marriage will be a source of great joy as "two become one." He also says that sex in the context of monogamous, lifetime relationships means babies will arrive in complete homes, no one will get sick, and no one will be left bleeding from the tearing of the glue bonds that sex always creates.

- God also says that in every case, sex outside marriage is morally wrong and—in the end—will be the occasion of pain. Our culture desperately tries to drown out His voice, but nothing can change truth.

Teenagers by the hundreds of thousands are joining movements that highlight making a promise to wait for sex until marriage. Millions more would do the same thing if important adults in their lives modeled and communicated a consistent message in that direction. Teenagers are perfectly capable of making promises and living consistently with those promises—and they will if adults will get over their own moral and practical confusion and give the young the clear direction and inspiration they need. America would be far better for it.

—*Richard Ross*
RELIGIOUS LEADER

94

I think we should give early childhood classes in kindness, compassion, responsibility, respect, and tolerance. We start them young in everything else; why not educate them in such basic tenets as how to be a decent human being? And make the parents come to a few of the classes. It's inevitable that in the early stages of implementing such social consciousness, we would have to deal with tired old prejudices and fears of anything different from us.

We seem to forget that we are a pluralistic society, home to people of many different races, nationalities, cultures, religions, and sexual preferences. Too many of us insist on believing ours is the right and just way and should be imposed on others.

And while I've got my moment on the soapbox, could we please take politics and morality out of the bedroom? Don't tell me what to do or not do in the privacy of my home, and stop using so-called moral issues for personal and political gain. Let's remember separation of church and state and stop letting opportunistic religious leaders buy off our politicians. Aren't political office campaigns supposed to be based on skill, record, and ideas? Pandering to people's moral concerns while tickling their thirst for scandal is a nasty and irresponsible way of avoiding the important issues, such as, can you do the job? Personally, I like the idea of our politicians being sexually alive—as long as women in office have the same right, of course! I think if people made love more, there would be less violence and hate. In fact, that old '60s slogan "Make love, not war" wasn't such a bad idea.

How about classes in how to be a good mate and lover, say around the age of eighteen? You think I'm kidding?

—*Candida Royalle*
EROTIC FILMMAKER

95

The easiest way to make America better is to stop spending enormous treasure and human effort on forced schooling of the unprivileged young. By "unprivileged" I mean the bottom 90–95 percent of our population, not the ghettoized poor. Public education, as it is called, is actually the most fantastic intellectual confidence trick of the century and probably of all time.

Compulsory schooling was a phenomenon borrowed from Prussia by the emerging industrialist classes of the four great coal-producing powers (the United States, Germany, England, and France) to prepare society for a highly centralized, mass production economy designed to replace the small entrepreneurial/agrarian economies of tradition. The development of coal, in conjunction with a reliable steam engine, made such a dystopian polity possible early in the nineteenth century.

Men could finally be like gods; at least a small fraction—perhaps 5 percent—could be, because high-speed machinery eliminated the *necessity* of regarding labor as fully human. The reality of laboring lives and parochial village concerns upon which graceful lives of wealth had uneasily rested up to that point could finally be discounted. But for this to happen, several things had to be managed.

First, an industrial proletariat—a landless, lightly rooted mob—had to be created. This was relatively easy to accomplish in England and on the Continent, where freedom traditions were squarely in the hands of a hereditary aristocracy. Where traditions of *noblesse* existed, they were overthrown by burgeoning commercial, industrial, and financial interests.

But in America a powerful economy and society had arisen on the tradition of independent livelihoods, fluid social classes, and the Reformation doctrine "Every man his own priest." Whereas elsewhere forced schooling was an underlining of the new moral world developing, in the United States it was essential to the *making* of the thing.

Forced schooling in America served a dual function: (1) the creation of a mindless proletariat stripped of its traditions of liberty, independence, fidelity to God, and loyalty to family and land; (2) the creation of a professional proletariat, suitably specialized to serve functionally in a highly centralized corporate/bureaucratic economy.

Next, a mass mind had to be created, a mind lacking critical dimension, dedicated to the proposition that one got ahead by pleasing authority, and trained to regard advancement principally as the road to increasing one's consumption. Forced schooling was (and is) the vehicle that drove the young to this end. The 20,000 walled and gated communities of America, a number rapidly growing, are only one of the tributes our disintegrating society pays to the class habits learned in school.

Over time, compulsory schooling in America has recreated the English class/caste system under the pretext of concern for the poor. It has dumbed down the American mind, artificially imposing a bell curve on the young as a justification of things as they are. It has crushed the average home owner with a stupendous burden of taxation to support a world that would have disgusted George Washington, Tom Paine, or Thomas Jefferson.

Forced schooling was imposed in America to turn back the promise of America's Revolution—to free the common man and woman to be whatever they had courage to be and to dream whatever dreams they pleased. Forced schooling is choking America to death, leveling it to a global standard. God help us.

Institutional schooling must be destroyed.

—*John Taylor Gatto*
AUTHOR/EDUCATOR

96

Most Americans, I believe, are deeply passionate about *something*. Politics. Technology. Art. Sport. Entertainment. Money. While most of us are long on passion, too many of us are short on commitment. Commitment to something . . . hopefully something socially redemptive. America's problem, then, is a commitment problem. To wit, the advice of my grandmother, whom we affectionately call Big Momma:

> *Once a task you've first begun, never finish until it's done.*
> *Be the labor great or small, do it well or not at all.*

—*Tavis Smiley*
AUTHOR/NEWS COMMENTATOR

Turn off the television.

Go outside.

Walk.

Walk someplace wild.

Breathe.

Breathe deeply.

Open eyes. Open ears. Look. Something just flew. Listen. The rustling of wind through leaves. Patience. A bird is perched on a branch of an aspen. Blue. Bluebird. An early arrival of spring. Sit down. Sit on a fallen log. Look up. The bluebird is still. Not for long. It flies, a flash of indigo against green. Green thoughts. Thoughts like water. The sound of water becomes clear.

Rise. Walk. Breathe deeply once again. Mind wander to the stream. Stream of desires. How is it we have so little time to wander in the woods, in the desert, on the beach, away from noise, away from cars, computers, faxes, and phones? Here is the stream. Kneel by the stream. Hands in the water. Water on the face. Refreshed. Rejuvenated. Rejoined. Nature. True nature. Mysterious. Unagitated. Whole. Hands on the earth, the health of the land is our own.

Return.

Return home, where our notion of community can expand to include all living things.

The land—may we love the land—our divine birthright and responsibility. *O beautiful for spacious skies.* America. The wild imagination of open spaces is another pledge of allegiance.

—*Terry Tempest Williams*
AUTHOR

ABOLISH THE PEREMPTORY CHALLENGE

For days, even weeks, before a trial begins in this country, each side's lawyers can maneuver and wrangle over who gets to serve on the jury. Foreigners think this is crazy, and they're right. Great Britain recently provided that the first twelve names randomly picked from the box should normally be the ones who serve, with the result that jury selection in Britain now lasts closer to a lunchtime than a lifetime. It's time we did the same.

"Peremptory challenges" let lawyers reject a certain number of prospective jurors, in some cases a dozen or more, without saying why. They underpin the $200 million jury-consulting industry, a vast business based on whispering into lawyers' ears, telling those with factually weak cases to boot engineers (too "analytic"), and advising on whether a soap-opera-watching Episcopalian retiree is better or worse for the case than a Subaru-driving, split-ticket-voting bank teller.

Lawyers in big cases accordingly launch questionnaires in which jurors—who aren't there voluntarily, remember—must disclose intimate data galore, including their incomes, whom they live with, their magazine-reading and churchgoing habits, and much more. (Privacy advocates, your beeper is going off!) Refusing to answer may be punishable as contempt of court.

Results in hand, the lawyers begin bickering while jurors cool their heels reading novels on benches. New York found that even modest cuts in peremptories would spare its citizens the equivalent of three hundred conscripted person-years annually—time spent not in hearing important cases but in being prevented from hearing them.

It might be worth a high price to get better and surer jury

outcomes. Unfortunately, the effect is to lower, not raise, the accuracy of jury findings. One major aim of peremptories is to bounce those who bring any sort of real-life expertise to the jury room. Another is to eliminate "opinion leaders" for the other side who might help colleagues see through manipulative trial tactics.

Juries are supposed to represent a cross section of experience. Yet peremptories allow the defense to exclude everyone who has fallen victim recently to a major crime, just as prosecutors can exclude everyone with a relative in prison. And given all the lip service "diversity" gets nowadays, it's downright incredible that the whole point of peremptories in case after case is to discriminate along otherwise suspect lines. (The Supreme Court has only recently, and nearly unenforceably, tried to ban the use of peremptories based on race or sex.) The crowning absurdity: lawyers come to court charging an employer, say, with age or religion bias and immediately begin kicking jurors off the panel based on their age or religion. It's another example of how our legal system punishes others for offenses it's constantly committing itself.

—*Walter Olson*
AUTHOR

cathy®   by Cathy Guisewite

ANY DEDUCTIONS THIS
YEAR FOR THE EXTRA
EXPENSES WOMEN INCUR
TRYING TO DRESS APPRO-
PRIATELY FOR THE TWENTY
DIFFERENT IMAGES WE'RE
SUPPOSED TO MAINTAIN?

NO.

ANY WRITE-OFFS FOR THE
UNPAID TIME WOMEN SPEND
CREATING RELATIONSHIPS,
WITHOUT WHICH THERE'D BE
NO FAMILY VALUES BECAUSE
THERE'D BE NO FAMILIES??

NO.

ANY ALLOWANCES WHATSO-
EVER FOR THE FACT THAT
OUR NATION WOULD
SCREECH TO A HALT IF IT
WEREN'T FOR THE UNDER-
PAID, OVERWORKED WOM-
EN CHEERFULLY WADING
THROUGH THE MUCK??

NO.

FORGET UNCLE SAM.
WHAT THIS COUNTRY NEEDS
IS AN AUNT SAMANTHA.

—*Cathy Guisewite*

CARTOONIST

100

If everyone would just shut up for an hour, we might be able
to think . . . maybe even about how to make America better.

—*Loretta LaRoche*

HUMORIST

101

America is such a violent society. People on the streets are
dangerously well armed, and the police (as evidenced in the
April 1997 North Hollywood shoot-out) have to make mad
dashes to the gun store to stock up. So many steps removed

from hand-to-hand combat, guns make killing a remote-control response. The best thing we could do for this country is take those 200 million handguns and make them obsolete. Or how about outlawing or controlling the sale of bullets? As the availability of ammunition (especially for assault weapons) dried up, guns would become less and less dangerous to society.

—*John Davis*
FILM PRODUCER

102

If you want to build a better America, volunteer. Volunteering is free. It's easy. And it builds the habits of the heart that lead to a better future for the next generation.

I started my political career by putting my beliefs into action as a volunteer. In the late 1960s, the Transportation Department wanted to put a sixteen-lane highway through my home, the Fells Point neighborhood in Baltimore. I volunteered to take on City Hall and stop the project. Thanks to a bunch of noisy, do-good volunteers who wouldn't take no for an answer, we kept them from paving over one of the liveliest neighborhoods in Baltimore.

Here's what I learned from volunteering:

Volunteering transforms people. It instills a sense of "yes, I can," and it creates a powerful antidote to victimhood.

Character and competence aren't limited to one particular social class, gender, or race.

By trying to save a community, by building a playground or painting a house or stopping a highway, you build a community. You build that community's heart as well as your own.

Consistent habits of the heart are the key to volunteering. You must volunteer every day, by practicing random acts of kindness and good manners.

Good public policy can encourage volunteerism, but it's ultimately up to each one of us to volunteer to do the things that make a difference and make America better. That's how you build a better America.

Volunteering isn't an event, it's a way of life.

—*Barbara A. Mikulski*
POLITICIAN

103

One hundred and fifty years ago, the slave owner's mansion was an island of comfort surrounded by a plantation of sweating slaves. It didn't last. Likewise, America can't last as an island of delight in a world of agony.

To make America better, we have to make the world better. That means higher wages. Unions. The right to speak your mind. Literacy. Stable populations. No more population explosions. Women's rights.

I'll be eighty years old in 1999, so, like most folks my age, I tend to be pessimistic. But if there still is a human race here in a hundred years, I'm convinced it will *not* be because of any one big organization, big church, big government, big political party, big corporation, or big slogan. Big organizations attract the power-hungry.

We will be here because of tens of millions of little organizations throughout the world. We'll disagree on so many things it'll be hilarious. Save this. Stop that. But we will agree on a few main things, such as it's better to talk than shoot. And bombs always kill innocent people, whether in Oklahoma City or Hiroshima. Likewise, chemical warfare and bacteriological warfare, land mines. And when words fail (they will), we'll use sports, the arts, good food. One woman told me, "Don't forget hot tubs."

In a frontier community folks will have to work together. In every neighborhood, in every house, on every block of every city, we will have to learn how to cooperate again.

—*Pete Seeger*
FOLKSINGER

104

America is, by far, the greatest democracy in the world. However, its role as a world leader will continually be diminished until it deals with the crisis that defines its urban communities. In order for America to become a better nation, it must first acknowledge that there is a crisis in urban America and resolve to solve it. The crisis will not be solved by merely building more jails to incarcerate those who have committed crimes; it will require investments in the two most critical areas that contribute to criminal activities: lack of education and lack of access to jobs.

It is obvious that the public education system in the majority of these communities has failed several generations of young people by not preparing them for successful global competition. The failure of the public system in these areas is evidenced by high dropout rates, low reading, math, and science scores, violence in schools, and overcrowding. I have consistently called for measures to challenge the public school system, including vouchers and charter schools, so that its monopolistic hold on our nation's youth can be broken and that urban public schools may reemerge as viable institutions for learning. Thomas Dewey stated, "Education is the great equalizer." That statement is no longer true for those students who are locked into urban educational systems.

Without addressing the failures of the public schools in urban America, we cannot hope to have the productive society that we strive for. A quality education has long been a cornerstone of achievement in this country, and too many of our children are being let down in this regard. Even as municipalities commit an increasing amount of resources to their educational systems, public schools continue to produce an inordinate number of dysfunctional graduates who are ill prepared to be competitive in the labor market. These young people, by virtue of their lack of competent vocational training, are on the fast track to either being a burden to our social service programs or being incarcerated. This nation cannot stand by idly and lose another generation of youths to inferior schools and hope that we will be able to compete with other world powers in industries that require proficiency in science and math.

When addressing the needs of urban communities, it is imperative to remember that these areas also need new economic strategies and investments to make them as thriving as their surrounding suburbs. In too many cases, there are no employment opportunities located near the places where poor and lower-income people live. It is impossible to conceive that in this time of economic prosperity, there are still large sections of urban America that do not have adequate supermarkets, banks, and other essential services. Urban commercial strips must not be ignored or redlined by developers and banks that are looking to participate in community redevelopment. It is evident from the thriving economies of commercial entities on the fringes of these urban communities that there is enough purchasing power within urban America to sustain them. The common excuses for not investing in these communities—crime and a lack of a talented labor pool—are no longer valid as these areas have been addressed in the past five years in most urban areas. The reversal in crime cannot be sustained, though, if there are no employment opportunities in these communities to give their residents, especially the young ones, a viable way to provide for their families. Investment in these communities should be one of America's top priorities if we would like to continue to be looked upon as the leader of democratic societies and not a country that has a wealthy privileged class and an impoverished underclass. Professor Michael Porter of the Harvard University Business School has indicated that inner-city economic development is a necessity and can be achieved through the creation of new models that are driven by market economies rather than by government and social service organizations.

It is my belief that as this nation moves toward the next millennium, it is imperative that America not continue to neglect the development of its urban centers. By concentrating on the needs of the educational and economic infrastructure in these communities, America can proudly say that it is still living up to its standard as the greatest democracy in this world.

—*Floyd H. Flake*
POLITICIAN

Imagine we lived in a world where election day was valued as much as Columbus Day and registering to vote was a requirement similar to registering for the draft. With this level of individual political responsibility, America would be a country *by the people, for the people.*

Based on recent elections and the legislation resulting from them, the most pressing issue facing this country is lack of participation in the political process. In New York City alone, there are 2 million eligible but unregistered voters. Some people do not think they can vote—because they are too old, once imprisoned, or homeless. But people adversely affected by recent changes in the government are the ones not showing up to vote. Of those who voted in 1994, 33 percent identified themselves as conservative, white evangelicals. Only 6 percent were under thirty years old, and only 23 percent made less than $10,000 annually. Only 19 percent of all Hispanics and 37 percent of all African Americans voted in 1994.

My motivation toward "educating" and increasing the electorate recently took a very realistic turn when I spent election day volunteering as a "door clerk for the handicapped." I spent the day seeing all too clearly the discrepancies that still haunt our country and being humiliated by your average Upper East Sider (for non–New Yorkers, this commonly used term denotes someone who is white, privileged, and rarely compassionate). I was shocked by the scant turnout and by the relative lack of diversity among the voters. Most were female, the majority were white, almost all were over the age of forty—and many were disgruntled. All of a sudden I saw the statistics come to life. I felt resentful toward the "elite" few who were motivated to vote, frustration toward those who just "forgot" or "couldn't be bothered," and sad for those who (yet again) didn't have easy access to it.

We really do wait until things are "that bad" before we become involved in making them "better." We need to start making the feminist link between *the personal* and *the political*. The facts that people don't have health insurance, that a proposed bill would discontinue the Safe and Drug-free Schools program, that we spend more money on promoting our military than on supporting our schools are just some examples of how our *personal* lives are directly impacted by these *political* decisions. We can no longer afford to let these things "happen" to us.

Now that the number of registered voters is on an upswing (74 percent of the voting-age population is registered to vote), *we need to focus on voter education*. We must ensure that we are voting for the person who is most likely to represent us and the issues we care about. Voter education could become a part of History 101, and registering to vote at the age of eighteen could be as exciting as getting your driver's license is for many people. We must fight for an honest exchange of information between and about candidates and encourage and support candidates who will represent our interests. Additionally, we must impress upon people that voting isn't the most we can do—it's the least. Casting our votes responsibly is the first step; what follows is holding politicians accountable for their promises and helping Congress look and think like the majority of Americans.

When all is said and done, fighting for reproductive freedom, affirmative action, and a national health care plan will no longer be necessary, nor will it be viewed as radical. This can only happen when America is a truly participatory democracy—when every voice is heard on election day and every other day, too.

—*Amelia Richards*
WRITER/ACTIVIST

106

We need to be a Gumpier America. Listen to Mom. Love someone unconditionally. Tell the guy in charge you have to pee. Walk fast before you run. Get a best friend named Bubba. Gosh, let's also talk to a few more strangers while we are waiting for the bus.

—*Steve Tisch*
FILM PRODUCER

107

"It is time for a new generation of leadership . . . for there is a new world to be won." These words of our great president John F. Kennedy have never been more relevant than in today's political climate. Bottom line: the political process—government's ugly stepsister—has been slipping since Nixon went medieval in the early 1970s, and is now at an all-time low. Today, political leaders spend endless hours "dialing for dollars" to pay for issue-deprived media campaigns and to fight with one another about whose transgressions were the most egregious. As a result, many Americans, especially young ones, understand politics to be skewed toward money and inexorably corrupt.

But we should not let our frustration with the political process turn us away from government. Government works— just look at Social Security, Medicare and Medicaid, our national highway system, or our public higher education. There is no question that our government provides us with services and opportunities that are unmatched by any other country. If government is to continue to be a force for good, we must demand changes that will shake the political process and return power to the people.

Here are two suggestions:

1. Scrap our Daddy Warbucks campaign finance system and make candidates responsive to concerned citizens, not deep pockets. Provide candidates with two options: the public will fund you to a reasonable amount, or, if you choose to spend more than that amount, you will receive *no* public funds and must raise all money privately. And make the networks and cable companies provide free media time—the only airtime candidates should be permitted to use. Incidentally, this system would replace the Supreme Court's *Buckley v. Valeo* paradigm (a court case that allows individuals to raise and use private money for campaigns) that is selling out our democracy.

2. Push for a constitutional convention where We, the People, choose citizens—not elected officials—from every community to evaluate the goals of government. A constitutional convention would address concerns such as whether health care, the ability to run for public office, and affordable, quality education should be birthrights for all Americans or merely privileges for the rich. This would be the best way to get ordinary citizens back into the driver's seat.

Government of the people, by the people, for the people . . . it's time to make it reality. Let's clean up the political process and restore confidence and purpose to the great American experiment.

—*Christopher Cuomo*
ATTORNEY/ACTIVIST

108

In a country that tends to be eager to note trends, there's one sweeping the country that hasn't been acknowledged: Women are leaving their marriages in droves. Well over 50 percent of all new marriages will end in divorce—and of those divorces, roughly 70 percent will be initiated by the wife. If any other institution had such pathetic stats—if more than half of all church members were leaving the church or soldiers the army—we'd scrutinize those institutions for flaws. We'd have programs set up to investigate: experts trying to fix the problems.

Yet even those aware of this epidemic continue to reiterate the myth of women's happiness in marriage. People can't let go of the idea that marriage is women's natural habitat, a cozy, nurturing institution in which wives inevitably will thrive. Yet study after study shows that men are the ones who flourish in marriage. Men, not women, wilt and die outside wedlock. Wives, by contrast, are one of the most depressed segments of the population—with a rate of depression three times greater than that of unmarried women, three to five times greater than that of married men.

Many a woman says she wakes up in the first year after marriage and finds she's changed; she doesn't feel quite like herself anymore. Attaining the coveted role of Wife, with all its responsibility, approval, and status, has effected small, insidious changes in the very parts of her that she treasured most—and that attracted her husband. She feels miscast. Her marital pleasure has morphed into stress, self-censure, self-doubt, and a sense that she must become a "better" wife.

How to make America better? Make marriage as nurturing an environment for women as it is for men and children.

Interestingly, women who don't undergo these insidious changes, who are more focused on pleasure than on becoming "better" themselves, are more likely to have marriages they want to stay in. Pleasure seems to be the basis, not the downfall, of a good relationship—and possibly the antidote to the divorce epidemic.

So, instead of dismissing "fun" as trivial or irrelevant to marital longevity, we could urge married couples to continue to make their own delight a priority. We could encourage women not to turn into Wives. Instead of talking to young women about goodness and duty, we could focus on fun and pleasure. If you were a young bride, which would you want to settle down with?

—Dalma Heyn
AUTHOR

109

GOAL-ORIENTED NEIGHBORHOOD POLICING: MAKING AMERICA BETTER AND SAFER

Having spent most of my life in law enforcement, the first thing that comes to mind for improving America is reducing crime. There are other areas that we need to work on, such as economic growth and improving our public schools, but until we get a handle on crime, we can't make progress in other areas. Safe streets and schools are the keys to improving our economic and educational climate, and the key to lowering crime is goal-oriented neighborhood policing.

What does goal-oriented neighborhood policing mean? The first component, "goal-oriented," refers to a style of policing that requires police managers to analyze local conditions, identify problems, then devise clear and concise plans to rectify those problems. For decades, the answer to nearly every crime problem from drugs to guns was simply to put more police on the streets. Sometimes more is better, but a uniformed presence alone is not enough. Even more important than how many police officers are hired is how those police officers are used. Whether you're on the battlefield or in the boardroom, formulating effective strategies is what makes the difference between winning and losing.

Of course, once plans are made and goals are set, it's also important to have a means of measuring progress. In the New York City Police Department, that means took the form of the CompStat process. We use state-of-the-art computer technology to track the incidence of crime, precinct by precinct, block by block, as well as the number of arrests that are made each week. We then use that information to make precinct commanders directly responsible for the crime that occurs in their neighborhoods. We look at the incidence of crime because all the arrests in the world won't matter if the overall crime rate keeps rising. We consider it a job well done only when crime goes down, not when arrests go up.

The second component, "neighborhood policing," is just as important as the first. No law enforcement agency can hope to do it alone. If the police are to be effective, they must have the support and the assistance of the citizens they serve. The way to get that kind of support is to foster mutual trust and understanding. Today's police officers have to be ready to deal with people who come from many different backgrounds. The only way to do that successfully is to employ courtesy, professionalism, and respect in every encounter with a citizen. Promoting that kind of model is as important a strategy for fighting crime as any other. When the public and the police are at odds, the only group that comes out a winner is the criminal class. When the public and the police work together, neighborhoods become safer and the stage is set for other improvements.

Goal-oriented neighborhood policing has worked well in New York City. In 1996, we reduced crime by 15 percent, and homicides were the lowest in three decades. I know it can work elsewhere.

—Howard Safir
POLICE COMMISSIONER

110

☛

—Ruben Bolling
CARTOONIST

TOM the DANCING BUG

-PRESENTS-

BY
RUBEN "WONK" BOLLING

5 SIMPLE STEPS TOWARD A BETTER AMERICA

① IF THERE CAN BE A DEATH PENALTY, SURELY THERE SHOULD BE A LIFE-EXTENSION REWARD. EACH GOOD DEED ENTITLES YOU TO ONE CLONE OF YOURSELF.

OPTIMAL ALLOCATION OF KACZYNSKIS:
ZERO TEDS   TWO DAVIDS

DIST. BY UNIVERSAL PRESS SYNDICATE

©1998 R. BOLLING   TOMDBUG@AOL.COM   W/O 1/25

② YES, SIMPLIFICATION SHOULD BE THE PRIMARY CRITERION FOR OUR TAX SYSTEM, BUT THE "FLAT TAX" IS STILL TOO COMPLICATED. JUST DIVIDE UP THE BUDGET AND SEND EVERYONE A BILL. (EXCEPT THE RICH -- THEY ALWAYS FIND LOOPHOLES ANYWAY, SO IT'S SIMPLER JUST TO LEAVE THEM OUT.)

"THIS IS SO MUCH SIMPLER!"

"NO MUSS, NO FUSS."

③ FOR A CRIME-FREE, CIVIL SOCIETY, WE SHOULD FINALLY GIVE THE "RIGHT TO BEAR ARMS" ITS FULL AND INTENDED MEANING -- AND GIVE EVERY CITIZEN PUSHBUTTON ACCESS TO AMERICA'S NUCLEAR ARSENAL.

④ WE LOST THE "WAR ON DRUGS" BECAUSE OF THE DRUGS WE CHOSE TO BATTLE. WE SHOULD DECLARE WAR ON DRUGS WHOSE USERS HAVE SOME REGARD FOR THE CRIMINAL JUSTICE SYSTEM. SO, LEGALIZE LSD, COCAINE AND HEROIN! OUTLAW ROGAINE, CHABLIS AND MARIJUANA (MEDICINAL ONLY)!

"FREEZE!"

"IT'S RECREATIONAL! I SWEAR!"

⑤ GIVE EVERY CITIZEN THE RIGHT TO POLLUTE 1/250 MILLIONTH OF THE CURRENT LEVEL OF POLLUTION. CORPORATIONS THAT WANT TO POLLUTE HAVE TO BUY THE QUOTAS FROM INDIVIDUALS.

"COME ON -- WE NEED 5,000 MORE WATER POLLUTION UNITS!"

"UNITED MILLS IS ON HOLD..."

111

HEALTH INSURANCE
FOR EVERY AMERICAN

Politics is the art of the possible. And sometimes figuring out what is possible is itself an art.

I believe strongly—and have for some time—that it is in our clear national interest to provide health insurance to every single American.

Our health care system is broken. It doesn't work particularly well for those who are fortunate enough to have coverage, and it's even worse for those on the outside.

Almost 41 million Americans have no insurance; one quarter of them are children. Millions more have skeletal policies that cover only catastrophic illness.

Most of the uninsured are hardworking, middle-class Americans who either aren't offered health insurance through their employer or can't afford the coverage that is offered.

For those without coverage, their health care choices are virtually nonexistent. But their lack of coverage, in fact, limits the health care choices of those with insurance.

Among uninsured people, illnesses that could be prevented or easily treated go untreated, become more serious, and require expensive emergency procedures and protracted hospital stays. The costs of that emergency care are passed on to the rest of us in the form of increased premiums, leading to fewer health care choices for all of us.

Why should we insure all Americans? Because it's in our economic interest to do so. Because all of us want to live in a society where basic human needs are met, not ignored.

The United States is the only industrialized nation in the

world without a comprehensive health insurance system that guarantees medical care for all of its citizens.

By tackling this admittedly thorny issue, not only will we guarantee affordable health care coverage to all Americans, we'll also signal to ourselves and the world that the United States is capable of doing something big.

—*Jay Rockefeller*
POLITICIAN

112

The problem with the world is us, and the prescription for all bad behavior flows from the same crime of unfairly taking power over others. From the beginning, one tribe has taken another into slavery and warriors have subdued those with smaller swords or slaughtered them and their families during dinner or sleep.

Why do people kill? Because we can. When we *uncreate,* we are like God. If we could remove this wrongful inclination from our genetic code, people would not wish to read books like mine, nor would I feel compelled to write them.

I am often asked why psychopaths are what they are and why mothers murder their children and husbands beat their wives and street hooligans kill for twenty dollars or perhaps a car. Remember the formula. It always applies. Every aspect of evil manifests itself in power. We are all about power and lust for it and will do anything to have it. We will steal and torture, lie and humiliate and cheat and laugh at pain. We will take our own lives violently to punish and injure those we leave.

Power is as grandiose as being a celebrity or the president and inspiring awe or as niggling as a secretary slighting the new person on staff. Oh, how good it feels to get that power rush through an unkind word or clever comment at another's expense or through money and, always, sex. Rape is power. Pedophilia and child abuse are power. Assault, mutilation, abduction, stalking are power. The ultimate overpowering of another living creature, of course, is murder.

We can leave the world a little better than we found it if we seek power with all our might, gain it fairly and rightly, and, most of all, use it judiciously and for good. Then our fruits will be charity, love, a kind word, a steady arm on rain-swept steps when one is old and infirm and lonely.

—*Patricia Cornwell*
AUTHOR

113

Growing up Asian American in America, for me, has meant having strong parents who stressed the importance of a good education. My family and I were immigrants to America. We arrived in Manhattan after a long ocean journey across the Pacific when I was eight years old. I entered the third grade not speaking a word of English. The initial years were difficult, but my parents never lost their confidence in the future. Education, they emphasized, would be the key to our advancement. And it was.

For the past thirty years, many colleges and universities have adopted admissions policies that had the effect of constructing incoming classes along national population ratios. Academic standards were loosened for some racial groups and tightened for others, all for the express goal of achieving some ideal racial composition. Today, these actions have sparked sharp debates on how best to achieve racial equality and whether discrimination can ever be justified in the cause of diversity.

The real issue, however, must be how best to prepare students to enter institutions of higher learning qualified to learn. The foundations of a good education must begin at the elementary and secondary levels, where, unfortunately, many schools have not proven capable of the task. Allowing parents the freedom, through a system of vouchers, to send their children to better schools engages and empowers the parents in the education of their children and compels inferior schools to improve their performance. School choice gives all children access to better education. This is one way to make America better!

—*Elaine L. Chao*
SCHOLAR

114

Ban all television shows where journalists or politicians shout at one another.

The food-fight atmosphere that infects so many television talk shows has had a coarsening effect on the political culture. The high-decibel nature of public discourse has been amplified by the noise level of the talk-show world, which rewards the most outrageous opinion mongers. The point is not so much to persuade as to posture, to score points, to slam-dunk the opposition.

The fatal flaw of these programs is that they oversimplify

complex issues by boiling them down to artificial, liberal-versus-conservative positions. Nuance and details are lost as journalists exaggerate their beliefs in an effort to become TV celebrities. Politicians, too, have learned that the way to get precious airtime is to deliver succinct attacks rather than seek common ground. These loudmouth shows have been a blight on the body politic. The audience should rise up and pull the plug on them.

—*Howard Kurtz*
REPORTER

115

As America celebrated Independence Day in 1996, my family and I attended a backyard barbecue on Chicago's South Side honoring four men who appreciated the real meaning of freedom.

Kenneth Adams, Verneal Jimerson, Willie Rainge, and Dennis Williams had just been released from prison after collectively serving sixty-five years for a crime they did not commit. Two of the men had been incarcerated on death row—Williams for eighteen years, Jimerson for eleven—and were awaiting execution when irrefutable proof of their innocence, and the guilt of four others, was discovered.

While many media accounts deservedly credited three of my journalism students (who uncovered new evidence in the case as part of a class project) for helping to create the storybook ending, in fact it took a far more complex and inspirational team effort to reverse one of the worst miscarriages of justice in American history.

The seemingly impossible happened when people from different professions and different walks of life finally got involved. And they weren't the type whom the public nowadays would expect to step up and make a difference.

There were a dozen high-priced lawyers who volunteered their time at the expense of their paying clients. There were television and newspaper reporters who stopped chasing celebrities to investigate the cause of four unknowns. There were whistle-blowers from an impoverished community who came forward to tell the truth at great risk to their personal safety. And there were the four men themselves, who had steadfastly maintained their innocence at the price of their liberty, repeatedly refusing deals that would have set them free in exchange for testifying against one another.

Now, on July 4, they came together, African Americans and Caucasians, wealthy and poor, to share their triumph and realize the endless possibilities that result from active participation for a common good.

But amid the revelry there was an undercurrent of anger and bewilderment: How had the criminal justice system so miserably failed these men? How many other miscarriages of justice are there? What can be done about them?

Tragically, the men fell prey to a combination of factors that I have commonly seen in wrongful convictions: law enforcement officials who rushed to judgment in response to public pressure to solve a horrible crime (an interracial gang rape and homicide), prosecutors who were more concerned with winning than justice, and court-appointed lawyers who did not have the resources or the skills to defend their clients.

It is hard to say precisely how often such circumstances converge. However, the evidence is clear that the problem of wrongful convictions has been exacerbated by the rapid expansion of our prison population (now topping 1 million) at a time when we are curtailing safeguards against mistakes. Even if the error rate in convictions is only 1 percent, there are approximately ten thousand prisoners who today are wrongly incarcerated, and experts estimate the number to be much higher.

This staggering violation of human rights can best be addressed by restoring time-honored legal protections: the right to bring evidence of innocence to court whenever it is discovered, the right to competent counsel, and the right to a thorough appellate review of capital convictions—pretty basic rights, it would seem, but among those gutted by self-proclaimed reformers who have capitalized on constituents' fear of crime (itself more media-generated than reality-based).

So I was filled with conflicting emotions on that Independence Day weekend. Four men, who had long been wrongly deprived of liberty and the pursuit of happiness, were finally home. But it was sobering to think that our legal system had been ready and willing to take the lives of two of them and that both would have been dead long ago under present-day "reforms."

Looking ahead, then, there is a challenge for all of us—to make America better by restoring fairness to the criminal justice system and by joining the fight to help those who remain unjustly behind bars, men and women who must wait for outsiders to make a difference.

—*David Protess*
PROFESSOR

116

GET EVERYONE WIRED

Here's the biggest thing that will happen in America—and the world—by the new millennium: hundreds of millions of computers will be connected to a global network and be able to exchange information, ideas, and entertainment. Stay awake, this is important! Almost every piece of knowledge or news will be available to every person anywhere who can use a computer. This will be bigger than television in shaping how societies work and economies grow. It has the potential to give every person equal access to information. It also has the potential to leave a lot of people behind—if they don't have the chance to get wired. America would be a stronger, more prosperous, and more equitable place if we dedicated ourselves to making sure that every high school student has a personal computer by the year 2001. It would not, in fact, be all that expensive. The alternative would be.

—*Walter Isaacson*
MAGAZINE EDITOR

117

How to improve America?

Now, that is one question no one has ever asked me to answer! First, I would change the process of how America's government is elected. Second, I would install a time-tested method of arriving at decisions for administering this country.

Thank God I don't have to educate America about Native

American processes used since the beginning on how we select clan mothers, chiefs, faith keepers, and healers. I'd still be talking and writing into the next millennium.

CHANGING HOW AMERICA ELECTS ITS OFFICIALS

All politically elected people are selected by the people who vote through the electoral system of running for office. All those elected are determined by the size of their budget and who champions their cause. The ones with the most money and the most influential friends are thrust into runoffs or primaries for a particular seat or office. Those who don't make it can still enjoy the possibility of an appointment to some high office by their party.

In this process, what happens to the person with the best ideas or the best vision or who was working on the good road? I'm sorry and our country is worse off, because without money those ideas will remain only visions elusive of ever being practiced.

The change, then, must be the first step to allow those people with vision to ascend in a system where those ideas can be employed without their being denied due to their financial status or political cronies.

1. Television, radio, and the print media all must provide equal access, without demanding the funds. Equal time and space must be given free to all who apply for public office.

2. All systems of transportation should be equally available to all candidates free of charge.

3. The money for the airtime and transportation should be

paid for by the XYZ companies who are paid the fees by the wealthy candidates, such as your publisher and railroads and airlines. Through these changes in the method of the initial process, those without the money would be ensured of reaching the final stage and even capturing the big prize.

ADMINISTERING THIS COUNTRY

Since the beginning with native people and indigenous people of the Western Hemisphere, clan mothers have made our system what it is: strong, true, and free of corruption. It is the clans and clan mothers who ultimately select the chiefs and faith keepers, who in turn select the young men and women to carry out the necessary duties to run the nation's business. No one gets to be chief solely by being popular in a campaign or having a lot of money to buy the clan mother vote. Most chiefs I know are lacking funds of great size, yet are rich with wisdom and walk the good road. They carry on the directives, without question, of all required by the clan mothers. It is, then, the clan mothers who directly and indirectly oversee the nation.

MY CHANGE

There should be a cabinet of five women to administer the national and international affairs of this country and act as a further voice of reason in the checks and balances. These appointments would be for life and would be first selected by the combined houses of Congress and then filled by the selection of surviving clan mothers.

They would guide the course of the country, using the president as their executive director. All matters would be approved by the Senate, House, and judiciary; legislation would ultimately need to be ratified by all five clan mothers before becoming law.

The composition of the five must be one Native American, one Black, one White, one Hispanic, one Asian American.

It could never be done, you say? I don't see us being very far away from changing some basic rules in this country. We can at least start with the trace of an idea. Who wants another Vietnam? Watergate? Wounded Knee? Or to be stuck with one leader not walking that good road? With clan mothers directing our course, the seventh generation would be assured of a good America to be born into.

—*Dennis J. Banks, aka Nowacumig*
ACTIVIST

118

THE CHALLENGE OF THE NEW MILLENNIUM: EDUCATING OUR YOUNG PEOPLE FOR TOMORROW'S MARKETPLACE

Although America faces an array of challenges as we prepare to embark upon a new millennium, in my view there is no single greater threat to our future economic prosperity, national security, and social stability than an uneducated workforce. In fact, if this nation is to compete and win in tomorrow's marketplace—driven and dominated by digitalization, deregulation, diversity, and globalization—we must develop a workforce that is more highly skilled and computer-literate than ever before.

In many ways, the dynamic forces shaping the new economy are already evident today. For example, in 1996, according to *Business Week,* the high-technology sector of our economy accounted for 33 percent of the growth in the gross domestic product. No wonder recent studies have found that in the next century more than 75 percent of our nation's kindergarten students will hold technology-based jobs that do not exist now. With this new generation of jobs will come a new frontier of competition. That is, the future success of today's young people will depend upon their ability to compete not only with their peers in Memphis, Atlanta, New York, Chicago, and Los Angeles, but with those in Beijing, Frankfurt, Buenos Aires, Kuala Lumpur, and Johannesburg.

As a public-policy maker at the national level, I have a responsibility to ensure that young people all across America are prepared for this new frontier of global challenges. To that end, I am a strong supporter of the federal government playing an increased role in our elementary and secondary education system, particularly when it comes to national achievement standards, school construction, and classroom technology.

According to the General Accounting Office, the price tag for rebuilding, revitalizing, and computerizing our nation's schools will far exceed $100 billion—a cost that states simply cannot shoulder alone. Every community across America, whether urban, suburban, or rural, has dilapidated and outdated schools that are literally crumbling to the ground. That means millions of young people—in cities such as Memphis, Miami, Portland, and Pittsburgh—are being deprived of the chance to learn in clean, safe, and computer-accessible classrooms. However, by making technology and infrastructure investments in our schools through the use of tax incentives and formula grants, the federal government can help states address these dire problems, without supplanting the primary role that the states traditionally have played in the realm of elementary and secondary education.

In the past, America has shown the leadership, courage, wisdom, and conviction to rebuild Europe through the Marshall Plan, propel a man to the moon and *Sojourner* to Mars, discover blood plasma, turn back the cold forces of communism, pave the Information Superhighway, and help define the principles of freedom, liberty, and justice for all. Surely, then, if we commit ourselves to working together, we can be enterprising and resourceful enough to ensure that every young person in America is exposed to the world of ideas so that they can take this great nation from what has been to what can be in the new millennium.

—Harold E. Ford, Jr.
POLITICIAN

119

As the mother of two young children, I feel a deep stake in the future of the America we adults are making for our children and for the generations that are to come. It's almost overwhelming at times to contemplate the troubles they will inherit from our ignorance or lack of vision, and it leaves me wondering, as a middle-class (nonfamous) working woman, what I can do to contribute to leaving something better than I found it.

Thinking in terms of improving the quality of life in America, one simple, rather embarrassingly old-fashioned idea comes to mind: civility. These days we deal and are dealt with in such a brusque, oftentimes rude and dehumanizing, manner by our fellow citizens. How often do we greet people on the street with a smile or a hello, how often do we really look into the eyes of people helping us at a store or restaurant counter and genuinely thank them for their help? People really don't expect to be treated with dignity anymore, and it's quite a mind-altering experience to actually connect with the people you encounter on your daily grind and see how the authenticity with which you interact with them is reflected back in such a humanizing way. In fact, it's quite powerful to turn cordiality and warmth on people who are expecting you to find them invisible and watch how much effect you have on their self-esteem.

I recently attended a lecture given by James McBride, the author of *The Color of Water*, his memoir of growing up in a poor black family helmed by a white Jewish mother. The audience—entirely white, well educated, and well off—asked Mr. McBride what they could do to combat racism. He said he didn't believe in committees or legislative action. He suggested that people just look at how they treat the people they run into in their day-to-day life, what level of equality and dignity they mete out on a personal basis. From this, he said, a real solution to racism and any sort of prejudice in our society could begin to bloom.

My children speak up. They salvo off hellos to the neighbors; they meet the glance of the man at the pizza shop and thank him heartily for their "slice." They offer help to someone in need of directions or information with courtesy. And they're surprised when someone is rude to them, when someone doesn't treat them with respect. I hope that all of us still have it in ourselves to make these simple gestures an expected fixture in our common life, these small yet profound ways in which any one of us can freely participate in making America better.

—*Tracy Mann*
MUSIC PUBLICIST

120

When Reginald Fessenden made the first public radio broadcast in December 1906, how could he have imagined Tesla's infant medium playing a role in the unification of America, as a muse of democracy and a key element in the groundwork of the civil rights struggle? His was a one-man show on which he fiddled his own version of "O Holy Night" and read a Bible verse to an audience of ships at sea.

By the 1930s, one in five households owned a glowing, church-shaped "wireless," and the mysterious unifying powers of radio became manifest. By then there was an *audience* out there, living in widely disparate circumstances and locales but all listening to the same programs, songs, and commercials. Orsen Welles, and then FDR, learned in their own ways that for all practical purposes the vast, unseen multitude functioned as a single entity. Once unified in panic by imaginary Martians, it then resolved to win the uneven struggle against powerful, malevolent opponents who were all too real.

In the 1950s, white teenagers discovered black music and all but forced it on the air with their burgeoning economic clout. In short order, Top 40 radio became a bubbling cauldron of ethnicity. Rock, R&B, folk, country, novelty records, dance records, all commingled on the personality-radio shows of Alan Freed, Cousin Brucie, B. Mitchell Reed, and the Real Don Steele, among others. The races were brought closer together. White musicians such as Al Kooper and Steve Cropper learned the blues from Muddy Waters and B. B. King (as a white youngster, my first real job was at Motown). Top 40's vital music mix inspired rebellion, and eventually, as Billy Joel has said, "It was rock 'n' roll that brought the wall down."

Today the airscape has changed for the worse as radio stations play to audiences discrete as segments of an orange: one station for rap, another for classic rock, this one for easy listening, that one for country, and so on. Recently one station in L.A. changed from an all-Beatles to an all–Broadway show format. Economic factors aside, the end result will be the demise of the homogeneous "us-ness" that radio and television created in the first place.

I asked my nineteen-year-old son, James, a music major at Bard College, if I was imagining things.

"The audience is so compartmentalized that it is a rite of passage in your own group to hate everything else," he said.

Make America a better place? Stop dividing us along musical lines: the black from the white, the old from the young, the educated from the blue collar. Put personality Top 40 back on the air. Make Dick Clark secretary of the interior. Keep your MTV. I want my *American Bandstand*.

—*Jimmy Webb*
MUSIC PRODUCER/SONGWRITER

THE COMMON GOOD

My Aunt Eula, who farmed long ago in East Texas, said something to me back then that applies to making America better today. She said, "The water won't ever clear up till we get the hogs out of the creek."

There's our problem! The hogs are in the creek, fouling our economic, political, and environmental waters, and our challenge is to get them out.

This is no easy task, since an ethic of hoggishness has come to prevail in all aspects of our culture. It is an ethic unabashedly celebrated by business and financial leaders and actively promoted through the policies of political leaders—an ethic that says: I got mine, you get yours; never give a sucker an even break; I'm rich and you're not . . . *adiós,* chump.

This philosophy, now being pursued with a vengeance by the elites on Wall Street and in Washington, rejects the founding American principle that we're all in this together, instead giving "private gain" primacy over "common good." It expresses itself economically in today's so-called prosperity, in which the financial gains being generated by the many are being hauled off almost exclusively by the privileged few. The Dow Jones soars, corporate profits skyrocket, and every CEO gets fatter than a butcher's dog—while eight out of ten Americans see their incomes and futures stagnate or fall. Sure, Wall Street is whizzing, these folks say, it's whizzing on us.

Likewise, this philosophy expresses itself politically through a corrupt and vacuous electoral system that operates as a pay-to-play game. This is why my party—the Democratic Party of Jefferson and Jackson, Roosevelt and Truman, JFK and LBJ—has abandoned the Kmart crowd and is hanging out with the same Gucci-and-Pucci set that owns the Republican Party. The result is a politics (and, consequently, a government) that leaves out or kicks out America's workaday majority—which is why more people now watch the Super Bowl than vote for president. Some people say we need a third party; I wish we had a second one.

To make America better, we need a mass political movement that appeals again to the common good and invites the workaday majority to start shoving the hogs out of the creek. I suggest that this movement should be rooted in the political philosophy of my daddy—a man who didn't know he had one.

When I was a kid, Daddy and a half-dozen other parents started the Little League program in my hometown of Denison, Texas. They got the land, cleared it, built the park, sponsored and managed the teams, announced the games on a squawking PA system, and ran the snow-cone concession. Even after I moved beyond Little League, Daddy continued to work at it, because it was not about his kid but all kids—the common good.

He believed in that concept of everyone pitching in, whether to build a kids' ballpark or a public library (a building I don't recall him ever entering, though he was proud it was there for the community). He applied his philosophy nationally, too, believing that everyone should be taxed so basics like health care could be available to all.

Not that he was some kind of do-good, touchy-feely liberal, for God's sake—indeed, he called himself a conservative. He had grown up on a Depression-era tenant farm and worked mightily as a small-business man to provide a middle-class life for his family. What he learned along the way was that "everyone does better when everyone does better."

That's what passes for political philosophy in Denison, and it remains the best I have found in all my travels elsewhere.

—*Jim Hightower*
RADIO HOST

122

Nothing brings people together like food. Eating is something we do every day of our lives that has community values right at its heart. If you eat a perfect peach—intense, ripe, irresistible—you'll begin to understand that when people truly care about what they eat, fruit is grown for flavor, agriculture is local, farmers respect the land, communities cohere, and families flourish.

Children need to learn what real food can be and what it takes to grow and prepare it. Otherwise, good food will remain a privilege of the few and not a human right. Of all human rituals it is probably the family meal that best transmits such basic human values as courtesy, honesty, and generosity, yet fewer American families than ever are sitting down and eating together. We are losing touch with authentic, simple pleasures, and our children are growing up without having ever fully educated their senses—or their consciences.

Producing, preparing, and sharing food teaches us that actions have consequences, that survival requires cooperation, and that people and nature are interdependent. With the family meal vanishing, we have to develop a curriculum in the schools that will teach these fundamental truths to our children. In my neighborhood in Berkeley, California, at the Martin Luther King, Jr., Middle School, parents, teachers, and neighbors are developing a program called the Edible Schoolyard where the students are involved in all aspects of caring for an organic garden, and also with preparing and cooking school lunches using the food they grow. I believe that every school in the country could have an organic garden integrated with both its academic curriculum and its school lunch program—if not a garden on the school's own grounds, then an association with a nearby farm or a community garden project.

A curriculum of gardening, cooking, and eating will teach good nutrition, good citizenship, and good stewardship of the land, while rewarding the learners with enormous sensual delights. And along with the immediate gratification of eating beautiful food from their own gardens, students will experience a deeper, moral satisfaction for having done the right thing for themselves, for one another, and for the planet.

Although we need such a national curriculum for the schools in order to renovate the goal of learning, we also need to physically renovate the schools whose facilities have become derelict and dangerous. We must correct what Jonathan Kozol has called the "savage inequalities" in education and make it a national priority that every child be taught as well as every other child. As William Julius Wilson and others have proposed, a federally funded WPA-style job program could provide a restoration corps to rebuild deteriorated schools in the same inner cities that suffer most from unemployment. Children deserve to be educated in places they can be proud of, in schools that are safe, physically inviting, and inspiring—and even beautiful.

As educators from Socrates onward have recognized, the goal of education is not the mastery of various disciplines but the mastery of oneself. An equal education will best teach children this self-mastery by preparing them to live responsibly in the world. And responsible living is learned best at the table, in the kitchen, and in the garden.

—*Alice Waters*

RESTAURATEUR

123

Reprinted courtesy of Tom Toles. Distributed by Universal Press Syndicate.

—*Tom Toles*

CARTOONIST

124

Being a woman, I find that my thoughts go immediately to our country's unfinished business—I am firmly convinced we cannot move forward in a successful manner until we "clean house."

I would address my remarks to the young man who so ably represents the magazine *George*, John F. Kennedy, Jr.

My request to you, John F. Kennedy, Jr., in order to heal this nation of its doubt and cynicism, would be to release the documents contained in the archives concerning the assassinations of your father and your uncle. The American people have a right to public inspection of these papers. Wherever they are and whatever they may be, these papers have been funded by our hard-earned money through taxation.

Give us credit for our intelligence, and don't treat us like unenlightened children! We have had enough conjecture. We all read *The Pentagon Papers* and were none the worse for its disclosures. We went through Watergate and almost impeached a president for just the second time in our history.

Do us the honor of respecting our ability to read the truth—no matter how brutal the facts may be.

Give us the "closure of disclosure" so we can use our hard-won right to vote, instead of leaving us forever in the vague limbo of an unresolved murder mystery.

Let us read the mass of collected evidence so we can be part of the justice system we all proudly declare is our unalienable right.

Who better to lead this crusade of the Disclosure Act of 1992 than John F. Kennedy, Jr., the son of the murdered president and the nephew of Robert Kennedy; Robert Kennedy, who gave us all such hope that the first murder in his family could be examined and possibly avenged?

Clean up our lingering doubts! Let those papers out of the archives. Let history be the judge rather than a few frightened men who have guarded this information for far too long. If we live in a dishonest past and present, how can we expect to live in an honest future? The unsolved murders of your father and your uncle stand as a metaphor for the lack of honesty in our present lifetime.

Own up to the American people with this information that we know exists and is being withheld, so we can get past this stumbling block to the next century.

—*Esther Williams*
SWIMWEAR EXECUTIVE

125

One thing we must do to make America better is reform the way we help people with disabilities who need some assistance.

Our current system of long-term care, as it is called, is provided through Medicaid, the state and federal health care program for poor people. But Medicaid requires people to become poor and remain poor as a condition of assistance, and it is heavily biased toward expensive institutional care, too often forcing people needing long-term care out of their homes and communities and into nursing homes and other costly institutions at taxpayer expense.

Though people of all ages have disabilities, the largest segment of those needing long-term care are seniors, and with the demographic tidal wave of baby boomers becoming older, the pressure on the current long-term care system will increase significantly. We need to reform this costly, inefficient, and often callous system of long-term care right away.

The answer is long-term care reform that focuses on flexible consumer-oriented services that allow people with disabilities to remain in their homes and communities.

Most of the long-term care in this country is provided at home by family members. Putting someone in an institution completely supplants that informal care. Providing targeted assistance can help people with disabilities remain in their homes and communities with their loved ones, and it can delay and even prevent the day when the person needing long-term care must enter a costly institution.

I think reform of this part of our health care system is a measure of how we value our people and what priorities we are going to set for our future.

—Russell Feingold
POLITICIAN

126

America, honey, you need a makeover! Listen, girlfriend, what are friends for but to tell you that you're a mess? You've got a good heart, but you are sporting some seriously outdated fashion trends.

Face it, doll, khaki is tacky. That militaristic look went out with the Cold War. And it's just too spendy for your pocketbook, when there're so many other things you could spend your money on, such as education and helping out poor folks.

About this corporate drag you're always going out in—America, dearie, Nike is not a designer label. You need to get yourself off this corporate bandwagon. Why'd you ever think it was a good idea to allow companies to have so much power? Support some local businesses for a change instead of these chains.

You've really got to cut down on the oil. All that smog—that dingy brown really just isn't your color. Free public transportation would be a more becoming style.

Everyone knows that cigarettes are coffin nails, but you're still spending all that money on tobacco subsidies. And you end up paying for the health consequences too.

Those red ribbons you're pinning to your lapel are a nice thought, but are you really doing all you could? You could go out and volunteer or get involved with needle exchange.

America, darling, I know you've got gay friends (like me, for instance), but you could really stand to get over your homophobia. I've heard you say that gay folks getting hitched is somehow threatening straight folks' marriages. And I've certainly heard bigoted things come out of your mouth about other groups of people too. You need to learn to do two things: mind your own business, but also treat everyone equally.

I'm not too impressed with those tacky polyester gowns you wear when you go to fund-raising balls. You get all dressed up, but don't you think it's a little hypocritical to get dolled up in such expensive drag when there're so many starving people in the world? In a way, I feel like I'm just feeding your vanity to even offer you these fashion tips when there are so many folks who can't afford even a single couture dress.

—*Larry-bob (Laurence Roberts)*
ZINE EDITOR

127

A few simple policy suggestions:

Renounce war and the capacity to make war, and stop all sales of arms abroad. That will immediately free at least $200 billion from the national budget. Then tax at 100 percent the trillion dollars added to the fortunes of the richest 1 percent of the country by the tax breaks they have received over the past twenty years. And establish a truly progressive income tax, from 90 percent at the very top down to 10 percent for middle-income people and zero for low-income people.

All that will create a huge pool of money, making it possible for the national government to do the following: guarantee jobs at adequate wages to anyone wanting to work; insist that these jobs perform the most necessary tasks our society needs; pay doctors and hospitals directly for all medical costs, ensuring free medical coverage to everyone; provide low-cost, good housing to everyone homeless or living in substandard conditions; clean up the water and the air; take the billions being spent for prisons and use it to double the salaries of schoolteachers; ensure good child care wherever needed; and create a non-GI Bill of Rights to pay for college education for anyone who can't afford it.

In other words, forget about being a Great Power. Eliminate the huge disparities in wealth. Be content with a peaceful, humane, modest country where neither the desperation of poverty nor the frenzy of monetary ambition becomes a cause for violence and madness. And the rights of aggrieved groups—blacks, Latinos, women, gays and lesbians, immigrants—can then be established in a kindlier atmosphere.

—Howard Zinn
AUTHOR/PROFESSOR

HOW TO REPAIR URBAN AMERICA

Talk of the "obsolescence of cities" seems to be fading for the moment; sharply declining crime rates in cities across the country are helping to spur the beginnings of a newly optimistic view of urban America. Even New York, long a familiar symbol of urban decay, is being recast as the "capital of culture," of "finance," indeed of "the world" by its tough guy, Mayor Rudolph Giuliani. And the media are celebrating the "renaissance" as avidly as they documented the decline. Record levels of tourism and soaring housing costs show that people are voting with their dollars. As cities ride the current wave of popular opinion and regain some of the cachet that they lost in their more-than-thirty-year decline, they have an opportunity to break free of the liberal pull of the policies and ideology of their past.

The age of the centralized, industrial metropolis has passed, but opportunities await those cities that can reintegrate their inner cities into the urban mainstream as they reweave themselves into the fabric of national life.

For the moment, the most important new opportunities for inner-city revitalization and employment are in retailing. With the overbuilding of suburban malls, developers and retailers (following immigrant entrepreneurs) are increasingly turning toward the untapped inner-city market.

Despite decades of liberal criticism of "dead-end" jobs, for most people upward mobility begins with entry-level jobs at low pay. At a time when one American in eight has worked at McDonald's at one point or another, "fast food outlets have replaced the army as the primary source of secondary socialization for people with limited skills," notes journalist Amity

Shlaes. Pizza Hut's chairman, talking about his stores in south central L.A., explained, "We teach people team building, time management, basic math, even how to assimilate."

The success of the new immigrants demonstrates that mobility must be pursued rather than provided. Whatever our desire for recompense, success has to be a matter of effort and accomplishment, not a gift of government. What local government can do, as it has to some extent in L.A. but less so in New York and D.C., is encourage the economic conditions that allow people to pursue their personal dreams.

Now, a century after the end of the Reconstruction period, when southern blacks were resubjugated under new forms of servitude, and twenty years after it was made clear that a second Reconstruction was shunting the sons and daughters of servitude into a genuinely dead-end welfare and social service economy, it's time to acknowledge that inner-city America will never be economically integrated until it fully participates in and benefits from the wealth-creating market economy. People everywhere in the world understand that wealth is created through market mechanisms; can we finally apply this to our own inner cities?

—Fred Siegel
AUTHOR/COLUMNIST

129

Americans are sadly lacking a sense of community. Community is *not* a romantic idea; it's a pragmatic coming together of people, and it's the only thing that really works. It's a natural human need, right up there with food, clothing, and shelter. We need it as we need air and water.

So what has happened?

One sad thing is how afraid Americans are of one another. Since this fear has most definitely not sprung from our souls, I've got to lay a huge chunk of the blame on the poor old media. So hung up on inflating their ratings, they often neglect the truth, consistently present images of the violent, the bad, and the nasty, and hype up pathetic stories to a titillating level.

How can we rally against something so all-pervasive?

The way I do it is to value the small/local, to become part of a community, to play my music, and to encourage people to look at life in a different way. As I travel around the country playing music—which, of course, is for a specific niche—I *do* see my audience as a community. And they (surprisingly diverse in age) are getting out of their houses and coming together, whether in rural New Hampshire, Seattle, or San Francisco. Quite apart from whether a song or any work of art supplies an out-front political message, the notion of people coming together to hear music or dance or see and talk about a play is really powerful.

This gives me hope for America forming a new sense of community. The only way I see things improving is when people get to know one another and discover common interests, common goals—without that we're in pretty tough shape.

—*Greg Brown*
FOLKSINGER

130

"I'LL HAVE WHAT THE GENTLEMAN OVER THERE IS HAVING."

—*Ophira Edut*
CARTOONIST

131

America's most pressing social issue—race—is greatly exacerbated by the erroneous assumption that harmony between Blacks and Whites is achievable only via the attainment of massive social integration. That is most unfortunate. While integration is clearly a valued process, it is not the promised land of social interaction; cultural pluralism is.

What is cultural pluralism? It is the acceptance and toleration of group differences; it is unity in diversity.

Today's working definition of integration is not achievable. That is because: (a) the only possible means of its realization is assimilation, and, for Black Americans, the melting pot is not and has never been a reality, and (b) the transplanting of Blacks beyond the geographic and cultural demographics that make them a "nation within a nation" is logistically impossible.

Structural integration, the association of Blacks in offices and other secondary associations, is a rapidly increasing reality. Personal integration, the binding together of the races in primary associations—families, churches, schools, etc.—is not. There are more Blacks living physically apart from other cultures today than ever.

But that should not bug or bother us. The opposite of segregation is desegregation, not integration qua assimilation as we have naively come to accept. Liberty and justice for all do not require the cultural homogenization of all.

Were we to make our goal the "fixing" of the Black community and not its "mixing" or melting into White America, we would be way ahead in our efforts to cure our nation's most perplexing social dilemma.

—*Calvin B. Rock*
RELIGIOUS LEADER

132

America has to make moves to become an honest nation. This cannot occur if the government is still carrying out its genocidal campaigns against the Indigenous Peoples of North America.

The U.S. government must stop using the Supreme Court to erode the treaties made with the Indigenous nations of this land. The next step would be to honor the Indigenous nations' right to jurisdiction, which would include the right to develop and regulate environmental policy within the boundaries of our nations as established by the treaties.

As an Indigenous Woman I live in an occupied land, invaded by pirates financed and claimed by European aristocracy. Eventually, those pirates established an illegal colonial government, with no regard to those nations that inhabited the lands before their invasion.

Genocidal campaigns were launched to eradicate the Indigenous Peoples who were living on the land before the invasion. Anything of worth was claimed by the colonial government. Eventually the colonial government entered into treaties with the leaders of the Indigenous nations that established the boundaries of those nations.

From early on, the colonial government violated the treaties it forced upon the Indigenous nations of North America.

To this day, the colonial government—now referred to as the U.S. government—has constantly violated those treaties. It has never provided the housing that was promised. Instead it has built inferior HUD homes, provided substandard health care, targeted Indigenous women with population reduction, usually in the form of sterilization, and removed our children from our homes.

Modern-day policies have included relocation programs that promised to educate and provide jobs if you left the land and moved to a major city. Once they got to the cities, they realized they had been abandoned and found no housing, no jobs, just more broken promises.

In the late 1970s, bills of termination were introduced into legislation to terminate all of the reservations in the United States. This was done so all of the natural resources the Tribes owned would no longer be within their control. Fortunately these bills were defeated when word got out that the sponsor of the bills had major landholdings under the names of family members, adjacent to a reservation that controlled the water rights. Water was needed to develop the land.

The right-wing racist, the "Father of War," openly admits his hatred for Indigenous Peoples and will never allow himself to honor the treaties his forefathers made with our Chief because he cannot stand that Indigenous nations may have something he cannot control. He must control it all, or no one will have it.

This land does not belong to us; we merely borrow it from the next generation.

—*Charon Asetoyer*
ACTIVIST

How can we make America a better place? What can a high-minded politician with vision and the gas of idealism powering him/her do? Careful reading of recent sociological studies, current events, and the dusty works of Havelock Ellis inspires in me but one new ideal. I think it is about time we move beyond the Sexual Revolution. I think it is time we separate the sexes once and for all. Adam and Eve's example in the Garden of Eden should have given us fair warning. The condition of men and women in the American military is warning enough. Men and women do not belong together unless properly chaperoned.

All the institutions where the sexes have been integrated are in trouble. The military, the universities, men's clubs—all have seen better days. There is no reason we cannot return to the all-female and all-male universities of yore. Surely if we wanted to we could field the fiercest all-woman army since the Italians' invasion of Greece. No woman who has tried to improve the cuisine of our heretofore all-men's clubs wants to continue the impossible task.

Statespersons, show some gumption. Get the boys out of the girls' hair and the girls as far removed from the lecherous boys as possible. Queen Victoria's vision of what we call "sexuality" was utopia.

—*R. Emmett Tyrrell, Jr.*
MAGAZINE EDITOR

134

This is an open letter to my teenage daughters about their future.

Dear Girls,

I've been asked to write about how I'd make America better, and it's *your* America I have in mind. You are two wonderful, lovely teenage girls, yet you are afflicted with a disease that is spreading rapidly in our country and around the world. I dream of a world in which your disease no longer exists.

Every day, three thousand children catch this disease: *they start smoking*. The percentage of teenagers who smoke is the highest it has ever been. Chances are, the cure lies within each of you—you must rid yourselves of this gross and harmful disease. I have exhorted you both to quit, and I will strive to see that others like you—other children and teenagers—never start.

An estimated 16 million to 17 million of today's kids will become regular smokers, and almost one third of them will die of smoking-related diseases. At your age, you can't fathom the meaning of mortality, so I must describe the dangers of smoking in a very graphic manner. The two of you should picture yourself standing next to a friend who smokes, and then consider that statistic. One in three of today's children who smoke will die of a smoking-related disease!

Cigarettes kill more than 400,000 people in this country every year. This exceeds the number of deaths from AIDS, alcohol, car accidents, murders, suicides, and drugs combined! The risk of you dying from this disease will begin to decrease on the first day you stop smoking, so I beg you to quit.

As an executive in the communications business, I am committed to helping to eliminate your disease. I will seek to ban all smoking in television programs produced and distributed by my company. I am aware that you and other teens absorb positive messages about cigarettes when you see television and movie stars smoking, and I will encourage the American entertainment industry to take a similar position. I will also urge television and movie companies to create and distribute anticigarette messages.

As a nation, we must adopt severe restrictions to prevent the spread of this disease and block cigarette companies from afflicting more of our children—a primary target of their marketing efforts. (Cigarette manufacturers spend in excess of $5 billion every year on advertising and promotion. That's more than $13 million per day!)

We must support all efforts to regulate tobacco and tobacco advertising and marketing, and not allow politics to water down any campaign to rid our nation and its children of this horrible disease.

I love you both,
Dad

—*Robert A. Iger*
TELEVISION EXECUTIVE

135

Turning the tide against alcoholism and alcohol abuse may be the most urgent way to improve American society in the next century.

As matters now stand, alcoholism is the number one health problem in America, as it is in Russia and many other societies. Fifteen million or more Americans are seriously addicted to alcohol. It is the dominant factor in their lives. This disease is now killing Americans at the rate of 125,000 annually—350 daily. One of those victims, who died at Christmastime 1994, was my daughter Terry. Her tragic death has deepened my own concern and knowledge about the ravages of alcoholism and the abuse of an ancient beverage that is generally pleasant when consumed moderately by people with no genetic vulnerability to addiction.

Alcoholism is a treacherous, seductive addiction that can hit any individual or family—rich or poor, educated or ignorant, strong or weak, creative professional or unemployed. It is responsible for filling more hospital beds and jail cells than any other factor. It causes more traffic fatalities, more child and spousal abuse, more rapes, more declining academic and athletic performance, more broken marriages, and more loss of jobs and productivity than any other cause.

One might expect the millions of bright and promising young people who fill our colleges and universities to be especially resistant to the abuse of alcohol. Such is not the case. Indeed, the practice of weekend binge drinking on a dangerous, excessive, and disruptive level has become the most serious problem on most of our college campuses, afflicting more than 40 percent of our students.

All these disturbing conditions call for a renewed consciousness and intelligent effort to deal with the abuse of alcohol in America. Parents need to be better informed of the dangers of youthful drinking and more aware of the signs of addiction in their children. Teachers and educators at the junior high, high school, and college level need to be especially involved in the effort to prevent, treat, and contain alcoholism.

It is important that every family and employer discover the

way to conduct an intervention with abusive drinkers who need to confront their alcoholism or excessive drinking.

On a public policy level and in our medical schools and treatment centers, we need more support for research, prevention, and treatment of alcoholism. Last year we invested $5.5 billion in research on cancer, heart disease, and AIDS. This is a wise investment, but we are devoting only a tiny fraction of that amount to alcoholism research despite the fact that this illness is often a contributing factor to the more heavily funded illnesses mentioned above.

Recently, Congress has eliminated treatment of alcoholism from illnesses that qualify for public assistance among the poor. This is an unwise and self-defeating economic move that should be reversed.

We are currently waging a war against illegal drugs coming into the United States from Central America. But the far more dangerous and destructive enemy facing America that we most need to confront to improve our nation is the abuse of a legal drug: alcohol.

—*George McGovern*
POLITICIAN/AUTHOR

136

WOMAN IN A BOX

On a clear, bright, early-autumn morning, the landscape of Manhattan at ground level is surprisingly beautiful—and provocative. On one corner, there are nannies with strollers and men and women carrying briefcases and cellular phones. They emerge out of apartment buildings with emerald green canopies and twenty-four-hour doormen. On another corner, just footsteps away, there is a skeletal, naked woman lying in a refrigerator box. Her sobs are audible even in the din of traffic. And in the interstices of these heart-wrenching sobs, she cries, "Help me! Help me!" Yet no one stops.

Passing her, on the way home from my run in Central Park, I hesitate. How many days has she been lying here in this box? How many days have I known she was here, suppressed this knowledge, and obliviously run past her?

I peer inside the box, am nauseated by the odor of feces, and begin to search for a police officer. There are no men or women in blue, and all the telephones in the vicinity are broken. I do not think to stop someone with a cellular phone, an obvious solution. Within ten minutes I am home eating my breakfast. And by the end of the day I have conveniently forgotten about the woman in the box.

I remember once, in Greenwich Village, there was a man, drunk, beat up, lying on the street, and people were stepping over him as though he were a rock or a log. I went to the pay phone on the corner, and when I explained there was an emergency, the young man refused to relinquish the phone. "Piss off," he said. "I'm looking for an apartment." I went into a café and had to beg to use the phone to call the police. It was perhaps five minutes or more before the manager agreed. And I thought then, we are the most heartless nation on earth.

After my encounter with the woman in the box—that was just two weeks after the death of Princess Diana in Paris—I telephoned Bernard Audit, a French attorney teaching at New York University Law School in the Global Scholar Program, and asked him about the French law—*Non-Assistance à Personne en Danger*—that was invoked in court when the judge charged the photographers. I had been astounded to learn there was such a law, a Good Samaritan law, and I wondered why we do not have such a law in the United States. Clearly, we need one.

There are profound philosophical understandings about the nature and obligations of citizenship implied in the French nonassistance law, M. Audit says, which evolved out of French social and political history, so different from our own. But there is also much we share, much perhaps we have lost or forgotten. A "person," as defined in the French law, is, for example, *any* person—princess or commoner, a woman in a box or a woman with a cellular phone—the law protecting both equally, a legacy of revolution.

In court, if we had such a federal law, we would all be guilty of ignoring the woman in the box.

—*Carol Bergman*
JOURNALIST

137

The Delphic Oracle advised Socrates "Know thyself"
Dying, Socrates said "All I know is that I know
  nothing"
Villon said "I know all there is to know except myself"
In youthful arrogance I stated "I know all there is to
  know
because there isn't that much to know . . . be rid of all
  the
nonessentials, maintain the essentials, and you'll know
all you need to know"
So to make for a better America
I say even if you do know all there is to know
know that this is nothing until you know yourself—

Know from whence you came and why—
Cease dumping upon one another—
And be kind, understanding, and regard people
as you regard yourself . . . we all face the universe
    alone;
terrible it is to become olding and lonely;
become wondrous or like all greatness, you will fade—

Civilizations have come and gone;
we're still on our first go-around;
Greece was but once; Rome the ancient one and
    Renaissance; twice—
What's most remembered of great civilizations?
Their poets, artists, philosophers, and few blessed
    leaders—
The individual usually plays a big part in this whorl of
    history—

Becoming older as poet
growing slothful and Buddha-bellied, and lost in a
    way
living as hermit for seven years in my apartment
I returned to Italy from the deathbed of my brother
    Ginsberg
hoping to find all that I naturally lost
but Italy wasn't where my ten-year dusting books of
    poems lay

I hurried back to America . . .
Crime has dwindled in the streets
(but they had to go ruin it and bring back Capital
    Punishment).

Anyway I'm back, and starting to work on my long-
awaited book
of poems . . . at least it gives me something to be
hermit about.

—*Gregory Corso*
PROFESSOR/POET

138

Want to make America better? Abolish multiple-choice standardized tests, I say! Think of it: more than 10 million of these
tests given each year, no one is immune or excused, even the
sandbox set prepping for preschool. You want to go to college,
business school, or law school, be an architect, financial ana-
lyst, or cosmetologist, the gatekeeper is how well you do on
such tests. Because these tests provide a number, a score, we
have a false sense of security and assume that there is some
scientific basis for their use. The problem is that the only
thing these tests predict is how well you will do on other multiple-choice tests! The truth is that they predict very little
about how people will do in real life. If we want a society of
professional test takers, of people who provide highly pre-
dictable and safe answers, I guess it's fine to rely on multiple-
choice tests. What I worry about is that these tests seem to be
stacked against just those sorts of people who might make a
difference, those who don't easily fit into a mold. Creative and
divergent thinkers who can see other possibilities are just the
ones who are often penalized by such tests. What if I can envision an answer that's isn't choice A, B, C, or D, what do I do?
Real life doesn't neatly fit into little bubble circles indicating

"one of the above." What happens to the man or woman who can think of a novel response that the more mundane test makers haven't even thought about? Rather than being rewarded, he or she is penalized and scores poorly. There is simply no test known that can judge or predict creativity, originality, or success in a chosen job, career, or profession. Let's end our national obsession with testing. When faced with a bulging folder describing the life and accomplishments of an applicant, on the one hand, and a simple score on a multiple-choice test, on the other, let's go for the real-life measure. Our society has much to gain by considering the full scope of a person rather than how well she or he happens to perform on multiple-choice tests. To make America better, we need our deepest thinkers, our most compassionate souls, our clearest visionaries. Simply said, we must focus on choosing the best people rather than the highest scores.

—*Dr. Sally Shaywitz*
PHYSICIAN/RESEARCHER

139

Over the last year or so, I've been very busy with three special projects, each close to my heart. One is an eyebrow-raising new album, *In a Metal Mood/No More Mr. Nice Guy*, a roaring big-band collection of heavy-metal classics. Second is championing the cause of Willy T. Ribbs, a man destined to be the Tiger Woods or Jackie Robinson of auto racing, in a quest to get him fully sponsored on the NASCAR racing tracks, piercing the last racial barrier in professional sports. And third is the production of *American Glory*, an unprecedented music video wedding the country's great patriotic songs with Norman Rockwell–type footage of our beauty and heritage as a nation.*

Each of these is a reflection of who I am and my intense love for this nation and our liberties.

Meanwhile, I've been making a speech around the country I call "Losing Liberty." Paradoxically, in this day of unprecedented civil liberties and acquired rights, it's obvious to me that America is losing its identity, its soul, its very character. People have become so afraid of stepping on toes, of being "politically incorrect," that we're becoming a homogenized, washed-out, intimidated, and bland people.

We're surrendering our freedom to express ourselves and our differences politically, religiously, and ethnically—in the name of the Constitution that was designed to protect those very liberties!

We're becoming so afraid of doing something "wrong" that we're becoming apathetic, passive, and noninvolved. We're even voting less and less, as if to say, "What difference would it make anyway?"

So what to do? Three things, maybe four. One, *care*—by God, if millions of Americans have *died* to preserve our privileges, we can at least care enough to use them!

Two, *be informed*—tune out Oprah, Rosie, and Geraldo once or twice a week; watch CNN and C-SPAN; and put down *People* and read *U.S. News and World Report*.

Three, *act*—vote, for Pete's sake; get involved in one or more organizations that are dedicated to reclaiming lost ground and rekindling the fire that used to be our American character.

---

*Editor's Note: Our contributor wrote this essay in July 1997.

And may I add a number four? *Pray*—read 2 Chronicles 7:14 for God's promise to America if we'll do our little part. The dream can yet be fully realized, the *glory* that was America *can* be regained.

—*Pat Boone*

ENTERTAINER

140

As all the many disorders, dislocations, and disempowerments that plague the people of the United States have been brought into such high and acute relief by the tragic death of the People's Princess, and as it has become all too abundantly clear that the gravest problem of all is the intolerable *distance* that separates Americans from their celebrities, the gulf that encourages all manner of unscrupulous chicanery on the part of unsavory celebrity middlemen, therefore be it resolved:

1. That an Estates-General of the Stars should be called to address this greatest question of our time, a body in which each of the six great celebrity communities (the fashion, cinema, athletic, television, music, and inherited wealth communities) will be equally represented and empowered with legislative and executive prerogatives, and will proceed to:

   (No, wait, one thing first: wherever they decide to hold the Estates-General, they must make both headlines and suburbanites *scream* with their rule-shattering outfits—I mean, nothing is more American than shattering rules, right? And nothing shatters rules and sees more efficiently to personal freedom than fashion, right? So costume must have a certain priority.)

2. Compose a National Mission Statement, a document that will rejuvenate our commitment to all the great goals that make our life as a country-community so meaningful and fulfilling, reconsecrating our nation as a Total Quality Democracy, where lifestyle righteousness is ensured by hundreds of locally designated National Excellence Teams;

3. Bravely pledge to stamp out things that are distinctly and identifiably bad, such as hunger and racism and classism and small-minded provincialism and all the attitudes held by that guy in the Amstel Light ads who wants to keep us from drinking Amstel Light;

4. Declare the year 2001 to be "Year One of the Disempowered" (the rest of the century following along in sequence: 2002 as Year Two of the Disempowered, etc.) and devise schemes by which the small, weak, feeble, and cute can enjoy enhanced, high-profile proximity to both A- and B-list celebrities;

5. See to much more rapid, efficient, and safe conversion of people's heroes into State Deities (i.e., through postage stamps, coins, statues, monuments, streets, parks, airports, the pattern they show when TV stations go off the air), regardless of such narrow concerns as nationality or living status;

6. Solve the question of campaign finance by declaring Commercial Sponsorship to be, officially and in perpetuity, the nation's designated economic order, beginning with the Estates-General of the Stars itself (the following

surfaces will be made available to the usual national advertisers: T-shirts, hats, telephones, the string and clips that hold reporters' credentials, tote bags, ballpoint pens, reporters' notebooks, portable fans, arena walls, and, for a premium, the entire Estates-General) and proceeding with all future elections, which will be referred to as "Revolutions" and sponsored by Nike.

—*Thomas Frank*
MAGAZINE EDITOR

141

In the nineteenth century, progressive thinkers made "girl advocacy" a part of their agenda for improving America in ways we ought to reconsider today.

In the 1870s, feminist Elizabeth Cady Stanton decried the ways in which young women slavishly followed fashion, and she spoke repeatedly about the need to encourage the creativity and spirit of female adolescents: "I would have girls regard themselves not as adjectives, but as nouns," she advised. Dioclesian Lewis, an eccentric Boston educator and health reformer, promoted practical rather than decorative education, good posture, and vigorous exercise because these were the best ways to prevent bad marriages and also prostitution. Young women with skills were not likely to end up in compromised positions, Lewis explained. (This wise observation came long before the current discovery of "self-esteem" as a critical variable in the development of adolescent girls.)

A great deal of Victorian thinking about girls was tinged

with elitism, repression, and efforts at social control, so I would not want to turn the clock back. Girls today are different than they were in the 1890s, and they have different needs and privileges, including the right to sexual expression. Yet many of the problems experienced by contemporary girls might be eased if we could recover the kind of broad moral commitment to them that drove conscientious parenting in the past, as well as strong community support of girls' social and emotional development. In 1900, many different kinds of women—at almost every point on the political spectrum—were committed to protecting and nurturing adolescent girls, largely through single-sex groups and associations in churches, schools, and the community. This meant that middle-class adult women were involved with girls other than their own daughters, something that does not happen often enough today except in our professional roles as teachers, social workers, psychologists, physicians, and nurses. At the end of the twentieth century, most of us who interact with girls are getting paid for it.

Dioclesian Lewis wrote, "My hopes of the future rest upon the girls. My patriotism clings to the girls. I believe America's future pivots on this great woman revolution." This may sound old-fashioned, but what if the women of the baby-boom generation began to feel the kind of moral imperative about girls that marked earlier generations of Americans? Couldn't we offset—or at least dilute—some of the crass commercial and sexual exploitation that characterizes female adolescent experience at the end of the twentieth century? We need to move off the stale idea that only conservatives or right-wingers want to "protect" girls or raise critical questions about contemporary culture's effects on their development. In fact, feminists and progressives need to begin to develop a code of sexual ethics that empowers girls in the Postvirginal Age. Ultimately, we need to face this fact: the way we protect and nurture young women remains a telling indication of our fundamental values and priorities.

—*Joan Jacobs Brumberg*

AUTHOR/PROFESSOR

Sylvia checked the social climate, then begrudgingly went to shave her legs.

142

© *Reprinted with special permission of King Features Syndicate.*

—*Hilary B. Price*

CARTOONIST

143

Young people in America today are faced with complex issues and challenges not seen by any other generation before them. Their worlds are constantly changing, and the events they deal with are not exclusive to poor and disadvantaged youths. Their issues, which become our concerns, traverse all economic levels, race, gender, and religion.

Their future includes, but is not limited to, being more competitive for a good education and rewarding jobs; resisting drugs and alcohol, gangs and guns; avoiding teenage pregnancies, domestic violence, and other health-related issues. They have to struggle with the question of "How can I make myself more marketable—what will separate me from the rest in terms of achievement?"

All these questions and concerns need to be heard. One way to make America better is by providing more of what these young people need: a dedicated ear. Someone to listen and to help make sound choices.

We, unfortunately, live in a society where competing interests have taken a toll on the family structure. From the extremely rich to the extremely poor, the youths of this country are not being heard. Families are suffering from a lack of time well spent and of sound morals and values—the basic tenets for effective growth and development of children.

Individually, we must step forward and commit ourselves to being sounding boards, not only for our biological children but for each and every child we come in contact with.

One doesn't have to be a role model, counselor, mentor, or source of economic help, but simply someone young people can call and talk to—someone they can count on to listen and who will not criticize or pass judgment.

This commitment will take thousands of us, working individually. It does not require a highly publicized effort. This should be part of the American culture, ingrained in our psyche as a great nation.

If each and every one of us were to make an effort to establish one-on-one contact with the next young person we encounter, the impact would be great. I think the number of violent offenses and counterproductive behavior by a growing segment of our young people would be greatly reduced.

Recently, I read a school's guidelines for student behavior. I was appalled at the unacceptable behavior categories because they contained penalties for the use and sale of drugs; bomb threats; possession of a deadly weapon, including explosives; extortion; bigotry; harassment of any kind; assault of an employee; and, a sign of the '90s, possession of a pager. This is why we need to take charge and make ourselves available to children. The majority of these offenses are felonies. Children in grade school should not be committing or exposed to these types of crimes.

We also have a responsibility to teach them the values that speak to respect for the life and property of others, as well as healthy self-respect.

I once heard a teacher say, "I tell my students on the first day of school, 'You have already earned an A in my class. From this moment until the end of the semester, it is my job to help you keep it.' "

It is the same with all youths. They start off on the right path, but very quickly the road starts to wind and curve. We have to be there at every turn to tell them how to maneuver and to encourage them to stay on a straight course. Equally important, we need to be there when, inevitably, they get off into the weeds. If we miss one curve, hoping that someone else will be there, that is when that child becomes vulnerable.

Our young people are America's greatest natural resource. Listening to and guiding them on a straight and successful course will make our country better into the twenty-first century and beyond.

—Beverly Harvard
ATLANTA POLICE CHIEF

144

The best way to improve anything about the world is to ask good questions. Since there is great confusion and even consternation about the role of technology in our lives, what we need are questions that will help us to know how to evaluate technology. Here are six such questions intended to provoke awareness of what technology can do and what it can undo. Question one (to be asked when considering the value of any new technology): What is the problem for which this technology is a solution? Two: Whose problem is it? Three: What new problems might be created by solving the old problem? Four: What people and institutions are most likely to be harmed by a new technology? Five: What people and institutions will most likely benefit? And six: What changes in language are new technologies generating?

Although different people will come up with different answers to these questions, it would be advisable for anyone who is asking them to keep the following two quotations in mind: First—Henry David Thoreau: "All our inventions are but improved means to an unimproved end." Second—Max Frisch: "Technology is the knack of so arranging the world that we do not experience it."

—*Neil Postman*

PROFESSOR OF CULTURE AND COMMUNICATIONS

145

THE *T&R* CHAIN-REACTION CORPS

My Better America is at the same time a great melting pot and a beautiful mosaic. A people rich in religious and cultural values who form the fabric of our democratic way of life. A people who stand up against hate, racism, bigotry, anti-Semitism, and all the anti-isms that would divide our nation. For when good people say "No" to hate, goodness prevails.

Each of us needs to become a *T&R* activist, personally practicing and promoting *tolerance* and *respect*. To that end, I would create a T&R Commitment Chain Reaction Corps that would reach out to parents and children, teachers and students, corporate executives and rank-and-file workers, politicians, journalists, law enforcement officials, athletes, and celebrities.

From the White House to the state house to city hall; from the boardroom to the assembly line to the farm; from the classroom to the playing fields, the message would go out that being tolerant and respectful is right, is American, is "in." There would be no formal membership, no dues, no oaths, no secret handshakes, no awards. Just the daily practice of T&R would make one a member in good standing.

Those who continue to believe in an America of their own image, who try to deter us and divide us, will surely fail because T&Rers will stand up, stand together, join hands, and say "No." Interacting the T&R way, one by one by one, should make America that better place we all seek.

—*Abraham H. Foxman*
NONPROFIT DIRECTOR

146

Wouldn't it be great if everyone could create his or her own world? You, see if that happened, you would have a lot of happy people coming together to create a perfect state, country, and world. If this world were mine, I would have rules. Make that one rule: mutual respect! Respect for the individual without regard to gender, race, religion, social status, or sexual orientation. And while we are at it, let's make Aretha Franklin's hit "Respect" our new national anthem.

—*E. Lynn Harris*
AUTHOR

147

The great national trouble is meanness. It has become accepted, legitimatized, rewarded. Meanness for its own sake, far from being scorned, has increasingly become the coin of the social realm. Those who refuse to deal in it find themselves outside the mainstream.

This is found in everything from political discourse at the highest levels of government to slogans on T-shirts on the streets of the smallest towns. There is a coarse bellicosity in the land that seems to thrive only because it is allowed to. Make a list of the dilemmas we as a nation face—gun violence, gangs taking over city neighborhoods, the wealthy living in fear of the impoverished and the impoverished seething with resentment of the wealthy, drugs being sold to children—and beneath the surface of nearly everything you will find one common factor, and that factor is meanness.

When the strong taunt the weak in sports contests, this is merely meanness disguised as something else. When Americans routinely treat strangers with a lack of civility—whether by using the foulest language in public places or by breaking the most elementary rules of daily life simply because they can get away with it—this is meanness as society's connective thread. Meanness goes beyond laws—you can't legislate against it, and indeed some of the most skilled practitioners of meanness are the very people who write the laws. They use it against one another—often with a vocabulary more polished than that heard on the streets but with the same devastating effect.

Which is to say: When a society turns mean and callous, it is difficult to go back again. When you choose to diminish someone, to make someone small, merely because you can do it, the person you are ultimately diminishing is yourself. Yet it goes on and on, the kind of thing that does not make headlines—and unless we figure out a way to reverse this, to start again on the path to routinely treating one another with dignity, the headlines will become even grimmer than they are now. The headlines will not specifically mention meanness—but that's what will be behind every word.

The only way to defeat this is person by person, day by day. There don't seem to be very many rewards for making this choice—sneering snideness, not voluntary civility and compassion, is the growth market—but we had better teach ourselves to start things moving in the other direction. If we don't, the real victims of the new national meanness will greet us every morning—staring right out of the mirror at us.

—*Bob Greene*
JOURNALIST

148

This world would be a better place if: Big Macs had neither calories nor cholesterol; cancer had a cure; race was never an issue; differences were appreciated; shoelaces never came untied; traffic jams and airport weather delays were unheard of; tee shots never hooked; news was beautifully written and accurate too; children looked up to Mother Teresa as much as they do to sports stars; we didn't need jails; rude people could be ticketed and fined; everyone loved to learn for the sake of learning; books entertained as many as television; farmers got the respect they deserve, teachers too; Congress was respected by the public and worked to keep that respect; big-band songs made the Top 40; apathy was unheard of; you could not only teach an old dog new tricks but make him computer-literate; children didn't have to worry; all parents were good ones; grandparents spent more time with grandkids; and you could have the fries too and not feel guilty.

—*Bill Barrett*
POLITICIAN

149

PUBLIC HYGIENE

Right before the 1996 Democratic Convention, the city of Chicago begged high-rise dwellers along the Gold Coast not to dump garbage out their windows. These wealthiest of Chicagoans live downtown, so their trash would be flashed all over the world.

Dropping garbage out the window? When they have maids and frequent garbage collection? It's not that the very rich are lazier or more shiftless than the rest of us—every park in the country is littered with trash, regardless of the race, class, or national origin of its users—just that their slovenliness seems more appalling. Every morning in the summer the beaches along the Gold Coast are hand-cleaned by people earning the minimum wage; similar people scrub out movie theaters following each show. The Gold Coast looks better than the poverty-ridden West Side because someone is always cleaning up after the rich.

We're obsessed with personal hygiene, showering, shampooing, and deodorizing once a day—or more. But outside the narrow sphere of our own bodies, we seem happy to leave our filth for someone else to worry about. This is true whether it's our parks, our lakes, or our countryside. For more than a century so many pollutants have been dumped into the south end of Chicago's lakefront that environmentalists estimate it would take five hundred years for the land to be restored to health. We're making a stab at cleanup, but only as a result of laws that were hard to pass and are proving hard to keep in place. No one voluntarily removes cyanide from industrial flux before pouring it into the ground or a lake.

That great observer of America, Alexis de Tocqueville,

wrote in 1840 that Americans were obsessed with the individual at the expense of the community. "Individualism disposes each [person] to sever himself from the mass of his fellows and to draw apart with his family and friends, leaving society at large to itself," he said, adding that such behavior "originates as much in deficiencies of mind as in perversity of heart."

It is pretty perverse to throw garbage onto the street, whether from a Gold Coast high-rise or a steel mill. It's as if we've retreated into such a narcissistic state that we can focus only on our own fanatically scrubbed images. If we could widen our gaze to take in our communities, who knows what problems we could take on? At a minimum, we'd live in a more pleasant country, and that would be no bad thing.

—*Sara Paretsky*
AUTHOR

150

We need to get over our hang-up about sex. If we would talk honestly and openly about sexuality and acknowledge that all of us are sexual beings, it would be much easier for young people to set boundaries or appropriately use contraceptives and/or condoms. Our unplanned pregnancy rate and rates of sexually transmitted diseases would go down. People would report sexual violence sooner, and guilty parties would be punished more quickly. Children who are planned and wanted at conception have a head start on life.

—*Margaret Pruitt Clark*
YOUTH ADVOCATE

151

A NATIONAL COMMITMENT
TO THE ARTS

Americans have a remarkably ambivalent attitude toward the arts. On the one hand, we celebrate and take pride in our most successful playwrights, actors, painters, and musicians. On the other hand, we are reluctant to recognize that the arts are an intrinsic part of our society and grant them the stature and support they need to thrive. The current effort to abolish the National Endowment for the Arts, led by conservative Republicans, is but the most recent manifestation of this attitude.

If America is to continue to be a major cultural force well into the next century, it must recognize that the arts are not just important to our society but a national responsibility, just as education, science, health, and the environment are national responsibilities. We need to stop squabbling over the National Endowment for the Arts (and its sister institution, the National Endowment for the Humanities) and develop an understanding and appreciation of the arts that transcends politics.

The conservative attack on the National Endowment for the Arts underscores the fact that before we can develop such an understanding and appreciation, we need to think far more about the arts than we currently do. The arts—painting, sculpture, dance, film, theater, opera, literature, and music, among many others—are part of our national patrimony, a vital element of what distinguishes us as Americans from the rest of the world; a reflection of our aspirations and goals, our anxieties and fears. The arts do not, however, exist in a vacuum. They require moral, intellectual, and financial support and, above all, talented artists capable of interpreting and reinterpreting our most deeply held thoughts and feelings. Often this results in works that challenge us to see and think in new ways. The most powerful and resonant of these can be as disturbing and unsettling as they are transformative and enduring.

The National Endowment for the Arts has nurtured hundreds of thousands of artists and institutions and in the process supported the creation of some of America's most important works of art. Along the way, a very small number of the projects it supported have offended some. That is the nature of the arts. The more important questions are: How does the National Endowment for the Arts fit into a national perspective? What are the other institutions and policies that need to be put in place to ensure that the arts thrive in America? These are not abstract questions; they have a direct bearing on our quality of life and our ability to think and reason.

The notion that the arts are only local or regional responsibilities, as many conservatives would have us believe, is as wrong as it is misguided. To be sure, cities and towns, just as states and local governments, have a role to play in nurturing the arts. Most have recognized this responsibility and realized the many cultural and economic benefits (from an improved quality of life to the income from cultural tourism) that follow from this.

What is required now is a broad-based national commitment to the arts, one that looks at how the arts can—and do—play a role in enhancing our life, in shaping the way we think and learn, understand and reason, and project ourselves as a nation to the world. This commitment needs to recognize both the educational and intellectual importance of the arts and place them within a larger national perspective that deals with ensuring that as we enter the twenty-first century we remain as competitive culturally and artistically as we hope to be scientifically and technologically.

—*Glenn D. Lowry*
MUSEUM DIRECTOR

152

NEEDED: SOME PRACTICAL NOSTALGIA

We are by now familiar to the point of boredom with the canonical imagery of the sixties: Woodstock and the Summer of Love, Elvis and the Beatles. . . . Worse than the boredom is the way these media fabrications crowd out the enduring political insights of that era.

How many people remember the brainstorming we did about the higher uses of our industrial abundance, like institutionalizing social justice in the form of a guaranteed annual income? Here is a welcome note of sanity to introduce into the money-mad chaos of the global economy. The liberal Lyndon Johnson had his War on Poverty, but the conservative Barry Goldwater ran for president in 1964 with a better idea: he advocated a negative income tax for the poor, an idea he had borrowed from his libertarian economic adviser, Milton Friedman. Across the political spectrum, from John Kenneth Galbraith to Richard Nixon, we were dialoguing ways to break the alienating link between enjoying life and earning a living. America was, after all, the affluent society. Why not make the human most of it?

Somewhere in the eighties, this beautiful Utopian élan, the sort of moral energy that affluence liberates, disappeared into a slough of social amnesia. The media continue to remind nostalgic boomers of the sex, drugs, and rock 'n' roll; they omit the daring vision that struggled to put a human face on the industrial system. Consequently, it is possible for right-wing think tanks like the Cato Institute to pretend that a society spending twice as much on gambling ($530 billion a year) as it does on Medicare cannot afford to help welfare mothers and disabled kids—nor the senior entitlements that every other industrial nation makes available. Their solution? Privatize all public programs and run them for profit. Greed, after all, is good.

As such corporate propaganda makes clear, the protest movement of the sixties left criminally much undone. It knew how to raise issues, but it was burdened with a fetishism for loose ends and unfinished business. After Watergate, protest paused. Or perhaps the hard work of building the Good Society has simply been put on hold until the boomers reach the safe plateau of retirement. When they get there and find Social Security under attack, they may be prodded into remembering that America's modest entitlements are the last surviving remnant of a guaranteed right to subsistence that even the United States Chamber of Commerce once touted.

If young America is looking for a cause, I suggest it review the literature of what we once called the Revolution of Rising Expectations, especially as it touched the lives of working- and middle-class Americans in the wake of World War II. What big dreams and bright ideas they will find there! But I would also suggest that today's twenty-somethings find a better model for political engagement than the protest movement of the sixties so permeated by narcissism and self-indulgence. Look back a full hundred years. The original American youth movement was progressivism at the turn of the century, launched out of the new land-grant colleges by freshly graduated professionals. That was a generation that knew how to get a job done! The Progressives could be very smugly WASP, but, armed with nothing more than brains, guts, and conscience, they took on Boss Tweed and the robber barons—and *won*. Teddy Roosevelt was a better example of crusading youth in the White House than John Kennedy ever lived to be. TR faced down the "malefactors of great wealth" with a patrician zeal for the public interest that puts contemporary conservatism to shame.

Today, Gingrichite Republicans, eager to uproot all the Progressives ever achieved, prefer to think of themselves as "populists." If there were ever a piece of intellectual banditry, this is it. Attacking the National Park Service and the NEA has nothing to do with historical populism. The real populists, mad-as-hell hungry farmers, were out to "soak the rich" and "share the wealth." They invented the income tax and government farm subsidies. If they had their way, they would have socialized the railroads as "public highways."

Conservatives are supposed to care about history. Well, the Progressives, the populists *are* history. They launched a century of bold American experimentation in making the avarice of the marketplace work for the common good. A new progressivism, a true populism at the service of countercultural values—what a great way to begin giving high tech a human face!

—*Theodore Roszak*
AUTHOR/PROFESSOR OF HISTORY

153

The United States locks up a larger portion of its population than any other country in the world. The number of people living behind bars is soaring and recently reached 1.7 million, making the United States' prison population *three* times as large as it was in 1980. Many Americans think this means that more hardened criminals are being tossed in jail. But in fact, this boom is largely the result of stricter sentencing laws, which have led to a huge jump in the number of people serving hard time for nonviolent offenses like drug crimes.

Prison has become a rite of passage for young people growing up in poor inner-city neighborhoods. Instead of being taught how to read and write, more and more young people are getting crash courses in prison survival. Nationally, one in three African-American men between the ages of twenty and twenty-nine is being supervised by the criminal justice system—either incarcerated, on probation, or on parole.

This explosion in the nation's inmate population affects even those people who do not know somebody in prison. Whether we like it or not, a larger portion of our tax money is being spent to support this crime control industry. Federal and state prison operating costs increased from $3.1 billion in fiscal year 1980 to $17.7 billion in 1994, according to the General Accounting Office. Across the country, this surge in prison spending has resulted in less money for public schools. Already, in California, corrections consumes a larger chunk of the budget than education.

Unless changed, these misplaced priorities promise a bleak future: more people will wind up in prison—making it extremely difficult for them to land a job once they are released—while at the same time the quality of our schools will plunge. The solution is to isolate the United States' criminal class. Nonviolent drug offenders now comprise about one third of inmates in state prisons. By sending these would-be inmates to drug treatment centers instead of prison, we would save money while also giving them a much better shot at rehabilitation.

—*Jennifer Gonnerman*
JOURNALIST

154

America will improve when we quit telling our children to fear strangers. I can't think of a more efficient means of producing a neurotic and paranoid society than to embed in its forming minds the idea that those one doesn't yet know are not, as Will Rogers put it, "friends one hasn't met yet" but are more likely harboring the ugliest aspirations imaginable.

Statistically, strangers do not present much of a danger to children. In fact, according to the Missing Children Help Center in Tampa, fewer than ten children are abducted and killed by strangers in an average year. Parents, on the other hand, annually slaughter around three thousand of their own children. Thus, it would seem that if the safety of children were our paramount concern, we would advise them to fear their parents and not strangers.

But I would rather advise American children to fear nothing. I would advise them to exercise a little caution, follow their instincts—which are usually superior to those of adults—and trust everyone until they have some reason not to.

We have an epidemic of fear loose in America that has devastated every element of our society. Let's make America better by planting young shoots of faith rather than suspicion.

—*John Perry Barlow*
LYRICIST

155

I'd repeal the Sixteenth (progressive tax) Amendment, which is inconsistent with the Fourteenth (equal treatment), and repeal the religion clause in the First Amendment (the establishment clause and the free exercise clause). Then sell tickets for the immolation of the officers of the ACLU, but this should not take place on Sunday.

—*William F. Buckley, Jr.*
AUTHOR/MAGAZINE EDITOR

156

LISTEN TO GIRLS

Listening to girls may seem simple. But truly listening to girls demands special awareness and openness, and it's extremely worthwhile. Listening to girls helps them become multidimensional, confident people in the public arena of their lives, classrooms, neighborhoods, streets, malls, media—and even influencing public policy. It enables girls to act on the culture that is constantly acting on them.

You see, ours is a culture that still focuses an insanely disproportionate amount of attention on girls' appearance. Media for teens show thousands of images and messages about being thin, clearing up zits, looking and acting the way that will best attract "him." Even parenting experts focus on girls' weight and appearance, while paying virtually no attention to them for boys.

This is a two-dimensional view of girls. There is more to any girl's life than appearance and dating. There are opinions, humor, dreams, thoughts, emotions, innovations, passions, beliefs, and hopes. When we truly listen to girls, we acknowledge these wider, deeper, and often ignored dimensions, bucking the cultural message that how girls look is more important than what they think. When we listen with an open heart and mind, we hear the range of her sometimes contradictory thoughts and feeling—often as familiar as our own. This bucks the message that it's more important for girls to be nice than it is for them to be honest with themselves and those they love.

When girls get caught up in the two-dimensional view of themselves, they become dependent on what others think of them or do to them—eventually manifested in failed relationships, early pregnancies, abuse, underemployment. Girls become objects, not subjects, even in their own eyes. And they become more of a problem than a resource for our country.

On the other hand, if we adults take girls seriously and truly listen to what they have to say, we will find ourselves uncomfortably challenged. Girls, especially in their preteen and early teen years, are merciless social critics (before cultural disapproval and self-doubt silence many of them). They are deeply attuned to hypocrisy, injustice, cynicism, dishonesty, superficiality, and inequity. When they assertively voice their cultural criticism, we call it childish whining or immature idealism run amok.

But when we have the courage as a culture to examine our actions and emotions, we will often find that girls have the goods on us. They've named problems we just didn't see ourselves. Could the roots of our blindness lie in the way many of us give up our youthful idealism to smooth our "crossing over" into adulthood in an often unjust world?

Once we listen to girls, the really hard part comes: Do we follow their voices down the path toward justice and equality?

—*Nancy Gruver and Joe Kelly*
MAGAZINE EDITORS

157

MEND THE HOLE IN THE MORAL OZONE

Tonight Show host Jay Leno does a lot of man-on-the street interviews, and one night he collared some young people to ask them questions on the Bible. "Can you name one of the Ten Commandments?" Mr. Leno asked two college-aged women. One ventured a reply: "Freedom of speech?" Mr. Leno to another young woman: "Complete this sentence: 'Let he who is without sin—.'" Her response: "—have a good time." Mr. Leno turned to a young man and asked, "Who in the Bible was eaten by a whale?" To this, he got the confident answer "Pinocchio."

I have been teaching college courses in moral philosophy for almost twenty years, and the young people Mr. Leno was interviewing are the kids I and other teachers of ethics see every day. They are decent, affable, well meaning, and ethically clueless. They come to us with no knowledge of their moral heritage. They have little or no acquaintance with the moral classics. So it's not too surprising that they are very reluctant to make any categorical moral judgments. "Torture wrong? Who's to say?"

Like most professors, I am acutely aware of the "hole in the moral ozone." One of the best things our schools can do for America is to set about repairing it. To do that they will have to confront the moral nihilism that is now a norm for so many students.

First of all, we must make students aware that there is a core of uncontroversial ethical ideals that all civilizations worthy of the name have discovered. Have them read the Bible, Aristotle's *Ethics,* Shakespeare's *King Lear,* the Koran, or the *Analects* of Confucius. Have them read almost any great work, and they will encounter the basic moral values: integrity, respect for human life, self-control, honesty, courage, and self-sacrifice. All of the world's major religions proffer some version of the Golden Rule, if only in its negative form: not to do unto others as we would not have them do unto us.

We must teach the literary classics. We need to bring the great books and the great ideas back into the center of the curriculum. We need to transmit the best of our political and cultural heritage. Franz Kafka once said that a great work of literature melts the "frozen sea within us." There are any number of works of art and works of philosophy that have the effect of thawing that "frozen sea" just a little bit.

American children have a right to their moral heritage. High school and college students should know the Bible. They should be familiar with the moral truths in the tragedies of Shakespeare, in the political ideas of Jefferson, Madison, and Lincoln. They should be exposed to the exquisite moral sensibility in the novels of Jane Austen, George Eliot, and Mark Twain—to name some of my favorites. These great writings are their birthright.

This is not to say that a good literary and philosophical education suffices to create ethical human beings; nor is to suggest that teaching the classics is all we need to do to repair the hole in the moral ozone. What we do know is that we cannot in good conscience allow our children to remain morally illiterate. All healthy societies pass along their moral and cultural traditions to their children. Why should we be the exception?

—*Christina Hoff Sommers*
AUTHOR

158

Benjamin Franklin advised, "Early to bed, early to rise, makes [one] healthy, wealthy, and wise." These remain ingredients for a happy, whole, and fulfilled American life. However, "early to bed and early to rise" has increasingly less to do with acquiring them. In fact, 100,000 of our children have no bed on any given night.

America could be a better place if every person had the equalities our Constitution implies to acquire health, wealth, and education. To be healthy requires education, to be educated requires health, and health requires wealth.

- Fifty-five million Americans currently are without health insurance. This translates into fragile and poor health for these Americans.

- One of every four children in America is poor, and one of every two African-American children is poor.

- The pitfalls of poverty begin even before birth. Wealthy babies are healthier and weigh more than poor babies.

Wealthy babies have better food and cleaner environments, better and cleaner schools, better books, and better enrichment programs, such as camps, vacations, museums, and art and music experiences, and hope abounds. Babies unlucky enough to be poor at birth fall behind by preschool and kindergarten and are sicklier, sometimes having not been immunized against childhood illnesses.

- Each year, an estimated 10,000 children die as a direct result of poverty.

- Affluent Americans have longer life expectancies than lower- and working-class people, primarily due to better access to health care (Office of Surgeon General, *Healthy People 2000*, 1994).

- It is estimated that as many as 35 percent of kindergarten-age children come to school unprepared to learn (American Humane Association, *Fact Sheet on America's Children*).

- Although 57 percent of all African-American children under three with a high-school-educated parent were poor, those children under three with parents who did not have a high school education had a poverty rate of 77 percent (National Center for Children in Poverty, 1996).

Health, wealth, and education seem to be inextricably bound in late-twentieth-century America. Business leaders and Republicans blame the poor, labor leaders and Democrats blame the system (Sidney Verba and Gary Orrem, *Equality in America* [Cambridge, Mass.: Harvard University Press, 1985], pp. 72–73).

We could make America better by putting our philosophies aside and providing the opportunities of wealth for the majority of poverty-stricken Americans. Americans are a can-do people. We can do no less for our citizens than other nations do for theirs, but we have never truly put our shoulder to the plow.

We can always find money for the projects we want, whether they are effective or not. We spend approximately $8 billion annually to prohibit marijuana, a drug that has never been documented to have killed one person. Yet we spend millions subsidizing tobacco farmers, whose product kills thousands per year. There is a hole created by circular thinking where all our money goes.

Between $13 billion and $400 billion per year can be saved by eliminating the war on drugs, which we have lost but not surrendered. (The higher number is from the Drug Policy Foundation, "The Cost of the War on Drugs," and Save Our Liberties of Sunnyvale, California). Medicalizing our drug problem would starve the crime fueled by drug trafficking, just as other countries have experienced without increasing drug abuse. I believe that we are bankrupting our democracy through waste of our resources.

The entire community must be involved in reinvesting our resources in the restoration of people's lives to wholeness and wellness. This is building a healthy, wealthy, and wise citizenry that can sustain our beloved democracy for all.

—*Dr. M. Joycelyn Elders*

FORMER UNITED STATES SURGEON GENERAL

It's a risky proposition, but I've always been attracted to the movement for a new Constitutional Convention. Thomas Jefferson thought it would be best if every generation had one. In truth, the Framers distrusted the people so much they had to meet in secret, behind closed doors, and James Madison was the only one who didn't dispose of his notes (the practice of paper shredding has a long legacy in American political history). Then as now, powerful interests—merchants, bankers, land speculators, planters, slave traders, and slave owners—lobbied hard and cut deals with the lawmakers. More than a century later, Senator Penrose (R–Pennsylvania), summarized the representative system for an audience of businessmen: "I believe in a division of labor. You send us to Congress, we pass the laws under which you make money . . . and out of your profits you further contribute to our campaign funds to send us back again to pass more laws to enable you to make more money."

The most damning thing that can be said about the legacy of the Constitution is that the American people have not used the gift of political democracy to further economic democracy. At the waning of a century that had seen the Square Deal, the New Deal, and the Fair Deal, most folks are now paying the price of a Raw Deal. As global free trade has increasingly taken center stage, the income gap between the world's rich and poor has accelerated and is now twice as great as it was thirty years ago. In the United States, income inequality has reverted to the levels of the 1920s, before the introduction of progressive taxation. The top 1 percent of families now possess 42 percent of American wealth, and the economy is governed by corporations whose ratio of CEOs' salaries to workers' wages is so astronomical as to mock any standard of fairness.

The Declaration of Independence and the Articles of Confederation had been documents of an active populace. The Constitution defined the populace as passive, reduced the formal duties of citizenship to a thin shadow of participation, and ensured that politics and civil life would be a perpetual quagmire of legal wrangling. What are the chances that a new Constitutional Convention wouldn't make things much worse? This is the only fear that holds us back. Unlike the strictly controlled town hall meetings our president likes to stage for the media, this could be a truly effective national conversation. It could be a grassroots exercise in civic participation that would put our current inaction to shame. It could be a time to talk turkey, rather than consume that poor bird in our weird annual ritual. And the outcome? That's for the people to decide, the way it probably ought to be. But for starters I'd bet that the vast majority would settle for some real control over the power of corporations. It remains one of the most stunning perversions of political history that under the Fourteenth Amendment, guaranteeing civil liberties to all as part of Reconstruction, corporations would come to be treated like persons and enjoy protection from oversight as if they were citizens with minds and bodies.

—*Andrew Ross*
PROFESSOR OF AMERICAN STUDIES

1. Personal responsibility.   We should all be willing to accept accountability for our actions.

2. Individual initiative.   The Wright Brothers invented the airplane in a bicycle shop. Thomas Edison envisioned a lamp that needed neither a wick nor oil. We should all strive to set an example and make a difference, rather than complacently following the status quo.

3. Self-reliance.   Only by relying on ourselves can we afford to help our neighbor. Individuals who always look to live on the generosity of others are hurting both themselves and their community.

4. Religious faith.   No people ever became greater by lowering its standards. No society was ever enriched or improved by loosening its moral code. Religion gives us support and constancy in a life filled with change and uncertainty.

5. Thrift.   We must know the limits of our own resources and live within our means. The federal government has burdened our children with a $5 trillion debt. My twelfth grandson was born in 1996, and he will owe $189,000 in *interest* payments on the national debt over his lifetime. We must save and invest for our future rather than limit our dreams of tomorrow by overindulging today.

—*Bill Archer*
POLITICIAN

161

Shortly after the 1993 Gay and Lesbian March on Washington, I was on the phone with my father, heatedly debating the issues: coming out of the closet, the need for same-sex marriage, serving openly in the military, and so on. Suddenly, in the midst of one of my movement-man rants, Dad stopped me: "OK, OK, you've got our attention. Now what do you want?"

"For you to join us," I said.

"On what?" he asked with a snigger. "Sex?"

"Well," I said with a gulp, "yes."

Winning Dad over on the notion that what he had most in common with his gay son was what we both did in the bedroom wasn't easy. I mean, who really likes to imagine his parents—or his children—doing the nasty? Especially when the nasty is sodomy?

Still, sex stands out as the one experience that both gays and straights can readily identify with—because we've almost all done it. In twenty-one states, sodomy laws still remain on the books. Some specifically prohibit oral and anal sex between gays, while many others also include "the offense of sodomy" between straights. And if that's not shocking enough, in 1986 the U.S. Supreme Court, in *Bowers v. Hardwick*, upheld the rights of states to enforce these laws.

My recommendation to make America better is to wipe sodomy laws off the books forever. And it's something we can do together!

If you don't believe these laws are still used by the authorities, tell that to Sharon Bottoms. In 1995, Ms. Bottoms was denied custody of her little boy solely on the basis that she was a lesbian. (The Virginia State Court of Appeals judge cited the state's sodomy law as the source of her being an unfit mother.)

Obviously, there are numerous reasons why these laws need to be removed, the most profound of which may simply be the sweeping subconscious psychological message they send to millions of Americans, gay and straight, that their lovemaking is a "crime against nature."

The main political reason, however, to abolish sodomy laws in America is to further separate the archaic ties between church and state. Implemented by our founding fathers, sodomy laws today represent Puritanism at its most radical and immature.

If we are to join much of the rest of the civilized world in the understanding that sex is God's most natural, accessible, and enjoyable vehicle of expressing love, we've got to make it legal. Maybe the church will learn something in the process, too. And maybe Dad will start returning my calls again.

—*David Drake*
WRITER/ACTIVIST

162

I'm a reporter, and as such I'm supposed to report other people's ideas more than I'm supposed to have any ideas of my own.

But even to me, it's obvious. How do we make America better? We make American education better.

You may want to consider that my brother, my sister, their spouses, several of their children, and my wife are all teachers, present or recent. But my respect for teaching goes back to childhood and the public schools of Houston, Texas.

If I had not studied with good teachers—if public education had not been available to me—then there's no doubt that I'd have wound up a laborer, like my father and his father before him. Honest, proud work—but backbreaking, low-wage work. Tough to raise a family, tough to make a difference. My father and grandfather managed it—I honestly don't know if I could have.

My brother, sister, and I were the first in our family ever to attend college. Because we were able to get an education, we had a head start in life. Opportunities. A chance to do the work we love.

I can't claim any expertise or recommend many specific measures to improve our schools. But I believe it's essential for parents to get involved in their children's education, with teacher conferences and, yes, PTA meetings a must. I believe it's essential for America to continue to provide its children with the best public education possible. Our future competitiveness, our future prosperity, our future happiness depend upon our ability to teach and to learn today.

—*Dan Rather*
REPORTER

163

Transportation: the American Freeway and our 10 billion gridlocking, lung-killing automobiles. Get rid of them, all of them, or at least the engines. Take all the cars we've already created and put them on tracks. Anybody can ride in any car they want, and all for a predetermined destination fee. One could ride solo or in the company of friends, family, and/or strangers. You would simply get in the car of your choice at the nearest public track station (which would be located at virtually every other corner), program in your destination, and zoom away in your own private little car. Billing would be monthly on your travel card, just like a phone or electric bill.

No more gridlock, traffic jams, drunk drivers, violent incidents over minuscule improprieties, stolen parking spaces, stolen cars, uninsured drivers, hit-and-run accidents, status symbols, and ego fantasies, no more "There was a lot of construction" excuses to bosses, no more pileups and ten-car accidents in rain, fog, snow . . . endless benefits, not to mention the ozone-depleting carbon monoxide and cheap suicide mode. No more going postal at 80 mph.

Read, write, practice musical instruments, make phone calls without driving all the drivers around you nuts, change your mind at the flick of a button rather than a swerve across three lanes, go out at any hour no matter what your age or ability, feel safe there won't be any hijacks, watch the world around you, meditate, stretch, watch a movie or the news, read a copy of *George,* try on the new Kenneth Cole shoes for the jazz gig you're en route to. Arrive human.

Please consider my idea. I live in Portland, Oregon, and it really is one big construction zone since 500,000 people decided they really wouldn't mind the rain if the traffic is better and real estate sooo very cheap. Ha.

—*Sally Van Meter*
MUSICIAN

164

If we're looking for a way to streamline America—to make it cheaper, more efficient, and more user-friendly—I think the most obvious solution is to downsize by wiping the slate clean and getting rid of states, or at least cutting back severely on their number. Our current state system just doesn't make sense in a nation filled with people who are born Georgians, grow up Californians, and retire as Nevadans. Why are we enslaved to a system set up for the convenience of the British Empire?

Think about how much money we waste by having fifty separate governors, state legislatures, state agriculture commissions, and water resource managers—each with a full army of bureaucrats who need telephones, office buildings, fax machines, computers, and parking lots. Is this really necessary in the late twentieth century? Do things change so much the minute you cross the border between New Hampshire and Vermont that each needs a separate government?

Think how much easier it would be to move if we didn't have to keep getting new driver's licenses and voter registration cards, if we didn't have to learn a new set of traffic regulations and ways to avoid paying state taxes. The least we can do is to create one national license plate, one set of taxes, one code of laws from Baja California to Bangor, Maine.

I'm well aware that this proposal runs counter to the latest political fad of returning power to the states, but I admit that I've never suffered from any romantic delusions about local government being more responsive to the citizenry. Maybe I've chosen the wrong states and localities, but I've never noticed that my local officials were much more concerned with my welfare than federal ones, although I have noticed that the collective IQ was a tad lower.

All this nonsense about states is a ploy by people who want power, and I admit it does give the power-hungry more of an opportunity—gee, fifty chances to become governor, or at least lieutenant governor. And having all these states is good for the flag makers, the license plate printers, and the map drawers. But what purpose do they serve for the rest of us? This isn't Europe, after all. We all speak pretty much the same language and eat the same kind of burgers.

So I think we should try redrawing the boundaries and replacing the fifty states we have with, say, ten maxistates. Okay, so nobody would want to be in the same state with California. Fine, leave it alone. But is there really any justification for not marrying New Hampshire, Vermont, Maine, Massachusetts, Rhode Island, and Connecticut? New Mexico, Arizona, Utah, and Nevada fit together naturally. And who could oppose attaching Delaware to Pennsylvania and Maryland?

And if the states' rights nostalgia buffs need some incentive, how about mandating that the capital of each new maxistate be the capital of the smallest former state and that the taxes reflect the lowest tax rate in the region?

—*Elinor Burkett*
JOURNALIST

165

The central mission of our society should be to encourage, motivate, and inspire every child to finish school, learn a skill, get a job, get married, and then have a baby. In that order.

—*Tim Russert*
TV HOST

166

Want to make America better? Then get off your butt and, as Nike says, just do it. It's time to take a lesson from Nike, because if Nike can sell us shoes in thirty seconds, we can sell a message of hope in three. All over America, there are people who are putting their time and talents where their mouths are, and they are effecting real change in our communities, our state legislatures, and the halls of Congress—from the ground up. Grassroots change is a real force in our political system, and it's doing more to shape this country than any "bridge to the twenty-first century" I've seen lately.

We can look to the environment as the great grassroots success story. Our air is cleaner—in the past twenty-five years, major air pollutants have decreased by one third. And our water is cleaner—since 1970, we have reduced the amount of pollutants released into our lakes and rivers by 2.2 million pounds per day. That's what I call progress.

Who do we have to thank for these improvements in the air we breathe and the water we drink? The American people. A 1997 poll shows that most Americans feel that they have been personally responsible for these improvements, by recycling their beer cans, by driving more fuel-efficient cars, or by supporting proenvironment candidates at the voting booth. People are taking the health and well-being of their communities into their own hands, and they're taking action to make things better—one car pool at a time.

Americans concerned about the environment are making their voices heard in a variety of ways, but few do it with the panache of Elden Hughes. While working to protect the fragile California desert, Elden took an unusual companion on his lobbying tours: Scotty, an endangered desert tortoise. When the duo paid a visit to one senator's office, they didn't wait for their scheduled appointment with some midlevel aide; Elden just plopped Scotty down on the floor and let him roam. Soon fourteen of the office staffers were on all fours. When the senator came out of the inner office and scanned the room at eye level, he saw no one and knew something was up. He looked down and saw his serious staff on their hands and knees, crawling after a turtle. With utter resignation he said, "Whatever it is, explain it to me later, it's OK." Senator Kent Conrad (D–North Dakota) then became a cosponsor of the California Desert Protection Act.

When the act finally came up for a floor vote, it was down to the wire. Activists knew they needed to generate support fast in order to gather the remaining votes needed to pass the act. Elden and company called up the Sierra Student Coalition, the student arm of the Sierra Club, and asked for its help. The Student Coalition quickly set up a dorm storm: activists on college campuses went up and down the halls of their dorms, telling their friends about the importance of protecting the desert and asking them to phone their senators' offices in support of the California Desert Protection Act.

Enough calls were generated to pass the act and preserve 7 million acres of desert habitat.

I'm sick of hearing about the cynicism that is pervading American politics, because I don't see it. For every Elden Hughes or Sierra Student Coalition dorm stormer, there are at least ten others passionately working on a whole host of issues. These are the examples I look to for improving America—the people who are out there shaking it up. Now is the time to take their example, now is the time to move forward. Now is the time for wildness.

—*Adam Werbach*
ENVIRONMENTAL ADVOCATE

167

THE PEOPLE'S FRANK

Senators and congressman write us for free using their so-called franking privilege. Well, why not a people's frank?

After all, the theory of the congressional frank is that it promotes public dialogue, that a more informed electorate is better able to govern itself. As Thomas Jefferson wrote on behalf of the frank, communications between elected officials and their constituents should be "free, full and unowned by any." This, Jefferson said, would "give the will of the people the influence it ought to have."

Why should the frank work only one way? Why not make it reciprocal? Why not extend it to citizens who want to let their representatives know what's in their hearts and on their minds, as Canada does?

Much has been written about how political action committees and previous campaign finance "reforms" such as spending limits have inadvertently functioned as a sort of incumbency insurance. But little has been said, except by challengers, about how the one-way congressional frank preserves the status quo.

The beauty part of the people's frank is that a limited test needn't cost the taxpayer a nickel. All Congress has to do is mandate that one half of each representative's current franking budget for mass mailings be allocated to citizens' replies. For starters, the law could require Congress to enclose franked return envelopes or postcards in every mass mailing. That would temporarily cut one-way mass-franked mail in half and seems a reasonable way to launch the experiment.

Such a reform is no more a panacea for democracy's malaise than are campaign finance reform, universal voter registration, free television time for all candidates, a "none of the above" option on every ballot, and lowering the barriers to third parties. But, as the old joke says, it couldn't do any harm. We call those we send to Washington our representatives. Yet each citizen is also a representative of the public interest and in that capacity should be encouraged to write to, rather than write off, the Beltway. If you agree with me, write your congressman today.

—*Victor Navasky*
AUTHOR/MAGAZINE EDITOR

168

I believe we must make it a priority to practice mutual respect and dignity. By engaging in meaningful dialogue about topics of disagreement, we can learn valuable information about one another. It should be mentioned that deeds and actions must follow the dialogue. When we watch shows such as *Crossfire,* we come away without a conclusion, mainly because our politicians are experts in spewing biased rhetoric.

My experience has taught me that ignorance leads to prejudice, panic, and hostility. We often fail to talk through differences, consequently, we take the easy way out, i.e., I am correct and the opposition is "all wet."

In closing, I would like to leave you with the philosophy my parents instilled in me at an early age: "First and foremost, always prepare yourself with knowledge and any history relative to the topic you choose to resolve." Often when minorities make well-researched suggestions and proposals, they make little or no impact in the arena of public opinion. Talk shows such as *The Capital Gang* and *The McLaughlin Group* seldom have minority regulars. Likewise, the talk group on BET should join this integration. The more we converse and work on the same level, the more we will learn about one another's customs and mores.

I hate to see our minority youngsters being saturated daily by the media, written and verbal, on the six and eleven o'clock news. For some reason, they constantly fill time spots with short segments about minority athletes and drug dealers. I would hope that somebody is aware of the long-range effect this will have on their hopes and aspirations.

It costs more to incarcerate a person than to send him or her to college.

—*Mo Vaughn*
ATHLETE

More American women are injured by battery than by rape, muggings, and accidents combined. Think of that! A woman is safer roaming the streets at night than snuggled up on the couch at home reading a book with her husband stewing in the den.

An American crisis? Yes, because so many of us who are tuned in to the media have heard it all (think of Nicole Brown Simpson and Hedda Nussbaum) but just don't know what to do. Haven't you seen some signs around you? Sunglasses and heavy makeup in the elevator? A cheerful coworker who becomes inexplicably depressed and suffers a limp due to recurring "accidents"? Or it may be thuds on your ceiling. And of course you have doubts ("Frank? He always has those annual barbecues . . ."). But remember, 82 percent of batterers are Jekyll-and-Hyde types. When acquaintances doubted that a person as likable as my batterer (whose main method of assault was to run at me and knock me down, as in a football tackle) could have broken my ankle and smashed out my teeth, the downstairs neighbors set them straight.

Not wanting to probe in people's "personal" lives, we often gape at the puffy eye and remain silent. But, as Keith Haring put it, "silence equals death"; we must reach out to these battered women (or men or children) in order to save their lives (and save America). It can feel so hard to do, so awkward, right? Well, here are a few tips on how to befriend a battered woman:

- Take her aside and quietly ask, "Are you safe at home?" or "Did someone hurt you?" If she doesn't acknowledge it, ask again next time.

- Keep telling her, "No one has the right to hurt you." Many battered women are brainwashed into blaming themselves. Comments such as "He must be crazy" have the power to break through the haze.

- Don't ask her what she did to provoke him. When a batterer reaches the boiling point in his compulsive cycle, the excuse can be anything . . . or nothing. My batterer once beat me up after we returned home from the opera because I'd toted a purse that he considered too large and "daytimey."

- Don't ask why she doesn't leave. She may be well aware that escaping is apt to escalate the danger. Instead, help her devise a safety plan.

So the next time you see a locker mate at the gym with a suspicious black-and-blue handprint on her thigh, start talking. It just may work.

—*Barbara Seaman*

AUTHOR/HEALTH ADVOCATE

Nina's Adventures — **LET'S CHANGE THE WORLD!** ©Nina Paley 12.23.84

—*Nina Paley*

CARTOONIST

171

America needs a political revolution. We are trying to govern in the greatest revolutionary period since the dawn of the Enlightenment and the democratic revolutions of the eighteenth century with political ideologies, parties, and institutions designed to protect the status quo.

Our outmoded governing institutions virtually guarantee that current policies and programs will continue to stagnate, since both institutions and policies were designed for an age that is quickly passing. Our parties have been overrun by special-interest factions, our policies are written in lobbyists' offices, and few who represent the national interest are heard.

Our best patriots, neither ideological liberals nor conservatives, will soon produce a new core political belief system around several classic ideals. First, restoration of civic duty and citizen responsibility in balance with rights and opportunities. Second, establishment of Jefferson's "ward republic" as the basic unit of government. Third, creation of a requirement (again from Jefferson) that each generation reaffirm its basic social priorities, laws, and constitutional principles. Fourth, establishment of a national standard that all new laws and policies meet the test of creating a better nation for the next generation. And finally, redirection of our economic, social, and political systems to establish the spiritual bond between humanity and nature that existed when the early Europeans first came to America.

Creating a core system of political beliefs from the best of our ancient heritage will be the greatest patriotic challenge since the American Revolution. We are at peace, and we are prosperous. We lack only the imagination, the dedication, the wisdom, and the will.

—*Gary Hart*
ATTORNEY

DRIVE CLEAN ACROSS AMERICA

Driving down the Avenue of the Giants in California, dwarfed by three-hundred-foot-tall trees on both sides of the two-lane road, I felt it was criminal to be coughing black tailpipe exhaust into the pristine ancient forest. The sad fact is that 130 years of logging have eliminated 95 percent of California's giant coastal redwoods; so few thousand-year-old trees remain that park rangers in the Pacific Northwest call the survivors by name. Tired of being a polluter and worried about global warming, I decided to find a way to have my vehicle stop emitting carbon monoxide.

After doing research on alternative fuels—electric, solar, hydrogen, and soybean—I decided that natural gas was the most practical and clean-burning. The U.S. Department of Energy flooded me with information extolling its virtues: natural gas produces up to 90 percent less carbon monoxide and 66 percent less reactive hydrocarbons than gasoline. There is an abundance of natural gas available throughout the Great Plains and Alaska. Convinced of its virtues as a realistic alternative fuel, I converted my vehicle to natural gas. Shortly thereafter, I proudly drove "Clean Across America." With environmental degradation a grim reality, consumers should abandon petroleum-burning engines in the twenty-first century for natural gas (or hydrogen fuel cells), thereby forcing the Detroit automakers and Texas oil companies to provide our planet with less toxic air. In addition, as emission levels of greenhouse gases rise in the United States, federal regulations must also increase. Citizens must demand clean air.

—*Douglas Brinkley*
HISTORIAN/AUTHOR

173

News anchorpeople must stop desensitizing the minds of Americans, especially the new generation, by trying to be celebrities, putting their own spin on the world and negating the emotions of what is felt of the news by the public with their silly chitchat.

Good news should be reported. Outstanding young scholars should be rewarded publicly, making it enviable to be smart and classy.

A group of one hundred or more young people chosen by a school submission to a board should tour some part of the world, subsidized by the government, so that they appreciate their country when they get back.

Give farmlands back to individual qualified farmers and let them sell their food to feed the governing body.

Minimize campaign spending—all networks must contribute equal time.

Release Leonard Peltier. Bring Native Americans back to being a part of mainstream America. Sponsor great Indian athletes.

Have English the main language in America again.

Prisoners should clean up American streets and oceans—build roads—work in nursing homes, dog pounds, and so on.

—*Connie Stevens*
PERFORMER

IT'S THE MONOPOLY, STUPID

Across the street from my home in Brooklyn sits the future of America's economy: Sarah J. Hale High School. Each day I watch the tide of students flow into school in the morning and out in the afternoon. As at the school I attended, the kids hang out, smoke cigarettes, act rowdy, and occasionally do something naughty. But whereas more than 90 percent of students at my high school graduated on time, this school manages only a 37 percent graduation rate. If Sarah J. Hale were a company—say, Delta Air Lines or General Motors—the 63 percent failure rate would have put it out of business long ago. Yet year in and year out, this school and a significant number of other urban American public schools fail to provide even a basic education to a substantial number of kids. Why do so many city schools perform so badly?

The problem is simple: monopoly. Poor families can choose from only one provider of educational services, the government. Consequently, byzantine school bureaucracies have absolutely no incentive to change. The same kinds of hassles most of us face with our local phone companies, the post office, and the IRS are also endemic to America's public school system. Again, the reason is simple: each of these institutions is a government-backed monopoly. The key to liberating poor children from unconscionably failing schools is competition. The battle for school choice will be the civil rights movement of my generation. Until poor parents have the same opportunity as the rich—to send their kids to non-government-run schools—nothing will change. As goes Sarah J. Hale High School, so goes America.

—*Omar Wasow*
POLITICAL COMMENTATOR

175

Listen, don't preach. The average eighteen-year-old makes no association between public policy, community leadership, or voting and the improvement of his or her life. We don't help matters. As adults, too many of us reinforce indifference in youths when we criticize their music and their culture. It's not that today's youths are disengaged, it's that we haven't been listening hard enough to know how to involve them. *We tune them out.*

Music can be a catalyst for dialogue between parents and their children. It can give teachers and politicians clues to the rapidly evolving concerns of younger constituents. We would be far better off paying attention to the views of young people rather than dismissing their opinions as ugly or stupid or ignoring them altogether. Our not-so-distant-future leaders depend on our *tuning youth in.*

—*Hilary Rosen*
BUSINESS EXECUTIVE

176

☛

—*Elisha Cooper*
CARTOONIST

177

ELIMINATE POLITICAL ADVERTISING ON TELEVISION

Everyone knows that American politics (we used to call it government) is being ruined by the huge amounts of raw cash needed to get into power and stay there. Even setting aside illegal contributions, what the Supreme Court now tells us is legal would have been considered grossly improper back in the good old days of Watergate. Now, it seems, writing checks for unlimited amounts of money, with no restrictions on how it might be used, is speech and therefore protected by the Constitution—as if Jefferson and Monroe would have been keen on the idea of businessmen pouring floods of unrestricted cash into the hands of politicians.

But has anyone questioned what they're actually *doing* with all that loot? I'm not a political scientist, but I do watch television, and it's obvious that the biggest chunk of it is going into producing brainless thirty-second spots that routinely lie and vilify in order to swing over the most impressionable (i.e., the dumbest) voters. Over the past few election cycles, the level of discourse in our public life has been abased to that of a playground rumble. In most elections, the voter is asked to choose between Candidate A, who aims to destroy the American family and has a sister in New York City who's a well-

FOR A BETTER AMERICA, PUT COWS IN SCHOOL UNIFORMS, TEACH THEM THE PLEDGE OF ALLEGIANCE, AND HAVE THEM SING THE NATIONAL ANTHEM.

known thespian, and Candidate B, who devotes all his energies to raising taxes and putting rapists and serial killers back on the streets. The elections for student council president at my high school were conducted in a far more dignified and enlightened manner. The process we have today is an insult to any thinking person—and has made it impossible for thoughtful people to become involved.

The quickest way to restore decency to the political discourse in America, and to reduce the obscene fund-raising that has corroded the electoral process, would be to eliminate political advertising on television. I don't care how it's done, and please don't talk to me about free speech: it may be speech, of a guttural kind, but it sure ain't free.

—*Jamie James*
AUTHOR

178

ELIMINATE THE SILLY BOXES

For a country that has dedicated itself to the principle of becoming "one nation . . . indivisible," I profoundly disagree with the practice of our government requiring its citizens to check little boxes that classify them according to skin color, ethnic background, or national origin and then to decide who wins and who loses in competitions for college admission, employment, and public contracts based on which box has been checked on application forms.

Not only do I object to the practice of conferring benefits or preferences on the basis of traits such as those mentioned above, I object to the box-checking practice altogether. In the transactions of our government, our skin color and the origins of our ancestors should be a private matter.

On June 11, 1963, President John F. Kennedy said, "Race has no place in American life or law." President Kennedy's comment—delivered to the American people at the height of the civil rights movement—not only represented the prevailing sentiment of that era, it articulated a vision for America that was conceived by our founders and continues to be embraced by an overwhelming majority of Americans.

The time is not too distant when the American people will be left with no choice but to confront and end the idiocy of the racial classification and box-checking business in which we now find ourselves. In addition to the moral and ideological reasons that ought to compel us to confront this practice now, there is another, more practical consideration that will soon render the box-checking business obsolete. I refer to the rapidly growing number of multiracial and multiethnic marriages and the products of those marriages.

The children—who frequently don't know which box to check and wonder why they need to check any at all—are one product. They and their parents are creating substantial political pressure for decision makers to address the reality of our changing population and how—or why—we racially classify people. "Diversity" has become its own change agent.

The other product of such marriages is the cultural attitude engendered by those who "intermarry." Such individuals truly become "color-blind" and intolerant of systems that classify people according to physical or ethnic traits; their attitude will someday be the impetus to lead America to eliminate the silly little boxes.

—*Ward Connerly*
EQUAL OPPORTUNITY ADVOCATE

179

*"A great civilization is not conquered from without
until it has destroyed itself from within."*
　　　　　　　　　　—historians Will and Ariel Durant

This profound observation gives us fair warning as we consider the future of America. To preserve our heritage and liberty, consider the lessons of history. The ideals that forged our humble beginnings into the greatest, freest, fairest nation in the history of the world will also keep it strong.

Families. No society in the history of civilization has survived if the family unit has deteriorated. There we instill the values of character, honesty, courage, discipline, and respect. Government policies must reinforce and protect the integrity of the family unit.

Spirit of entrepreneurship. People have come to America for more than two hundred years for the opportunity to work hard and give their children a better life than they had. If American capitalism is to prevail, government policies should not stifle and overregulate the initiative and sacrifice of individual talent.

Patriotism. Throughout history, Americans have been willing to fight and even die for our freedom. The only way to repay those who have sacrificed is to pass the commitment to our country through to future generations. Only then can they hold our democracy together, always remembering that peace comes through strength, not weakness.

As America has grown, we have been blessed, but we must

never take our blessings for granted. We must be vigilant in our pursuit of democracy and in keeping pace with an ever-changing world. We must combine the technological advances of the twentieth century with the bravery, integrity and wisdom of the founders and builders of our earliest years as a nation. This will propel America into the twenty-first century with the strength to endure.

—*Kay Bailey Hutchison*
POLITICIAN

180

How to make the United States a better place? It's simple (though not easy): redistribute the wealth. For starters, guarantee a minimal annual income—$25,000, say—to every American.

The gap between rich and poor has gotten shockingly wide, and there are many more poor than rich. "God's will," some will say. After all, the Bible tells us that "the poor you shall always have with you." Not being biblically inclined (nor God-privy), I can't help but doubt the (self-serving) banality of the explanation. Besides, I've known far too many people with brilliance of various kinds who never had the chance to convert smarts into tangible assets. No, the poor are not dumber than you and me; they just haven't had our access to privileged head starts.

The Social Darwinists among us—and nineteenth-century values are alive and well in much of the land—would insist that those who win the race for wealth are those who are the most "deserving." But the personal qualities that usually translate into economic success are often the least attractive ones humanly—qualities like avarice, connivance, manipulation, ruthlessness. Not that everyone who makes a bundle is a bastard. Some simply inherit it from wealthy families. We are a nation that purportedly believes in "earning one's bread by the sweat of one's brow," yet such protest as we hear about "giveaways" relates to Aid to Dependent Children, not to corporate welfare.

Nobody needs three houses and five cars. But lots of people need a clean, dry apartment, enough food on the table, basic medical treatment, and education. So the downside of guaranteeing everyone an annual income (since the economy is unable to guarantee decent jobs) is that a few of the rich might be taxed down to two houses and four cars. Tough.

—*Martin Duberman*
AUTHOR/PROFESSOR

181

ROLL BACK COLLEGE TUITIONS TO WHAT THEY
WERE IN THE YEAR (1955) THAT BILL GATES WAS
BORN, AND HAVE HIM MAKE UP THE DIFFERENCE.

—*Stan Mack*
CARTOONIST

182

I've never forgotten a science fiction story I read as a teenager. It described a society with a national child lottery held every four years. Every child's name was put into it, and children were randomly redistributed to new families.

Babies were not part of this lottery. A family got to keep its newborn child until the next lottery, but then it became part of the national child swap. The cycle was broken every third swap, and kids were sent back to their original parents until the next lottery. So by the time you were considered an adult, at age twenty-six, the most time you could have spent with your birth parents was ten years. The other sixteen were simply the luck of the draw—maybe your new parent would be the head of a gigantic multinational company and the most powerful person in the country, or you might find yourself the child of a family living in a trailer park.

The whole idea sounded horrible to me, but people in the child-swap society took the lottery for granted. They didn't try to hide their children or send them away to other countries; child swapping was simply part of their culture. But one thing the lottery did was to make the whole society very conscientious about how things were arranged for kids. After all, you never knew where your own child would end up after the next lottery, and in a very real sense everyone's child was—or could be—yours. So the kids did OK and the society itself was harmonious.

What if someone wrote a story about what American society in the late twentieth century takes for granted in the arrangements for its children? Well, we take for granted that some kids are going to have much better lives than others. Of course. We take for granted that some will get the best medical treatment and others will be able to get little or none. We take for granted that some kids will go to beautiful, well-cared-for schools with excellent libraries and computers for every child and others will go to schools where there are not enough desks and textbooks to go around—wretched places where even the toilets don't work. We take for granted that teachers in the beautiful schools will be better paid and better trained than those in the poor schools. We take for granted, in so many ways, that the children whom the lottery of birth has made the most needy will get the least. "After all," we say to ourselves, "it's up to each family to look after its own. Probably these other parents just don't care."

Maybe it's time for America to adopt a child-swap system. Let's start with national political figures and their children and grandchildren, with governors and mayors and millionaire businessmen. Then let's see what happens to our schools and health care system—and our shameful national indifference to children who are not ours. I bet it won't take more than a lottery or two to set things right.

—*Sandra Feldman*
EDUCATION ADVOCATE

183

TEENAGER
AMERICA

In the time scale of nations, America is a teenager—full of energy and precocious successes, striving to find itself, and somewhat worried about . . . its pimples. Like a youth aspiring to improve, America should shape its personality according to its best qualities and talents while learning from its mistakes and from its elders. America's central mission seems clear enough from its history and people: to persevere and advance freedom and compassion within its borders and across the world. Too often, however, this focus is missing, with egoism and greed, disguised as rugged independence and free-market capitalism, gaining over the loftier goals. To learn from its elders, America should look at their experiences—something we seldom do. Why is it that education in the nations with the highest educational scores is pursued at the national level and involves uniform exams, while in the United States it is pursued locally and without uniformity? Endless arguments on how best to educate our children are pursued by many different communities without reference to the hundreds of years of experience in education of our foreign peers.

America, you are already doing well. But you will do even better if you stay inwardly focused on advancing freedom and compassion and outwardly open to the experiences of other nations.

—*Michael L. Dertouzos*
AUTHOR/PROFESSOR

184

CELEBRATE AMERICA 2000

America tends to be optimistic. What makes America distinctive and unique is that we have agreed to live together as a variety of people with different religions. It is not "my" America, it is "our" America. So what does America stand for?

"A": Attitude . . . America's positive attitude is what makes America great and why we have achieved so much. Our single greatest and most valuable export remains the product of hope.

"M": Mission . . . America's Declaration of Independence is the mission statement of our country.

"E": Education . . . not indoctrination. America has always made education its top priority. Responsible parents must give children the best possible education because education gives the capacity to release creative energies. There is, in America, a systemic compulsion to excellence. Education contributes to excellence. Let education continue to give the next generation the compulsion to excel.

"R": Religion . . . We have not wiped God out of our country. We are "one nation under God."

"I": Individualism . . . which comes through religion and the dignity of the person. Positive religion produces individual self-confidence. The resurgence of individualism is producing the basis for a strong optimism for America's future.

"C": Civility . . . Individualism with the compassion of God's spirit produces civility. Civility is community. Civility produces volunteerism.

"A": Achievement . . . It is the responsibility of Christian leaders to motivate people to succeed. "If it's going to be, it's up to me."

We focus on success, and the skeleton of success is service. Find a need and fill it. Find a hurt and heal it. Find a problem and solve it. Then prosperity is dignified.

If you call yourself an American, you can add the letter "N" so that the last four letters of "American" read "I CAN," and together we can create a stronger America than we have ever seen before.

—*Robert Schuller*
RELIGIOUS LEADER

185

For a first-generation immigrant such as myself, America looks so good that being invited to suggest how to make it yet better is almost like asking me to improve on Henry Moore's sculpture. Yet, it is a failing of both India, where I come from, and America, where I now live, that there is nothing to lose and everything to gain from taking an ego trip. Indeed, in both cultures, to borrow from Gore Vidal who doubtless speaks from the immediacy of his experience, requited self-love is the sweetest of human emotions. So, by George, you will get from me what you have asked for.

It is a cliché that the United States is a nation of immigrants. This endows it with the most humane policies of any nation today when it comes to refugees, legal and even illegal immigrants. And yet this generosity has frayed as the clamor against illegal immigrants, in particular, has grown. But these are poor scapegoats for problems that accrue from other, deeper causes such as the social disintegration in the inner cities. America would be a better place if this bashing of illegal immigrants was stopped and these hapless human being were not driven into exploitative work situations.

And America would equally be a better place if the vastly increased multi-ethnicity of our current society were given a stronger place in our public life. As I sit through Christian ceremonies on public occasions, now punctuated by an occasional rabbi, I think back to Mahatma Gandhi, who opened his public meetings with prayers taken from all of India's religions. Religious toleration and equal treatment of all faiths in public life are two different things, and America can profit from Gandhi's wonderful example.

—*Jagdish Bhagwati*
PROFESSOR OF ECONOMICS

186

HOW TO MAKE AMERICA BETTER:
FIVE MODEST PROPOSALS

1. Launder campaign contributions legally. Political contributions should be funneled through a central bank that distributes the money to candidates without the donor's name attached. You still get to exercise your free speech rights, your candidate still benefits from your financial support, but the system is cleansed of the influence-buying that sullies today's campaigns. Until this plan can be implemented, newspapers should publish the name of each legislator voting for a bill alongside a list of the corporations or interest groups that contributed big money to him or her and now stand to gain or lose by the bill (example drug or insurance companies). Show us the money trail.

2. Make all public transportation free. Ridership on buses and subways would increase which would mean fewer cars, less traffic congestion and air pollution, more mobility for students and elders. Financial savings would result from the elimination of personnel in change booths, collection, accounting, turnstile machine maintenance, and prosecuting fare beaters. Further funds can be raised by increasing bridge, tunnel, and highway tolls and the gasoline tax.

3. Mandate parenting education in the schools to ensure healthier family dynamics in the future. By the age of sixteen, all children should have had three semesters that teach them the basic timetable of child development; how much work and selflessness are involved in raising a child; and such fundamental skills as diaper changing, baby bathing, and disciplinary strategies. Students who complete the course will receive a "Certificate of Parenthood Preparation," without which no young person will qualify for a driver's license or marriage license.

4. While you party, let no one starve.   Borrowing an idea from an organization called Mazon: The Jewish Response to Hunger, Americans should tithe themselves an amount equal to 3 percent of the total cost of each Thanksgiving dinner, wedding, or other celebratory event in their lives and send a check for that amount to a food pantry or hunger organization.

5. Make voting compulsory.   Because the proof text of democracy is the ballot box, and full representation can never be achieved until all voices and all constituencies are heard, voting should be compulsory. Paying taxes is not voluntary; serving on a jury is not voluntary. By the same token, voting should be an obligation of citizenship. No American should be able to get a marriage license or passport unless he or she voted in the last election.

—*Letty Cottin Pogrebin*
AUTHOR

187

☛

—*Dan Piraro*
CARTOONIST

Reprinted courtesy of Dan Piraro.

The right to vote is cherished by every American, yet with each election fewer and fewer Americans are exercising that precious right. Barely half the eligible voters cast ballots in a presidential year. Off-year elections produce an even lower turnout. Why? The voters aren't dumb. They have figured out that most of the time their votes don't count. More than 90 percent of incumbents in Congress are reelected on a regular basis. In four out of five elections, voters have only one choice of candidate who has any real chance of winning. Special interests pour money into the lopsided races, ensuring their continuing influence on members of Congress.

America's population is becoming increasingly diverse. In the next century, whites will slip from the majority to become the largest *minority* of the population as Latinos and African Americans gain larger shares of the population. The membership of Congress has not kept pace with these demographic changes. Yes, Latinos and blacks are represented, but not in numbers proportionate to their population. And women, a numeric majority in the country, remain sorely underrepresented.

There is a way to simultaneously guarantee a more representative Congress and to give people a real stake in electing that Congress. The solution is to replace the present winner-take-all voting system with a new system based on proportional representation. Instead of one-member districts for the House of Representatives, the map could be redrawn to create districts of three, four, five, or more members. Voters would cast ballots for the party of their choice, with seats being apportioned according to party strength, or rank candidates in order of preference. Either way, minorities within these larger districts would stand a much better chance of voting for a winner.

In Senate races and the contest for president, voters would rank candidates 1, 2, 3, and so on. If no candidate obtained a majority on the first ballot, the candidate with the fewest votes would be eliminated but would transfer his or her second-choice votes to the remaining candidates. This process would continue until one candidate gained a majority.

In the presidential elections of 1992 and 1996, Democrat Bill Clinton faced not only Republican opponents George Bush (1992) and Bob Dole (1996) but the strong independent candidacy of Ross Perot and opposition from the Libertarian Party, which gained ballot access in all fifty states. Clinton was unable to win a majority in either election. If the second-choice ballots of the losing candidates had been counted, Clinton would have either become a majority president or been upset by one of his challengers. Either way, voters would have had the satisfaction of knowing their ballots really counted.

The Center for Voting and Democracy, headed by John Anderson, himself a maverick independent candidate for president in 1980, is the leading advocate for this bold way of injecting vitality and fairness into our election system. It has worked well in other democracies around the world. It would work well in the world's leading democracy.

—*Tom Brazaitis*
JOURNALIST

"A culture of disbelief" is how Professor Steven Carter of Yale University describes today's America—a nation where devoted people with faith in the living God are often ostracized and ridiculed.

Perhaps America would be a better place if we revisited our roots of faith that made this a strong nation from its inception.

I encourage Americans to see firsthand the monuments of our nation's pioneers. A visit to our Capitol building offers visual reminders of the vital role religious belief played in founding America. The Rotunda features a painting of the *Mayflower* pilgrims, kneeling in prayer on the deck of their ship with the New Testament of Our Lord and Savior Jesus Christ open before them.

There's also a scene featuring missionary Mother Joseph, kneeling in prayer with architectural tools surrounding her—symbolic of the eleven hospitals, seven academies, five Indian schools, and two orphanages she helped erect in the Pacific Northwest.

A statue of the Reverend Dr. Martin Luther King, Jr., reminds us how racism has plagued this nation, yet God gives us leaders to challenge us to put aside differences and love one another as God has loved us.

Each of these paintings and statues serves as a reminder—of where we came from and where we are headed as a nation. Take time to "see" those whose lives have inspired us. Recognize our heritage of faith. Then celebrate the virtues of that faith that resonate from Frederick Douglass's words: "The life of a nation is secure only while the nation is honest, truthful, and virtuous."

—Don Argue

RELIGIOUS LEADER

190

Imagine an America where the elites of this nation finally figured out that it is in their self-interest to develop *all of its human capital to its fullest potential.* Suppose this realization took root and focused on the most isolated, impoverished, marginalized ghettoes, reservations, barrios, and small rural communities in this land. Imagine that these institutional elites figured out that America has squandered so much of its intellectual and social capital by neglecting to adequately develop the capacity of those who just happen to be poor and nonwhite. But most of all, imagine if America were able to see its poor youth as its biggest asset. Rather than scapegoating teenagers and young adults for the nation's problems and depicting them as deficient and problematic, adults of all races and classes would begin to mentor, nurture, and support young people. Instead of teens being on death row or incarcerated with adults, maybe we would begin to recognize that young people really do represent the future of this nation— our communities, organizations, institutions, and economy. Wouldn't it be a radical notion for American leaders if they figured this one out?

—Lisa Y. Sullivan

ACTIVIST

To ensure an enduring democracy, we need to revisit the multicultural and environmental roots of our democratic traditions. While the founders of American democracy emulated the separation of powers, federalism, and vesting of sovereignty in the people of the Iroquois League, not all of the Iroquois League's visionary ideas were incorporated into our government. Thus, we should once again look to Native American models to revitalize our democracy. The Iroquois League's tradition also fostered respect for Mother Earth. Iroquois chiefs were charged with "protecting seven generations past, those in the bellies of women, those on this earth now, and seven unborn generations in the future." Imagine if U.S. leaders were admonished to think of their responsibilities in those terms today? Since North America is a unique synthesis of Native American, European, and many other peoples, the last five hundred years have been a multicultural experience. Thus, factoring stewardship of the environment into our political equation would be a significant challenge to our democratic system. A Native American elder told me, "The White people think they own the earth, but Indians know that Mother Earth owns them." Such Native American environmental insights are crucial to reinventing ecocentric and democratic traditions for the twenty-first century.

—*Donald A. Grinde, Jr.*
PROFESSOR OF HISTORY

192

TUNE OUT, TURN OFF, AND DROP IN

It has practically become a media truism that information technologies such as the Internet will improve our democracy—if not save it outright—by making available more information and encouraging the formation of virtual communities. A public able to access the Library of Congress will vote smarter, and Americans able to associate with people from the other end of the world will gain a greater appreciation of other cultures. Or so the argument goes.

Of course, many of those preaching such let-them-eat-data solutions to our nation's problems are the ones who have the most to gain from a more wired world. Truth is, twenty-four hours a day of C-SPAN haven't made more people write letters to their congressmen, and the wealth of information already available on the Net isn't encouraging more citizens to vote. Indeed, most Americans already have access to more media than even existed during much of recorded history. Fascinated by the facts at our fingertips, mistaking them for knowledge, we indulge our info-addiction at the expense of action.

Done right, democracy is not a spectator sport but a participatory one—and it works best when people are involved in their local communities, not ones that exist only on screens. We need to tune out the fifty-seven channels of cable that bring the world to our doorstep and get involved in community boards. We need to turn off the Internet and its endless esoterica and volunteer for food banks close to home. While we're at it, we should drop in on the neighbors and see how they're doing.

—Robert Levine
MAGAZINE EDITOR

"Make America better": it sounds like a daunting task—some would say improbable, if not impossible. Many people want to make a difference but fail to take any action because they believe their solitary act won't make an impact. I have seen how an ordinary person's simplest act can make an extraordinary difference and have a lasting impact.

My mother, Lucimarian Tolliver Roberts, was raised during the Depression in Akron, Ohio. In grammar school she was fortunate enough to have someone recognize her potential. That person was Wilma Schnegg, my mother's teacher. Wilma Schnegg was not a particularly attractive woman, but to the students she warmly embraced as they entered her classroom, Miss Schnegg was beautiful. She was a teacher who would forever change Lucimarian's life. Miss Schnegg, the school's enrichment teacher, saw something special in Lucimarian and told her so. Miss Schnegg told young Lucimarian to continue making good grades so she could one day go to college and have a professional career. This was not just a passing conversation. Every year, through grammar school and later high school, Miss Schnegg was there encouraging Lucimarian. She was one of the first people to call and congratulate Lucimarian in June 1942, when the *Sunday Akron Beacon-Journal* announced that Lucimarian Tolliver was the recipient of the John S. Knight Academic Scholarship. My mother would go to Howard University, graduate with a bachelor's degree in psychology, and marry another industrious student, Lawrence Roberts . . . my father. Lucimarian today is a polished woman whose credentials are awe-inspiring. She was the first woman to serve as the president of the Mississippi Coast Coliseum and the first woman to chair the Mississippi

Board of Education, and she currently serves as a member of the New Orleans Board of Directors of the Federal Reserve Bank.

Miss Schnegg had no idea that helping my mother get a college scholarship would lead to her meeting my father at Howard. She had no idea that marriage would afford my mother the opportunity to see the world as the wife of a Tuskegee airman who would eventually retire as an air force colonel. How could Miss Schnegg have known that because she taught my mother the importance of an education, she would have four children who would all go on to to college and have professional careers? Not only did Miss Schnegg encourage one child named Lucimarian Tolliver, but she improved life for generations of others.

Miss Schnegg just wanted to help *one* child. My family has founded an organization based on that premise called Each One Save One. What many children lack is not money but hope.

Wilma Schnegg tossed a life preserver to Lucimarian Tolliver, and the ripple effects will be felt for as long as she has a descendant on this earth. Each one *can* save one and in the process make America better.

—*Robin Roberts*
SPORTS COMMENTATOR

194

The United States of America defined the twentieth century as a century of freedom and opportunity, helping hundreds of millions of people walk in freedom—free from the tyrannies of communism, Nazism, and fascism. To ensure that the next century is an American century as well, we must motivate our culture to attain its highest and best, rather than accommodate our culture at its lowest and least.

Too often, government has discriminated against the very institutions that succeed in inspiring people to attain their highest and best. America's charitable and faith-based organizations can frequently succeed where government has failed: in moving people from dependence to independence. Yet laws and interpretations of the law have blocked these institutions from realizing their full potential.

In the new welfare reform law, I had the privilege of authoring the "Charitable Choice" provision. This part of the new law allows states to contract with charitable and faith-based institutions to transform lives by helping people move from dependence on government to the freedom and dignity of work. Maryland, Michigan, Mississippi, and other states are already making use of this pioneering law. They are seeing the success that comes from fully enlisting the energy and creativity of the private sector.

We must continue on this course. Whether in drug treatment, juvenile rehabilitation, or job training, the law should allow people to seek their highest and best in the way best suited to their needs. By involving charities and faith-based organizations in developing solutions to our social and cultural problems, we will take a giant step toward a better America.

—*John Ashcroft*
POLITICIAN

Recently, newspapers, magazines, and television news programs across the country have been filled, almost on a daily basis, with stories of unimaginable horror about teenagers leaving newborn babies abandoned on trash heaps, murdered in bathrooms and motel rooms, and left in closets. One story tells of a young man, knowingly infected with the HIV virus, who continued to infect numerous sexual partners until he was identified as the person responsible for a mini-epidemic involving ten people for certain, and perhaps many more. Authorities say that up to eighty young men and women may have been affected through primary or secondary contact with him.

We read of young women who deliver full-term infants without having been aware that they were pregnant. In my own clinic, the Adolescent Health Center, a part of Mount Sinai Medical Center in New York, it is not unusual for young women to see a physician because they believe they have a "stomach virus," only to be diagnosed as being six and seven (sometimes even more) months pregnant. There are times when a young person will even be accompanied by a parent, who is also ignorant of the fact that her daughter is in the third trimester of an unplanned pregnancy.

What is behind these bizarre and heartbreaking occurrences? Why, in this rich and powerful nation that prides itself on being "advanced," is there so much unplanned teen pregnancy, STD, and sex abuse? There are many reasons for these events. However, a large part of the problem stems from the lack of communication between parents and their children about sex and sexuality. Without accurate information lovingly given, our young people are stumbling in the dark. Things that *must* be spoken about are remaining unsaid, and the results, as we see, can be tragic.

Children must have clear, correct information about sexuality in order to make wise choices. Study after study reveals that while young people learn from friends, school, and the media, they'd really like to get the answers about sexuality primarily from their parents! With that in mind, I have compiled a list of some crucial dos and don'ts that I hope will help people talk with their kids about sex:

DO:

- Normalize sexuality. Sex is an integral part of people's lives no matter what their values or views.

- Acknowledge your own fears and concerns. We may be adults, but most of us didn't grow up feeling comfortable with and talking with our parents (or anyone else) about sexuality.

- Talk about sex. Use whatever time or tools you have: at dinner, watching television, driving in the car. They may roll their eyes and feign embarrassment, but really they'll be pleased to know.

- Tell your kids that it's okay not to know everything (or be totally "cool") about sex. None of us knows everything.

- Be clear, specific, and factually correct. Your kids have the right to unbiased information about puberty changes, reproductive health, sexual intercourse, sexual orientation, pregnancy and parenting, HIV, and STDs.

- Teach your family's values about sex, but don't preach. If you think your kids should wait before they have sexual intercourse, tell them—gently but wisely. Offer them positive alternatives to sexual behaviors you wish them to not engage in.

- *Talk about protection*—the different kinds, where to get them, where to go for information. Show them condoms; go on a shopping trip with them to the local pharmacy.

- Get help if you feel uncomfortable—by taking a sexuality class, attending a workshop, talking to other parents, reading a book.

DON'T:

- Assume that they're too young to know. If they're asking the questions, they want and need the answers.

- Assume that boys know everything they need to know. Research shows that American boys know far less about sexuality than girls.

- Believe the myth that the more your kids know, the more they'll do. Studies reveal that the more information and the more discussion young people have about sexuality, the less likely they are to engage in unsafe sexual practices.

- Think you have to be an expert. You and your children can learn together.

—Dr. Cydelle Berlin
ADOLESCENT-HEALTH ADVOCATE

SEARCHING FOR COMMUNITY: A BETTER WAY

The Cuban passport issued to me forty years ago shows a little girl not quite three years old, with a protruding lower lip and a scowl I now recognize in the faces of my own daughters. The photo marks a turning point in my life—my family's move to the United States in search of economic opportunities no longer available to them in the island that had been home for several generations. That defining experience poses a complex question: Can an immigrant suggest ways to make America better when the very fact of immigration implies that what we have come to is inherently better than what we left behind?

Forty years of assimilation later, my answer is an unequivocal "Yes!"

It is, perhaps, ironic that in forging a common national identity based on individualism, Americans have lost a genuine sense of community—a far graver sin, in my opinion, than the loss of family values proclaimed by many of my clerical colleagues. The dominant culture has lost the intricate network of relationships that both transcend and enhance the biological families. We have lost both the support and the mutual accountability that come with knowing that we are part of a fabric larger than our individual selves.

Immigrant communities, having stubbornly and gloriously refused to give up our ways, have much to teach the dominant culture about what it is to be connected to one another in ways that strengthen not only individuals but the larger society. Latino culture is rooted in the larger community, the extended family, the circle that reaches out rather than drawing in.

How can we make the country of our adoption better? By bringing more, not less, of our culture and traditions into the process. By expanding our communities to embrace all others. This is the gift we bring.

—*Reverend Martha M. Cruz*
RELIGIOUS LEADER

197

America's already a great country. A terrific country. We have freedom and opportunities that exist in no other place. It's not perfect—and I wouldn't begin to pretend to know the reasons underpinning our various problems. But I do know that one terrific way to unite people is through a common goal. We all share a stake in America's future. The idea is that we need to get involved. This is true whether you start a company, work on a grassroots campaign, or volunteer in your local Boy Scouts chapter. Private philanthropy is a great American tradition. It doesn't matter whether you're devoting time or money. In every city and in every town, there is something you can do. I'm not suggesting you donate a certain percentage of your annual salary or spend a specified number of hours per month feeding the homeless or reading to a child. I'm just encouraging a wider participation in a distinctly American pastime. Get involved! There is nothing more satisfying or fulfilling—and there's certainly nothing that unites our country more than the heritage we leave to our children.

—*Michael R. Bloomberg*
BUSINESS EXECUTIVE

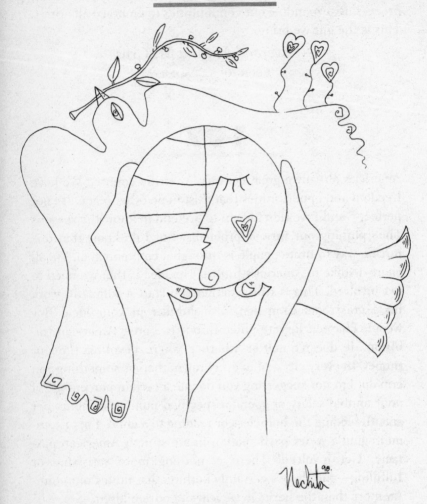

One of the most important things we need is peace. It's great to do community work—but sometimes we forget how important peace is. Another thing that would make America a better place is children my age—younger and older. . . . We need to embrace positive and good news . . . because we sometimes are fascinated by bad news. Embracing good news brings good news. Focusing on bad news brings bad news. We need responsibility, positive attitude, and determination to make the world a better place.

—*Alexandra Nechita*
CHILD PRODIGY

199

ABOLISH GOVERNMENT
CLASSIFICATION BY RACE

The single most important reform that the American nation needs is the outlawing of government classification of American citizens by race.

For almost four centuries, American citizens and residents have been assigned to one of several racial categories that were based on racist ideology, not sound anthropology: white, black, mulatto, Oriental. In the early 1960s, liberal integrationists sought to eliminate the use of racial labels by the government. Unfortunately, as affirmative action became the favored method of redressing the inequities of America's caste and class society, many reformers were persuaded by the argument that eliminating racial labels would make monitoring of racial progress impossible.

Our present system of racial labels—white, African-American, Hispanic, Asian/Pacific Islander, and Native American—was devised in the 1970s by the Office of Management and Budget. It represents bureaucratic logic, not social reality. Those who propose a "mixed-race" category take the pernicious idea of government-certified "races" for granted.

More than a quarter century of race-based public policy programs has failed to address the most intractable legacies of American slavery and segregation. The liberal integrationists of the 1950s and early 1960s, like Martin Luther King, Jr., who wanted to help poor whites as well as poor blacks, were right: we should abandon divisive, zero-sum policies of counting by race in favor of color-blind reforms aimed at helping the disadvantaged of all races. And the government should cease reinforcing popular stereotypes by mislabeling Americans, who in reality belong to only one race: the human one.

—*Michael Lind*
JOURNALIST

200

Let us adopt as policy the slogan of the Midwives Alliance of North America: "A midwife for every mother." What would that mean?

A *MIDWIFE* FOR EVERY MOTHER

The English word "midwife" means "with woman." A midwife is a childbirth professional whose work goes beyond "catching babies." Some midwives are nurses, but many are not; they come from a long tradition of women who work with mothers, teaching and guiding them through pregnancy, birth, and early motherhood. A midwife nurtures a woman's strength, helping and supporting her through the sometimes difficult transition to motherhood. Unlike obstetricians, who are trained within medicine as surgical specialists, midwives are focused on birth as a normal, healthy process. Yet midwives also have the skills needed to identify problems and help women get whatever medical help they or their babies might need.

A MIDWIFE FOR EVERY *MOTHER*

Having a baby is not a medical event; it is part of a woman's life, part of her family's life, part of her growth and development as a woman and as a mother, part of her sexuality, part of her spiritual and psychological life. Midwives think about a woman not as a "host" or "maternal environment" or "maternal barrier," as the obstetric literature refers to her, but as a mother-in-process, a woman becoming (or becoming again) a mother. A birth that makes a woman feel comfortable with her body and her baby, and trusting of herself and her partner and family, goes a long way toward giving her a good start on mothering.

A MIDWIFE *FOR* EVERY MOTHER

A midwife helps a woman get what she needs—from society, from her family, from her medical caregivers. Everything from helping the woman's partner/husband to give her a back rub while in labor to helping her get food stamps to seeing that she is respectfully informed and consulted when there are problems with her newborn falls within the purview of the midwife. She is the advocate of the woman, standing beside her and being there for her.

A MIDWIFE FOR EVERY MOTHER

A woman in pregnancy and birth needs to develop a trusting relationship with *a* midwife (or two or three in partnership); she cannot form such a relationship in huge practices, where caregivers come and go. Consistency of care is important: it is how a midwife comes to know a mother and how a mother comes to know and trust a midwife.

A MIDWIFE FOR *EVERY* MOTHER

Midwifery is not just for "low-risk" women, those who can give birth easily. Women who face pregnancy complications, who have had difficulties in previous pregnancies, who face the birth of babies with problems, these women too need the supportive, nurturant, teaching help of a midwife. No woman is too young, too old, too sick, or too "at risk" to need the kind of care midwives give.

A midwife for every mother would mean giving women—and their babies, partners, and families—respectful, empowering, loving births and the best possible start to families.

—*Barbara Katz Rothman*
PROFESSOR OF SOCIOLOGY

201

Honesty in politics is a necessity in order for the American people to trust and respect their politicians. Many politicians talk out of the side of their mouth, promising one thing, then doing another. It is essential to hold politicians accountable to a high standard of ethical conduct *during* their campaigns as well as *after* their election.

We must motivate all Americans to *vote*. Americans should be responsible voters and participate much more in the process of electing government officials. As a people we need to educate ourselves thoroughly about who is running for office and exactly what the politics of those candidates are before casting our vote. Very often officials are elected by a *minority* of eligible voters. Far too many people check off on the party line or just take a guess because they are uninformed. That is not voting. It is our duty as Americans to take an active part in the process of electing our government officials, not just be mindless drones.

Also, we need to dump the Electoral College for presidential election. The president should be elected by the people directly. We need to know that our vote goes to the candidate and not to a committee.

—Daniel L. "Digital Dan" Lawrence
RADIO PERSONALITY

202

The United States is a country created from genocide: the systematic annihilation of millions of native peoples.

Begun in the seventeenth century and continuing to this day, the American holocaust is estimated to have exterminated more than 80 million people in North and South America, and 10 million in what is now the United States.

The borders of the continent were no bar to American aggression. In 1893, the U.S. military overthrew our Native Hawaiian government. In 1898, the United States annexed Hawai'i, Guam, Puerto Rico, the Philippines, and other possessions against the resistance of the indigenous people. Thus did the United States enter the twentieth century as a global power.

The Native peoples who survived this American holocaust remain in captivity today. Therefore, all indigenous nations now under American hegemony have both a moral and a legal claim to the following:

1. Acknowledgment by the U.S. government of past wrongs, including invasion, occupation, and forced annexation of Native lands and peoples.

2. Restitution to the Native peoples. Where treaties are in place, this would entail honoring all conditions, particularly return of lands and waters.

    Where treaties were not signed, a formal process for restitution must be created. In the case of my people, Native Hawaiians, this process has concluded with a 1993 federal apology. All entitlements in the original congressional apology regarding the overthrow of our national government in 1893 were deleted. Thus, there is a continuing need for serious reparations, including of land and monies.

3. Compliance with international instruments such as the U.N. Declaration on the Rights of Indigenous Peoples.

Genocide can never be repaired, because murdered human beings can never be replaced. But the United States can begin to honor the dead by making substantive restitution to the living.

—*Haunani-Kay Trask*

UNIVERSITY DIRECTOR OF HAWAIIAN STUDIES

203

THE NEED FOR NEW LEADERSHIP
IN BLACK COMMUNITIES

For much of our history, black Americans lived under a racial caste system whose nature was similar to the status-based society that existed in Europe in the eighteenth century. Before the civil rights revolution, one's chances of economic, social, and political advancement were not determined by talent, initiative, and industry. The prospects of the overwhelming majority of blacks were severely limited by state-sponsored segregation and hard-core white racism. However, racial discrimination is no longer an insurmountable obstacle for black Americans. Market forces, enhanced legal protections, and changes in the attitudes of white Americans go a long way toward explaining why racial discrimination is no longer an insurmountable obstacle for blacks.

Traditional civil rights groups, such as the NAACP and the Urban League, deserve a considerable amount of credit and praise for their historic role in leading the charge against de jure segregation and convincing many white Americans that their racist attitudes and discriminatory actions were at odds with the ideals embedded in the Declaration of Independence and the Constitution. However, these same organizations are guilty of ignoring the fact that racial discrimination is no longer an insurmountable barrier to economic, political, and social advancement for black Americans.

Many black communities are struggling against ineffective public schools, disintegrating families, rampant crime, and the ravages of drug addiction. For many blacks residing in these communities, these problems, not racial animus, constitute an insurmountable barrier to advancement. In the main, traditional civil rights groups have limited their efforts to the preservation of racial preference programs. While these programs unfairly accelerate the advancement of those blacks who possess "middle-class" values, they do not address the needs of the black children who are forced to attend dysfunctional public schools in our inner cities, nor do they address the spiritual decay that manifests itself in high rates of crime, illegitimacy, and drug addiction. The blacks who face these problems are in dire need of effective aid.

The government is ill suited to play a dominant role in solving the spiritual and social problems that plague urban centers. Traditional civil rights advocates, many of whom are ministers, not only have failed to address these problems, they have attacked anyone who has raised the issues. Traditional civil rights groups appear to be unwilling or unable to alter their mission so that it places a heavier emphasis on market-oriented, community-based approaches to solving some of the problems that are preventing many blacks from advancing. But all is not lost. A new generation of leadership is developing in black communities. The new civil rights agenda promoted by the Center for New Black Leadership and other community-based groups focuses on the spiritual and economic problems in black communities.

Faith-based organizations and community groups are forming relationships with the inner-city residents who are in most need of help. This relationship is vital. Someone must convince black teenagers that having a child out of wedlock is wrong. Churches are playing a greater role by encouraging churchgoing married couples to provide guidance to black children before they have children out of wedlock or are lured into criminal activity. Local churches and grassroots organizations are also using their political muscle to persuade politicians to create pilot projects for publicly financed school vouchers that are restricted to the economically disadvantaged.

We must work to remove the remaining barriers to advancement in black communities. We must provide disadvantaged blacks with the values and skills needed to pursue the American dream. We cannot claim that the civil rights movement was a complete success until we accomplish this task.

—*Gerald A. Reynolds*
NONPROFIT DIRECTOR

204

In today's America, people move quickly from one company to the next, one project to the next. Here a small business, there a large corporation, here a nonprofit. Increasingly, people are employed in these jobs through temp agencies.

Economists project that the number of temp workers will double by 2005. According to the U.S. Department of Labor, the temp agency Manpower Inc. is already the largest private employer in America.

Now, nothing is inherently wrong about temp work if the jobs (a) pay well, (b) provide health benefits, retirement savings opportunities, and paid holidays, and (c) recognize the right of people to organize and negotiate for their standards of living. Temp work, however, provides (d) none of the above.

So my solution for America's economic future is to make all members of Congress—and their staffs—temp workers.

You see, we need two things: (1) real talk about what makes a good job and (2) real reforms to change more of today's bad jobs into good jobs.

Setting goals for good jobs and working toward them used to be a collaborative process among government, the private sector, and individuals. People were relatively well organized because they stayed in one workplace for years. This organization brought decent incomes, weekends off, the minimum wage, safe working conditions, pensions, health care.

Today, in the new "nonstandard" work environments, people have fewer protections, such as the right to press for wage increases or health insurance—and less power to do anything about them. One of America's strongest legacies, shared prosperity, is rapidly eroding.

Temp workers are at the very bottom. They—we—have a lower standard of living and less long-term opportunity than traditional full-time workers. The industry is particularly rigged against women and people who do not graduate from college.

I believe that temp workers should have health benefits. Even if the government has to step in and mandate a subsidized benefit package, temp workers should have health care. If they did have health care, companies seeking greater economic flexibility and efficiency—a worthy goal that moves America forward—would still use temp workers. But companies making a choice based on the wrong values—replacing good jobs with temp jobs in order to cut benefits—would lose the financial incentive.

At the same time, people who want to work temp for their own flexibility, as well as people who do so because nothing else is available, would have basic health care. And that would make America a much better place to live in.

—*Hans Riemer*
NONPROFIT DIRECTOR

205

MAKE AMERICA BETTER
BY REDUCING ILLEGAL DRUGS

The greatest resource America has is the creative energy of our youth. Just as the external environment is a web of interdependent systems, so too is the physical world within each individual. Drugs upset—sometimes irrevocably—the chemical balance that determines personality. Drugs sap the strength of children and of our country as a whole. Reducing illegal drugs would make America better by improving public health, education, and productivity while supporting families and communities.

Here are five ways to enhance American freedom through reducing the number of people enslaved by dangerous substances:

1. Use mass media to teach children about toxic and addictive drugs, including alcohol and tobacco. The Office of National Drug Control Policy has asked Congress for $175 million to fund an advertising campaign that would "sell" a drug-free lifestyle to young people.*

2. Offer more treatment through the criminal justice system, workplaces, schools, hospitals, and clinics so that Americans whose lives have been damaged by drugs have an opportunity to recover.

3. Reduce the number of Americans behind bars by expanding drug courts along with treatment programs within prisons. Our country now incarcerates more citizens than

*Editor's Note: Our contributor wrote this essay in August 1997.

any other Western nation, and illegal drugs contribute enormously to the cycle of crime.

4. Reduce violence in our streets, teen pregnancy, delinquency, and domestic abuse by fighting illegal drugs that contribute to these problems.

5. Increase the life span of Americans by decreasing drug-related deaths from overdoses, car crashes, diseases such as AIDS and lung cancer, hospital emergencies, and violent crime.

—*Barry R. McCaffrey*
POLICY MAKER

206

We fret about "teen" violence, complain about "inner-city youth" or urban "gangs," express shock at drugs and violence in suburban schools. Yet news reports never mention that, whether white or black, inner city or suburban, these bands of marauding "youths" or troubled "teenagers" are all young men.

Meanwhile, thirtysomethings on the make wear power ties, chomp on enormous cigars, and down power lunches in the world's largest display of postindustrial impotence—as if power were a fashion accessory. Others rally with the evangelical Promise Keepers or march with a million black men on the streets of Washington, D.C., while their fathers troop off to the woods with Robert Bly on a mythic quest to retrieve their lost manhood.

American masculinity is in crisis. The meaning of manhood has been loosed from its traditional anchors: the patriarchal family, the all-male workplace, an expanding economy with room for men on the move.

What are men looking for out there in the woods, at religious rallies, in urban streets? In a word: soul. The three largest men's movements in America today—Promise Keepers, mythopoetic retreats, and the Million Man March—are spiritual movements, concerned with allowing men a deeper, more emotionally resonant, spiritually meaningful life.

This deeper, richer, more resonant life is American masculinity's Holy Grail. For two centuries, we've shipped out, run off, headed west in search of a new start, an opportunity to prove our manhood. "I reckon I got to light out for the territory," observed Huck Finn, "because Aunt Sally, she's going to adopt me and sivilize me and I can't stand it."

I have but two words for American men: *Come home!*

Feminism accomplished half a revolution, freeing women from the requirement that they stay home and care for children. Today that's increasingly a woman's choice, and most American women are struggling to balance work and family life.

But if women were imprisoned in the home, men are exiled from it, unable and unwilling to complete the transformation feminism began.

This is not a jeremiad that lays all America's social problems at the foot of absent fatherhood, a dubious and empirically shallow proposition. Nor is it one of those disingenuous calls for tightening divorce laws as a way to keep marriages together. We need strong laws to keep men responsible, not to keep bad marriages together. Responsibility is more than a lifestyle option.

Responsibility is the way for men to live the lives we

want—animated by close relationships with our wives, our partners, our children, our friends. We can't have those lives by running off to the woods, only by coming home and doing our share of the mundane chores that really constitute nurturing: sharing housework and child care. In short, we need more Ironing Johns, not Iron Johns.

It's also about the lives we want for our children. As women work outside the home, our children, both boys and girls, will grow up to know that competence, ambition, and skill are qualities that *grown-ups* have, not something men have and that women may sporadically exhibit. And if men share housework and child care, our children will grow up knowing that nurturing is something that grown-ups do, not something that women do routinely and men do only at half-time on Sunday afternoon.

Coming home also involves taking a public stance. Though we tend to think of "family-friendly" workplace reforms—on-site child care, flextime, parental leave—as "women's issues," they are more accurately *parents'* issues. As men identify as parents, *we* must support them so that we can be involved parents.

Jefferson envisioned democracy as a delicate balance between rights and responsibilities. American men have spent so much time and energy recently focusing on their rights, we've forgotten that it is responsibility that connects us to our communities, our friends, our families, our selves. Coming home will both support women's efforts to balance work and family and allow men to live the lives we say we want to live. "Feminism," wrote novelist Floyd Dell eighty years ago, "is going to make it possible for the first time for men to be free."

—*Michael Kimmel*
PROFESSOR OF SOCIOLOGY

Ensuring that all children have access to safe places, challenging experiences, and caring people on a daily basis would make America better, both today and in the future. We can achieve this goal by instituting high-quality universal preschool for all three- and four-year-olds and by providing school-age children with a better selection of after-school activities.

Preschool education, if high quality, prepares children for success in elementary school; it is associated with less grade failure, less special education, and higher achievement test scores. The effects, such as lower rates of juvenile delinquency and fewer problem behaviors during adolescence, can be long-lasting. High-quality preschool surrounds young children with caring adults and challenging experiences in a safe setting.

Engaging after-school activities for elementary and middle school children counteract disengagement from school and offer alternatives to risky behaviors, such as drinking, smoking, and early sexual activity, during the typically unsupervised time after school. As with preschools, suitable after-school activities provide youths with the opportunity for challenging experiences and caring relationships with adults in a safe setting.

All community institutions, including schools, religious institutions, community centers, medical centers, and businesses, need to reach out to the children and youths in their community to guarantee them access to these opportunities: caring adults, challenging experiences, and safe places.

—Jeanne Brooks-Gunn and Jodie L. Roth
PROFESSOR OF CHILD DEVELOPMENT; RESEARCH SCIENTIST

Suggestion: A high-speed passenger rail system; a bullet train linking the major U.S. cities together.

Rationale: Time is people's shrinking commodity. As our nation's population continues to grow, the arteries of our current modes of transportation continue to clog. Perhaps it is time to look into high-speed rail.

To meet the daily travel needs of the American public, as well as the domestic and foreign tourist industry, America must consider alternative modes of transportation. The answer is not to build bigger airports or planes in order to accommodate the storage and transport of additional travelers on their way to Whereverville but to provide an alternative, safe, and rapid way for them to arrive there. Let's keep in mind that there is a large percentage of the traveling public that literally hates to fly—are scared to death of it and would be much more comfortable on the ground if they didn't have to go at a snail's pace.

The current move for high-occupancy vehicle (HOV) lanes, while providing small populations some travel convenience, carries a high state and federal price tag. Restricted lanes are excellent public relations venues, showcasing our tax dollar at work. And in some states, such as California, joint-venture funding between state and private sources is providing high-speed commutes.

But reality sets in when you see half a dozen vehicles pass you in the HOV lanes and you are stuck in the fast lane of a parking lot with twenty thousand other cars. Additional roadbed opened to the traveler boosts our economies by providing employment, but it pales in the reality of our pressing situation.

High-speed rail makes good sense from every viewpoint.

But who should pay? I think everyone would have a role to play, from the user to the investor. Joint-venture capital between the airlines and the rail system might be one of several options. That venue is already in place and may just need expansion. Money could also come from the private sector, as in the case of the HOV lanes in California, where the user pays via an electronic register.

Tens of thousands of people would experience the benefits of work with a challenge again. Caution: Don't overautomate it; rather, put live bodies at workstations along the way. Let the locals have ownership. There might even be a small exodus from the cities back to rural America, a blessing all America could enjoy. City renewal could be a side benefit, as the wave of the future streaked into town.

There is something romantic about traveling on the rails. Think about it: high-speed rail is a commute that just might put time back into the hands of people. Why not try and revive it in the good old United States of America?

—*Thomas R. Neslund*
NONPROFIT DIRECTOR

If history, especially the history of the last fifty years, has taught us anything, it is that any successful social change must first recognize, then flow in, the direction of technological change. One can no more ignore the digital revolution today than one could the Industrial Revolution two centuries ago. Yet, despite the increasing lip service politicians, academics, and social activists give to semiconductors, computers, and the Internet, few have shown any appreciation that we are, in fact, in the midst of one of the most profound social, economic, even philosophical transformations in human history. They are swimming against a gigantic wave they don't even know is there and cannot understand why they are perpetually proven wrong.

So before we can make America better, we must first identify the underlying forces that are driving the country forward. The electronics industry, the only sector of our economy consistently proven right in its predictions over the last five decades, has long known what these forces are. And upon that knowledge it has built the richest and most powerful manufacturing sector the world has ever known. The most important of these forces is Moore's Law, the doubling of the power of computer chips that takes place every two years. If, in 1960, you had understood only Moore's Law and nothing else about the dynamics of American life, you would have had a better chance of predicting the state of this country on the verge of the millennium than with any other piece of knowledge.

Moore's Law still dominates modern life. But other, equally powerful, forces are appearing now as well. They deal with the Internet, microcontrollers, networks, and, perhaps soon, biotechnology. This suggests that the extraordinary pace of change we are experiencing now may pale before what is to come. A second lesson of history is that technological change is never restricted to new products and services. Rather, it emanates outward like a shock wave, first to companies and institutions, then to society and culture, and ultimately even to the way we see ourselves and the world. What begins as technological revolution always ends as philosophical evolution.

We are only halfway through this process. To determine how to make America better, we must not only predict what America will be a decade or more from now, but, much harder, imagine *who* we will be in that future. And that understanding will come only when all of our citizens, not just our technologists and high-tech entrepreneurs, understand the true nature of the dynamo at the center of our society. Only then will our educational programs, tax policies, social services, health care, and every other facet of public life in the United States be aligned with the direction of change.

Until then, we will be flying blind.

—*Michael S. Malone*
AUTHOR

—*Tom Tomorrow*

CARTOONIST

211

MENTORS: PRIORITY NUMBER ONE
FOR AT-RISK KIDS

What real-world solutions are there for the growing number of young people who find themselves on the streets of America with nowhere to go and no support from friends and family—and with fewer and fewer government-sponsored programs available to assist them?

After more than a decade of providing shelter and basic care to homeless youth, the staff of Covenant House have recognized that a desperate need exists for longer-term assistance among the older youth. To meet this need, we have developed an independent living, job-training program designed to provide young people with the chance to change their lives as they become more confident about themselves. Integral to fostering this growth is the relationships the residents develop with their mentors.

Mentors are volunteers who, despite their busy schedules, have freely chosen to do what other adults in their experience have not done for them. Through caring, candid relationships, mentors contribute significantly to the personal and social growth of the residents.

Volunteering is inherent in the American character. Alexis de Tocqueville, the French political historian, noted this American trait more than 150 years ago, when he wrote, "When an American asks for the cooperation of his fellow citizens, it is seldom refused; and I have often seen it afforded spontaneously and with great good will."

Volunteering is not a slogan, event, or one-day fling. Mentoring is a special form of volunteering that builds a sustained, productive, and caring relationship between an experienced, accomplished adult and a young person in need of guidance, support, encouragement, and advice. It takes a special kind of person, especially if one is mentoring a teenager or young adult.

If Americans expect our hurting young people to pull themselves up by their own bootstraps, we owe it to them to try to teach them how to tie their shoelaces.

I often reflect on a little lesson I learned long ago from our Judeo-Christian heritage: "On the street I saw a small girl cold and shivering in a thin dress with little hope of a decent meal. I became angry and said to God: 'Why do you permit this? Why don't you do something about it?' For a while God said nothing. That night He replied quite suddenly, 'I certainly did something about it. I made you.'" You can make an enormous difference in a young person's life, but you must do something about it!

—*Sister Mary Rose McGeady*
NONPROFIT DIRECTOR

212

How to improve our political situation?

How about doing away with ourselves? This has never been an extremely popular notion, but current evidence suggests that it makes perfectly good sense. Stephen Hawking has theorized that the reason we don't routinely hear from creatures from other planets is that once civilization reaches a certain point, it destroys itself. His argument goes as follows: Our destructive capacities have increased by leaps and bounds within the last fifty years or so, yet we still have basically the same DNA we had in the jungle hundreds of thousands, if not millions of years ago. Jungle DNA plus atomic weapons. A bad combination.

The hope is that we could modify our DNA in such a way as to make us less lethal to ourselves and others. Not everyone will agree with this, so there will be fighting, maybe even war. There will be those in favor of modifying our genes and those against it, the Dolly-ites against the anti-Dolly-ites, and the Dolly-ites will win.

Awaiting us, presumably, is a new genetic future. Or maybe, like Rodney Brooks, the MIT robot scientist in my movie *Fast, Cheap and Out of Control,* we can abdicate our role on the planet in favor of some new, emergent silicon-based life-form.

—*Errol Morris*
FILMMAKER

213

At the end of the twentieth century, the notion of an omniscient state leading us to a new Eden has been exposed for what it is: a formula for stagnation and misery. Technology has outstripped the capacity of any bureaucracy to control the exchange of ideas, inventions, or investments. The speed-of-light dynamic now driving markets and nations might best be described as "digital capitalism."

What this will do to America's social structure is still unclear. Certainly, the wealth of nations has gone from quantifiable accumulations of material resources to the ceaseless, incalculable flow of information and its finished product, knowledge. But will digital capitalism help us erase the brutal discrepancies between rich and poor? Will it be an ally of freedom and equality?

As I see it, the digital networks spreading across America and the globe can generate unprecedented levels of opportunity. Yet this won't happen as a happy accident of technology. No matter how versatile our machines and software become, their impact will be determined by human intent and agency. If we extend the reach of justice and fairness, it will be because we have decided to use technology to that end. If we succeed in reducing the suffering and conflict in the world, it will be because of our willingness to fight against fear, ignorance, and mistrust.

Any hope we have of using digital capitalism to the benefit of America's future—to help people cross the borders of race and class, to advance the cause of inclusion—must actively involve the country's corporations. Their sum possession of enterprise and imagination is among America's most potent resources.

Today, at the beginning of a technological revolution that will affect our world as forcefully as the printing press and internal combustion engine once did, there is a real chance for corporations to help shape the future. Without altering their competitive focus, they can find better, more effective ways to empower the women and men within their ranks to put their expertise and experience at the service of local communities.

Volunteerism is already a national buzzword, and the last thing we need is yet another round of verbal endorsements of the *idea* of volunteerism. Instead, the time has come to make community participation a fundamental ingredient of American business strategies. Part of the shared commitment of corporate America must be to ensure that those who wish to serve have the means, know-how, and support they need to get involved.

Digital capitalism has the potential to give us a better America—a nation not just richer materially but with more freedom, compassion, and understanding. Technology offers the tools. History will tell whether we have the will and the moral purpose to use them wisely.

—*Gerald M. Levin*
BUSINESS EXECUTIVE

214

America will be a far better, healthier place for our children when we are able to keep tobacco out of their hands—and their lungs. Each year, more than 430,000 Americans die from smoking-related diseases. Five million of the children living in this nation today eventually will die from a smoking-related disease. But people who develop lung cancer, emphysema, or heart disease from smoking are not the only ones who are harmed by tobacco. Children who breathe secondhand smoke are more likely to suffer from pneumonia, bronchitis, and other lung diseases. And children who have asthma and who breathe secondhand smoke have more asthma attacks.

Each day, 3,000 children smoke their first cigarette—that's more than 1 million annually. At least 3.1 million adolescents are current smokers. The average teenage smoker starts smoking at the age of twelve, and is a daily smoker by the age of eighteen. Two out of every three adolescents who are using tobacco at age eighteen become an adult user.*

---

*Editor's Note: This essay was written in July 1997.

Young people develop a tolerance for, and become dependent on, nicotine as quickly as adults do, and young people have a difficult time quitting.

We need politics to prevent tobacco use among young people, including:

- Tobacco education in the schools

- Restrictions on tobacco advertising and promotions

- A complete ban on smoking by anyone on school grounds

- No sale of tobacco products to minors

- Tax increases on tobacco products so young people cannot afford them

Through measures such as these, we can help ensure that our children will breathe easier.

—*John Garrison*
PUBLIC HEALTH ADVOCATE

215

Stop "giving back." Nothing nauseates me more than watching a celebrity or business leader declare (most publicly and with cameras on and cameras clicking) that he/she/they have achieved such status that now it's time to "give back," for they have *so* much. These saccharine gestures allow the principal to adorn him/her/themself/selves with a self-proclaimed Irving Thalberg Award. Give me a break!

Trying to make the world a better place shouldn't be a goal

that we acquire only after we feel that the system has so enriched us that we can afford to look in the rearview mirror to take a second look at society's roadkill. "Giving back" should give way to "giving forward."

"Giving forward" means that responsible corporations or personality icons should focus part of their *ongoing* activities toward the public good: figure out what can realistically be accomplished and then apply the personal/corporate agenda to make things happen.

That's the way we ran Lifetime, and our viewers and customers knew we were "for real." Just as corporations envision a share price at some future date, media's corporate goals should reflect responsibility for positive change and education. Companies that tell you their profit pictures do not allow themselves the ability to respond to society's problems are saying they lack "response-ability."

While the CEO of one of America's top ten electronic media companies, I dedicated Lifetime's editorial power to the fight against breast cancer. We have focused heat and light on the issue. We chose a strategy of awareness, advocacy, agitation, and aggressive action—from distributing breast self-exam cards to creating an on-line petition protesting HMO policies for postmastectomy treatment. Our viewers' signatures and letters found their way to the White House and Capitol Hill. We built this call to action into the DNA of our corporate culture.

Using our medium to bring about positive change allows our employees, customers, and distributors to take part in a crusade and feel that we're making a contribution today. The players on "Team Lifetime" know that we have the ability to respond ("response-ability") to use television to help address crucial issues.

If each of today's and tomorrow's networks were to recognize that their ability to add value to the media landscape *requires* them to incorporate "giving forward" and the self-discipline to focus on effecting positive change, we'd be living in a much better world.

By incorporating a prosocial agenda into their goals, individuals and corporations can ensure that serving the community is a meat-and-potatoes issue, the main course—not a dessert that comes as an afterthought.

We in the media have an *obligation* to leave the world in better shape than the way we found it. That responsibility exists in both good times and bad. An argument can even be made that in bad times our responsibility increases when budgets tighten and society's safety nets loosen. Thus, the responsibility to lend a stronger voice and a helping hand also increases.

My advice is: Pick an issue. Get something done. Do it now, not when you think you can afford it more.

—*Douglas W. McCormick*
BUSINESS EXECUTIVE

216

I believe we should renew our commitment to being a nation of citizens with political courage.

History has taught us that people empowered with political courage can accomplish extraordinary deeds and sustain them. They can create and nurture democracy—and stand against tyranny in foreign lands. They can tear down racial and gender barriers—and provide opportunity for those willing to seize it. They can invest in an economic future for their children greater than the one they inherited from their parents.

Yet as we near the end of the twentieth century, we've become a nation of citizens increasingly disenchanted with our government's ability to do good and our leaders' ability to do the right thing. This is hardly surprising.

Serious issues are ill served by seven-second sound bites. Urgent problems are too often eclipsed by a relentless pursuit of more trivial matters. Both have hindered our government's ability to solve difficult problems and our people's ability to trust our government.

To meet the challenges of our time, we need energized, informed Americans who demand political courage from their leaders. We need honesty and an honest dialogue. We need elected leaders to be candid with the people they serve. They need to be able to vote against their constituents' desires and short-term economic interest on occasion and challenge our people to sacrifice for things that truly matter.

Our citizens, in turn, have a responsibility to look beyond the seven-second sound bites and the provocative headlines to read the fine print. Our citizens need to educate themselves on the details of complex issues and understand the effects of acting—or not acting—on the strength and security of our nation. Then they need to summon the political courage to place the public interest above all else—and demand *at the polls* that their leaders have the courage to do so as well.

We are not a great nation because we've traveled the easy road. As Robert Frost reminded us, "Two roads diverged in a wood, and I—/I took the one less traveled by,/And that has made all the difference."

—*Charles S. Robb*
POLITICIAN

217

OUR FUTURE IS TIED
TO THE FUTURE OF EDUCATION

I am grateful for the opportunity to write about my vision of the future for our great country. If one examines the biographies of Americans who have won a Nobel Prize or who have been recognized for their contributions to the advancement of science or technology, one will find people of diverse ethnic, racial, and economic backgrounds. One thing most of these luminaries share, however, is that they were beneficiaries of a strong public education, an education that stimulated their curiosity and challenged them to dream. Many people of my generation can remember a time when most school-age children could proudly recite Albert Einstein's "$E = mc^2$," Einstein's elegant statement of his Theory of Relativity. Today, if asked what the Theory of Relativity is, many students would probably respond that it is a network television show.

It is extremely unfortunate that education seems to have lost its place of importance on our national agenda. As a member of Congress, I am often saddened—and sometimes angered—by the apparent lack of concern of the Republican majority with the welfare of our nation's children and the state of our educational system. Ironically, many of the members of Congress who consistently vote against critically needed funding for education do not hesitate to vote to spend billions of dollars for new weapons systems. While I consider myself a strong supporter of national defense, I cannot in good conscience—and contrary to common sense—be any less ardent a supporter of and advocate for our nation's educators and students.

If we are to have a bright future, it is essential that Americans recommit themselves to the principle of a quality public education for every child. Congress and state legislatures must provide needed funds to pay for construction of new schools, the purchase of new equipment, and the hiring of new teachers. At the high school level, greater emphasis needs to be placed on providing students with classes relevant to our increasingly high-tech society. While many high school students will want to attend college, others may be more attracted to opportunities for vocational training. These students should have access to job/school cooperative programs, in-school vocational training classes, and other creative programs.

The CEOs of major corporations often express their concern that they may not have a pool of potential employees capable of performing jobs in high-tech areas. Obviously, it is in the self-interest of private companies to support public education, both financially and through programs such as mentoring and student internships. At the undergraduate and graduate levels, the private sector should endow teaching chairs, fund scholarships, and support university research.

In closing, I am reminded of Vice President Dan Quayle's address at a United Negro College Fund event, when he said, "What a waste it is to lose one's mind. Or not to have a mind is being very wasteful. How true that is." Never has there been a statement that more clearly emphasized the importance of education.

—Eddie Bernice Johnson

POLITICIAN

I know all the things that would make America better. But it's more like a wish list than anything that might truly happen. Still, I think we need a vision, so here are two items, at least, that are on my wish list:

I wish: *the family might be built back together, across America*. A professor of mine at Harvard many, many years ago said that The Family goes through a historic cycle, with three phases: Clan, Domestic, and Atomistic. To use the family car as a metaphor, here, Atomistic is where each family member goes off in his or her own car on a Sunday afternoon, Domestic is where all the family members pile into one car and go for a Sunday drive, and Clan is where there is a caravan of cars, made up of related families and relatives, going for that Sunday drive. You get the picture. Clearly, The Family is in the Atomistic phase across much (though not all) of America. It is in this Atomistic structure of the family that so much of the mischief we decry—crime, drugs, promiscuity, lack of a sense of purpose in life—finds its source. To cure these problems, we must first cure The Family. I pray that those places where the Domestic family structure is still to be found may flourish and grow and multiply, so that it becomes the dominant form of The Family once again, all across America.

I wish: *the love of wisdom were taught throughout the land*. I mean in schools, in churches, synagogues, and mosques, on TV, radio, and the Internet, in newspapers, magazines, and books, and in the home. In other words: everywhere. In case you are in doubt as to what I mean by wisdom, let me briefly explain. There are three kinds of stuff floating around in people's heads: information, knowledge, and wisdom. Information is bits and pieces of data, unrelated and unorganized, such as: some plants bloom at night. Knowledge is systematic information, organized and applied to practical situations, such as: how to operate or fix computers. And wisdom—well, wisdom is knowledge that has context or perspective and "weight" to it, about what's important and what isn't, such as: "You don't limit your life to the problem you have. You learn to get your life to work. You just find new bridges." (That's Lulie Gund's wisdom about life with her husband, who is blind.) We are a nation intoxicated with information, having a love affair with knowledge but not much acquainted with the value and importance of wisdom. Youngsters don't prize it, adults don't seek it, and elders (who often have it in abundance) are generally treated with total disrespect. "Geezers" is society's favorite characterization of them, rather than "wise ones." Were we to learn to love wisdom, we would turn around much in America, including our educational system, and we would all have a new definition of our goal in America: to acquire Wisdom—which includes, of necessity, Compassion and Love for all.

—*Richard N. Bolles*
AUTHOR

219

HELP AMERICA PASS THE EMPLOYMENT NON-DISCRIMINATION ACT

Picture this: You've been a good and loyal employee for years. You've always earned good job performance reviews, and the quality of your work has been outstanding. Yet one day your boss tells you you're being fired because there's a rumor going around that you are gay. You have always been very private about your sexual orientation—more so, in fact, than your heterosexual colleagues. Yet there is that pink slip staring you in the face, as you wonder how you'll continue providing for your family. You try to get some help through the courts, only to find that what happened to you is not against the law.

Sadly, too many of us don't have to imagine this scenario, because it is far too real. Federal law does not yet protect hard-working American families from job discrimination based on sexual orientation. Outside a handful of states that have statewide nondiscrimination laws that include sexual orientation, Americans are losing their livelihoods to this kind of discrimination, only to find they have no law to turn to for justice.

Fortunately, you can do something to right this wrong and make America a better place for everyone.

Urge your U.S. senators and representatives to support the Employment Non-Discrimination Act (ENDA), a bill to protect Americans from job discrimination based on sexual orientation. ENDA would apply equally to lesbian, gay, bisexual, and heterosexual employees, ensuring equal rights on the job for all. While prohibiting discrimination, ENDA also prohibits quotas and preferential treatment. It would *not* apply to religious organizations, small businesses, and the military.

ENDA enjoys bipartisan support, but Congress needs to hear from you if it is to become law. Regardless of how you may feel about other gay issues, this is a bill worthy of your support. It is about the fundamental American value of fairness. Whatever your views, you can make America a better place by helping to pass ENDA, because you don't have to agree that homosexuality is right in order to act on the knowledge that job discrimination is wrong.

One of the most fundamental American values is that we

can disagree without treating one another disagreeably. More than three decades ago, we made the laws of our land reflect that value when we passed the 1964 Civil Rights Act. So now, for example, when disagreements over religion escalate into discrimination, the law is there equally for everyone, regardless of religion. The law preserves our values by not taking the side of one particular viewpoint over another. So, too, should it be with the issue of sexual orientation: the law should be there equally for everyone. I hope you'll join me in helping to make America better by urging Congress to pass the Employment Non-Discrimination Act.

—*Candace Gingrich*
HUMAN RIGHTS ADVOCATE

220

Henry David Thoreau once said, "For every thousand hacking at the leaves of evil, there is one striking at the root." I am convinced that the key to striking at the root of the tremendous challenges we face in our great nation is to apply the lessons we learn from a compass.

To make this point in my teaching, I often get up in front of an audience and ask them to close their eyes. I say, "Now, without peeking, everyone point north." There is a little confusion as they all try to decide and point in the direction they think is north.

I then ask them to open their eyes and see where people are pointing. At that point there's usually an eruption of laughter because they see that people are pointing in all directions—including straight up!

I then bring out a compass and show the north indicator, and I explain that north is always in the same direction. It never changes. It represents a natural magnetic force on the earth.

Now, just as there is a magnetic north—a constant reality outside ourselves that never changes—so also are there unchanging natural laws that ultimately govern the consequences of all human behavior. People can move about and make choices based on their own desire and will, but the north indicator is totally independent of their desire and will. Not a single person's vote on which direction is north can change true north.

Consider the following illustration of this idea: How many of us have tried to lose weight a thousand times? Well, no matter how you go about it, eventually you come to see that in order to achieve permanent and healthy weight loss, you must align your habits and your lifestyle with natural laws, the principles of proper nutrition and regular exercise that will bring the desired result.

Apply this thinking to a major issue in society, such as health care, and you would ask, "If we were really serious about health care reform, what would we primarily focus on?" Almost everyone acknowledges that we would focus on prevention. But the social value system regarding health care, which ultimately drives medical practice, is primarily focused on the diagnosis and treatment of disease rather than on prevention or lifestyle alteration.

This same analysis carries into education reform, welfare reform, political reform—actually, any reform movement. Ultimately, people come to realize that the essence of real happiness and success is in aligning our public and private lives with natural laws or principles. This takes both humility and courage and produces integrity. I have found in more than twenty years of teaching this throughout the world that nearly everyone—regardless of religion, race, nation, or culture—knows in their hearts what these laws and principles are. They are truly universal, timeless, and as self-evident as trying to achieve trust with another without being trustworthy oneself.

Finally, I am convinced to my core that if we as a society work diligently in every other area of life and neglect the family, it would be analogous to straightening deck chairs on the *Titanic*. I offer three powerful, practical suggestions to strengthen our families:

First, involve everyone in your family in developing a family mission statement that identifies your purpose and values. Second, set aside a regular time each week to be together as a family for planning, solving problems, teaching values, and having fun. Third, have regular one-on-one dates and bonding times with your loved ones.

—*Stephen R. Covey*

AUTHOR

221

STOP PRETENDING

As everyone knows, American cities are a mess. The list of culprits is a long one and includes the city planners who gutted urban neighborhoods in the name of urban renewal, the social reformers and their modernist architects who replaced residential streets with superblocks of high-rise housing projects, the big-city mayors and the transportation engineers who pushed highways through—instead of around—cities, and, of course, Henry Ford, who figured out how to build inexpensive cars in the first place. There is plenty of blame to go around.

Identifying historical villains has become something of a national pastime—everyone is someone else's victim—but we should not let one group off the hook so easily: ourselves.

We have let our cities decline, in large part, because of our indifference. Americans have always been ambivalent about their cities. After all, no less a person than Thomas Jefferson once said, "I view great cities as pestilential to the morals, the health, the liberties of man." In fact, he was wrong about the urban threat to liberty; his rural southern yeomen were a much graver menace to human freedom than the dwellers of New York and Philadelphia. Moreover, his distrust of cities was curiously at odds with his personal life. He spent five enjoyable years in Paris. There, he became a devotee of Parisian urban delights such as neoclassical architecture (which he copied in his own house at Monticello), Louis XVI furniture (which he bought and shipped home), and *la cuisine bourgeoise* (whose recipes he assiduously recorded). Jefferson may not have wanted cities, but he definitely wanted what cities had to offer.

We persist in the misguided belief that American civilization resides elsewhere than in cities. The majority of Americans have been urban since 1920, yet it is the small town and the family farm that continue to be held up as paragons of American virtue. Popular culture extols the unsophisticated. At least in the 1940s, our singing idol was Frank Sinatra, a wiry street kid from Hoboken; today it is Garth Brooks, a genial rustic in a cowboy hat. A sort of regression has set in. Americans drive pickups and trucks instead of coupes. They wear baseball caps instead of fedoras and denim instead of gray flannel. When will we stop pretending? We are a grown-up, urban people, and it's time we started acting our age.

—*Witold Rybczynski*
PROFESSOR/AUTHOR

Perhaps the best thing we could do to reaffirm both our national unity and our culture of equal opportunity is to eliminate bilingual education programs.

Bilingual education was a hopeful experiment of the 1960s. Thirty years later, the evidence is in: the programs are bilingual; most of their graduates are not.

In today's Internet-connected world, English is increasingly the language of opportunity not only in the United States but in the world as well. Yet consider the words of Ernesto Ortiz, a South Texas Mexican American: "They teach my children in Spanish in school, so they can be busboys and waiters. I teach them in English at home, so they can be doctors and lawyers."

Most immigrant parents are determined that their children learn English. Yet instead of giving these children the English classes they want and deserve, we give them bilingual education. And when they graduate, we give them bilingual ballots and bilingual welfare applications. These kids know that they have been cheated. They will be a potential powder keg for American society in the same way that Quebec is a powder keg ready to detonate Canada's national unity.

As John F. Kennedy said during the first presidential debate, "I think we can do better. I don't want the talents of any American to go to waste."

—Jim Boulet, Jr.
NONPROFIT DIRECTOR

Stop trying to stamp out new or risky products or activities. Don't demand that the world stay still. Tolerate the open-ended future.

We all want to live in a better world, but we often don't appreciate where it comes from. Progress depends on an uncertain, trial-and-error process of experiments that sometimes succeed and sometimes fail. Too often we are too afraid—or too intolerant—to let people take their own risks or try new things. Or, paradoxically, we rig the experiments so they're sure to "succeed," which is hardly how *real* experiments work.

There's a serious cost to demanding a risk-free, certain world. Sometimes it's financial: Congress guaranteed that depositors wouldn't lose money in savings and loans, no matter what sort of risks the institutions took in their quest for greater returns. So instead of shopping around for good management, depositors just looked for high interest rates. Depositors got the money, the S&Ls took crazier and crazier risks, and, in the end, cleaning up the mess cost $481 billion, about $417 billion of it from the taxpayers. By trying to stamp out depositors' risks, federal insurance actually encouraged bad experiments to continue.

More often, however, the demand for a risk-free world crushes new ideas. American women have less reproductive freedom than Europeans not because of the antiabortion movement, as strong as it is, but because of the lawsuits, Food and Drug Administration hurdles, and fear mongering that have stifled contraceptive innovation. Even birth control that isn't particularly risky has been scared out of the U.S. market.

The personal computer industry, by contrast, could get started because it was out of the public eye. The buggy, early-generation computers and software were sold to hobbyists who were so excited to have their own computers that they were happy to take chances on not-yet-perfect products. They didn't demand progress without risk or choice without responsibility. They provided the critical opportunity—and feedback—that let this new technology develop, to all our benefit. (Ever think about the first contact lenses? Now, *they* were scary. But I'd hate to live without their descendants.)

Letting people take chances isn't just about business. It's about tolerance and responsibility. Not everybody has the same approach to dangers: making the world conform to a single, safety-first standard—as the very loud public health lobby demands—also makes it a poorer, less interesting place. We should just say no to people who insist that everyone must wear a seat belt because they do, that no one should snowboard because it's dangerous, that every new product must be 100 percent foolproof before you can buy it. Making the world better means letting it change, and that requires taking—and tolerating—risks.

—*Virginia Postrel*
MAGAZINE EDITOR

224

PASSION IS WHAT THE SUN FEELS FOR THE EARTH

Have you ever watched the sun rise? To do so is to bear witness to the re-creation of the world. But early rising—apart from getting a jump start on the day—reminds you what you're supposed to be *doing* during the day. Living. Loving. Learning. Leading. Letting go of everything holding you back from returning, through your authentic gifts, "a portion of the world's lost heart," as the poet Louise Bogan so beautifully puts it. To sit silently in the shadows as the earth is seduced into being, coaxed into becoming, and slowly roused from her slumber by a lover—at once ancient and new—is to succumb to passion's embrace at a safe distance. You need not turn your gaze away in fear as you do when strangely familiar eyes suddenly begin to recognize your face. You need not begin reciting the mind's pernicious litany of reason when risk invites you for a cup of coffee. All you need to do at dawn, in the dark, *all you must do*, is pray. Pray that you may know once, or once again, passion before you die.

Passion. When you think about "passion," what immediately comes to mind besides clandestine bodice-ripping clichés that have given the romance of living a bad rap? *Wild. Chaotic. Emotional. Selfish. Indulgent. Permissive. Excessive. Obsessive. Swept away. Out of control. Bad to the bone. Beyond redemption. Fatal attraction. Unpredictable. Unrestrained. Un-American activities.*

Precisely. Which is why I believe that if, like our founding mothers and fathers, we want to restore America to its rightful place—as our spiritual home as well as our primary place of residence—we need to give ourselves permission to revel in our passions. Notice I do not suggest merely the occasional indulging in passionate impulses but *reveling* in them, as in *revelation*. And what will be revealed as you carouse and celebrate your good fortune to carry an American passport, which bestows upon you the unalienable right to pursue your passions and not deny them? How about the truth that will not only set you free but change the rest of our life for the better, as well as this country's destiny?

Passion is embodied prayer or embodied despair. We are conceived in passion and die in passion; everything in between is our choice. Passion is holy—a profound Mystery that transcends and transforms through rapture or rage, renaissance or revolution. A sacred fire burns within each soul and humanity, whether we're comfortable with this truth or not. Passion is what the sun feels for the earth. Heat and light. And just as the earth cannot exist without either, neither can Americans, no matter how self-reliant or arrogant we may be, and as a nation we are both. Pick up a newspaper in any city or town in this country every morning or turn on the evening news at night. Forget the headlines. Read between the lines. Listen with your heart. The tectonic plates are shifting beneath us, and below this thin cool crust is a molten core of transformative energy. But every day the same force that in the beginning created this magnificent country destroys it as passion erupts in cruelty, brutality, and violence. Why? How can this be?

Could it be that the same sacred pulse meant to keep us alive turns on us with a vengeance, a rogue cell enraged, determined to bring the collective body down because it was excluded, left out in the cold, left to wither away and die? Could it be that Divine Providence disapproves of our smug, savvy, and sophisticated attempts to defy the laws of Heaven and Earth by keeping a lid on not only our own passions but those of others? Could it be that if we do not give outward expression to our passions we will experience self-immolation as individuals and a nation: the spontaneous combustion of our souls? Violence may be random, but it is not senseless. Violence is calculated and cunning because it catapults us through horror into an exile of existence, the realm of the unspeakable. If the eyes of a hungry child, homeless family, abused woman, or abandoned man dying of AIDS do not grab our attention, then violence, the vigilante of the vanquished, will. We think we're just getting up in the morning to do whatever it is we think we should be doing to "make it" in America, when what we're really doing in every conversation, encounter, argument, or decision is searching for that flicker of flame to guide us through the darkness that surrounds us. The darkness of complicated need. The darkness of indifference. The darkness of ignorance. The darkness of pride. The darkness of prejudice. The darkness of our own second guesses. But Nelson Mandela admonishes us, and rightly so, that it is "our Light, not our Darkness, that most frightens us." However, he reassures us that "as we let our own Light shine, we unconsciously give other people permission to do the same." So it is with reveling in our God-given, prophetic, and profound passions.

Passion is the muse of meaning. It's the primordial, pulsating energy that infuses all of life, the numinous presence made known with every beat of our hearts. The gift of each day on this earth offers us another opportunity to live passionate lives rather than passive ones, if we will bear witness not only to the sun's rising but to passion's immutable presence in the prosaic, in poetry, and in politics.

—*Sarah Ban Breathnach*
AUTHOR

225

—SARK
ARTIST/AUTHOR

MAYBE

MAYBE We'll paint MARSHMallows purple, or Free circus elephants. MAYBE we'll ride on A chocolate Merry-go-round, or MAKE tennis shoes for CAMELS. MAYBE we'll FIND A CHILD WHO Feels unSAFE AT HoME and take Her out of there right away. MAYBE We'll MAIL so many letters to GOD, that everything Gets All Healed up MAYBE we'll take All the Mean People, and use them to Fill up the ozone Hole. MAYBE WHEN we see A SIGN THAT SAYS "DRAWBRIDGE" We'll Get out and Do A lovely Bridge sketch. MAYBE We will MAKE Airplanes out of the SAME MATERIAL THAT the "BLACK BOX" is MADE of. MAYBE We'll live in reAL COMMUNITies, equal For everyone. MAYBE 100% of the people will vote, and START A new WORLD. MAYBE everyBody is an angel, God, animal, nature, All rolled into one Bundle of nerve and tissue, lip and Bone. MAYBE we'll All stop FIGHTING and trying to Be right. MAYBE there will Be NAP rooms everyWHere, and cars will run on Kisses. MAYBE DReAMS Are reAL and AIDS is only A Diet candy. MAYBE All the HoME-less will Move onto All the GOLF courses. MAYBE schools Are filled with iMAGINATION, and prisons Have nutritious Food and spiritual programs. MAYBE We Are All Free, SAFE and well loved. We All want the SAME things MAYBE we·All·love·everyone

©SARK 93

The greatest danger America faces is that our bonds of extended community are loosening. I think the best way to make America better is to address that issue head-on.

One way of doing that would be the creation of more local community coalitions whose goal is to be institutions that care for the entire community—not just people of one class or race or religion but everyone in the community. These organizations would build coalitions between diverse constituencies to:

- do community betterment projects
- give technical assistance to those wanting to start or expand local businesses or nonprofits that will provide new jobs in the community
- take on problems in the community by providing mediation services and working toward community consensus
- help recruit volunteers for neighborhood schools and local service agencies
- do advocacy on behalf of those in the community who currently have little power or skills to have an impact on office holders
- do training and consulting for local nonprofit organizations on how to strengthen themselves

If we had more of these kinds of broad-based, multipurpose, community-strengthening coalitions, our communities would be better places to live in. And if these local coalitions were networked together nationally, so that ideas and projects and skills could be shared throughout the nation and so that people in these local groups had a stronger voice in our national affairs, America would be a better place to live in.

—*Michael Lux*
NONPROFIT DIRECTOR

227

TAX POLLUTION INSTEAD OF WORK

Our tax code primarily taxes income and work—things that we want to encourage—rather than pollution, which we want to discourage. A revenue neutral tax shift could put some tax on pollution and provide a tax break for employment.

Currently, the tax code actually favors raw resource extraction over recycling and discourages efficient use of resources. The code even rewards the mining of lead and mercury. With pollution taxes, businesses would have every incentive to reduce their emissions—all without the need for new regulations.

There are plenty of burdens in the tax code on employers to discourage them from hiring additional people—all the Social Security and medical costs. By shifting the tax burden, we could achieve a cleaner environment while employing more people.

In summary: Don't increase taxes, just shift the burden on what is taxed so that good behavior and employment are encouraged and polluting behavior is penalized.

—*Brent Blackwelder*
ENVIRONMENTAL ACTIVIST

America is too tolerant of violence. It is part of us; we accept it as normal. We hardly even question it. Spousal abuse; the neglect, abuse, and murder of children; drugs; mass and serial murder; organized crime; rape—there are our headlines, yet we picture ourselves as the most civilized nation on earth. How so?

Crime syndicates from Sicily, China, Japan, Korea, and Russia come here where their violent professions can flourish. Americans, they reckon, are accepting of what they have to offer.

We do have the science to detect and fight crime and violence. We don't have to permit criminals and drug dealers (and terrorists) in if we don't want them. We can identify the worthy citizens from other cultures and welcome them while barring or jailing for life the individuals that wish our society harm. (We are not going to rehabilitate them, so why turn them loose on ourselves again?) No nation has more to offer people of goodwill. It is ironic that no nation is more vulnerable to those who wish us evil.

Suggestion: We should be totally intolerant of violence whether it originates among ourselves or is imported. Either way, violence is an evil we should no longer accept as a normal way of life. There is no doubt that America would be a better place if violence were not considered the norm but instead treated as the aberration it is.

—*Roger A. Caras*
ANIMAL RIGHTS ADVOCATE

229

I believe it is time for America to formally review our U.S. Constitution to reassess its efficacy within today's complex, global society. A new constitutional convention should be convened to accomplish this task.

Without question, the U.S. Constitution is one of the wisest and most farsighted documents of governance ever created. Its principles were drawn from centuries of experience in government, and its authors were men of exceptional vision—Benjamin Franklin, James Madison, and George Washington, to name a few.

But the fact remains that our Constitution was written more than two hundred years ago, and its assumptions about societies and individuals' rights within them were drawn from the authors' understanding and experience of society as it had evolved to that time. Visionary though they were, the Constitution's writers could never have imagined, much less provided for, the kinds of situations and challenges that modern society presents today.

Balancing the Internet and free speech, global terrorism and the rights of criminal defendants, the rights of the homeless and undocumented aliens—these are the kinds of pressing and provocative issues that challenge our Constitution today, and that will continue to mount in the future. While the constitutional-amendment process allows for limited changes to be made, it does not provide for the kind of comprehensive review and updating that is needed at this point.

We should begin with a fresh articulation of what Americans want their country to be, and then review each of the Constitution's articles against that vision. The present historic document comprises 4,543 words, drafted by 55 individuals in under 100 working days. The goal of a new constitutional convention should be to produce an equally thoughtful but modernized version of that document—on a comparably ambitious schedule.

—*Michael J. Critelli*
BUSINESS EXECUTIVE

230

Meet your neighbors. By taking time to get to know the folks next door, we come to view them (and by extension others) as individuals—not as members of a group defined by race, age, sex, or religion. We develop a stake in the community we can most affect directly and that most directly affects us. We come to respect and appreciate property rights and boundaries that promote harmony. And we gain healthy perspective on the barrage of daily headlines that portray the world's problems as insoluble.

—*William H. Mellor*
NONPROFIT DIRECTOR

231

America would be immeasurably improved by a stiff dose of selfishness.

Throughout our history we Americans have prided ourselves on our generosity toward others. We have showered assistance on other countries. We have welcomed the "huddled masses." We have saved the world from communism.

In recent years all this largesse has prompted a backlash. Today 82 percent of Americans say that the chief goal of U.S. foreign policy should be "creating jobs for Americans."

Some people criticize the United States for its current self-absorption. But I think we ought to be unashamed of acting in our self-interest.

Because the clearer we are about our self-interest, the more obvious it is that it requires us to remain engaged with the world. Engaged not only economically but in advancing our values, our commitment to freedom, democracy, and human rights.

How, after all, are we going to create jobs if we remain isolated from the international community? Trade and investment around the world require political stability, but if a country violates labor rights, ignores the rule of law, and persecutes its own citizens, chaos is eventually inevitable.

Want to keep your son or daughter out of a shooting war? Nothing makes such conflict more inevitable than ignoring violations of human rights around the world. Care about how your taxes are spent? If the United States had spent $300 million in 1994 to stop the genocide in Rwanda before it got out of hand, we would not have had to spend $1.2 billion *a year* in humanitarian and refugee aid to deal with the aftermath. Worried about environmental disasters? Tragedies like Chernobyl are almost guaranteed when people in the know are afraid to tell their governments the truth for fear of punishment.

The list goes on and on. Like it or not, America and the world are stuck with each other. Supporting democracy and human rights is not just a matter of morality. It is the bold requirement of an enlightened self-interest.

—*William F. Schultz*
HUMAN RIGHTS ADVOCATE

My early childhood includes memories of World War II and of the relative, a Holocaust refugee, who came from Germany through Shanghai to live with us during the War. (For my generation, "the War" means not Korea or Vietnam or the Cold War, but World War II.) Consider, too, that when my father was at Stanford, he could not join any of the social organizations because he was Jewish, and those organizations, at that time, did not accept Jews. Indeed, I can remember, as a child, my mother thinking of going to lunch at a downtown San Francisco hotel with a friend of hers who was African-American, and their discussing whether they would be served. When my colleagues Justices Sandra Day O'Connor and Ruth Bader Ginsburg graduated from law school, they had trouble finding jobs—because they were women. So did Senator Diane Feinstein. The world has changed, often for the better. I think it is very important to remember that those changes did not occur magically—that they represented individual, and collective, pioneering efforts. We need to remember those efforts both because so many of us now benefit from them and because there is so much still to be done. You still can choose to be a pioneer.

—*Stephen Breyer*
UNITED STATES SUPREME COURT JUSTICE

*(From a commencement speech
given at Stanford Law School)*

233

To improve this nation of ours, I would suggest that after the completion of the fifth grade every student be required to spend the summer in a third-world country. International travel is an eye-opening experience that leaves an individual with patriotism for the United States, a deeper sensitivity to mankind after having seen human suffering in person, and a fervent appreciation for what our nation provides us.

International travel will leave the students with a burning impression of how fortunate they are in America. Poverty—rampant poverty, children running and playing in trash heaps half-naked with flies infesting the area—has to have an impact. Dozens of children and adults with physical handicaps on one block begging for food or money leaves a haunting image. A constant military presence in one's everyday life leaves Americans taking it for granted that electricity and water are endless and demonstrates how dependent our society is on electricity. Most important, travel outside of the U.S. emphasizes the freedoms that we as Americans treasure: freedom of speech and association, and participation in the American political system. And by answering the question "Where are you from?" and responding "the U.S.," Americans are bound to be told, "You are so lucky to be an American."

Compassion for other human beings is what this nation needs. We need to begin this process at an early age. We all need to work toward a caring nation—one that sees humans as humans and does not differentiate based on the color of one's skin or one's religion, gender, national origin, or sexual preference. If we have seen and experienced what others yearn for, we will appreciate and protect what we have in America.

—*Daphne Kwok*
NONPROFIT DIRECTOR

234

THREE WISHES
FOR THE MILLENNIUM

An optimistic dream wrested from the jaws of the apocalypse: First of all, the arms race had become so maniacal that eventually it turned itself inside out. When everyone on the planet could kill everyone else a billion times over, ancient forms of sacrifice began to reemerge: a global potlatch ensued in which individuals and nations competed to toss heaps of weapons from high cliffs into the sea. A frenzied display, a peacock's preening of power and accumulation, a blind cathartic outpouring of the world's most deadly wealth. And then suddenly one day, a short and shining moment when there wasn't a single Saturday-night special, not one grenade launcher, not an ounce of plutonium to be found. People still rushed to make slingshots of their tuning forks and to render rotisserie skewers into poison spears, but just for a moment the trauma subsided, mass destruction took a little holiday, the world heaved a sigh, and peace crept in under the bolted steel doors like an erotic little shiver.

Second of all, in that still inconceivable gap, a gush of good news, a rush of glad tidings. An angel of the Lord appeared on high, directly over the George Washington Bridge actually, and announced that the children born of that moment would be blessed indeed: all the babies on Earth, for just that one season of peace, would somehow inherit enormous mental powers. Some scientists who had been looking down instead of up discounted the sighting as mass hysteria—something in the water, maybe—but the prophecy was made manifest despite them, for the faith of the people was abiding. And lo, there they were, a generation of geniuses! Every single last one gifted, exceptional!

Education suddenly became the priority of a new world order, and good kind teachers were paid what CEOs were once paid in the Ignorant Ages. CEOs had to make do with a nice comfortable hourly wage (plus a bushel of apples at the end of every quarter just to reassure them that they were still very much loved). Meanwhile, the children were playing chess by the age of three on chessboards distributed as a public service, they were speaking three languages by the time they were four thanks to personal tutors supplied them by the state, they were curing world hunger by the age of ten because politicians were under a mandate to take their concerns for the world seriously. Best of all, they did it all while humming complex jazz riffs born of rich mathematical understanding gained from long jam sessions with their personal firr masters.

Finally, because these wonderful babies born of peace were known to have very fragile bones, spanking was absolutely outlawed. Parents and caregivers were put to the test of finding nurturing, nonviolent ways of disciplining their young charges. Purely incidentally, as a happy side effect, the determined scientists found that new realms of creativity open up in the adult brain when one is made to cajole, wheedle, joke with, or inventively constrain a child. Patience blooms. Adult IQs rise. Children smile.

—*Patricia J. Williams*
PROFESSOR OF LAW

235

Adolescent pregnancy is not about sex. It's about poverty and opportunity. If each adult would reach out to just one young person, male or female, and personally invest in helping to expand that individual's options, we could, as a country, confront this problem.

—*Donna M. Butts*
NONPROFIT DIRECTOR

236

Just Do It.

There is one simple, but crucial, way to make America a better country. It is to require arts education as a central part of the curriculum in every school.

Acting on an age-old American knee-jerk prejudice that the arts are only a frill, school after school in this country of ours—driven by a simplistic view of economic priorities, and uncured of the hangover of a Puritan ethic—has drastically reduced, or cut out altogether, instruction in music, dance, theater, and the visual arts. It is time to rethink.

One fundamental reason is that, in recent years, those who think most searchingly about thinking have revised our understanding of what constitutes cognition. Gradually the work of Harold Gardner at Harvard (multiple intelligences) or Theodore Sizer at Brown (a new curriculum in the "essential school") is permeating our consciences at the local level. The old question was "How intelligent is this child?" The new question is "How is this child intelligent?"

The arts require what an old hero of mine, Serge Koussevitsky, music director of the Boston Symphony of my youth, used to call "arteestical discipline." The arts are challenging, they require practice and focus, and, even more fundamentally, they are a way of knowing, of analyzing or ordering, of communicating, that builds essential life skills. Along the way they put a premium on creativity and the imagination. These attributes are more and more in demand in our increasingly competitive global economy. It is no longer enough for our workforce to be prepared solely to perform some repetitive task on an assembly line.

Mounting evidence from serious research indicates that children who take arts classes in school outscore those who have not: sixty points higher on the verbal SATs, the College Board reported in 1996, for example, and forty-two points higher in math. Preschool children with piano instruction outscored those without it by 34 percent on intelligence tests administered by the University of California at Irvine. The "Mozart effect" has begun to make an impression even on politicians who had assumed that arts-bashing was in their political self-interest.

There are so many other benefits of core exposure to the arts that do not lend themselves to quantitative measurement. Children's self-confidence goes up; the classroom atmosphere becomes one of excitement and fulfillment; drop-out rates decrease; cultural differences become understood; after-school programs entice at-risk children off the streets. And if our future elected officials and future paying audiences all share an understanding of and commitment of the arts, the lasting and fundamental quality of our civilization can only go up.

As Secretary of Education Richard W. Riley has put it, children may be 20 percent of our present, but they are 100 percent of our future. What kind of a future can America expect? Only what it deserves, but one, potentially, whose society has been afforded the essential benefits that can be uniquely and richly provided by a required grounding in the arts as an integral part of our children's education.

—*J. Carter Brown*
ART MUSEUM DIRECTOR

237

What the world needs is a good intellectual whitewashing, a fresh coat of common sense to cover up all the embarrassing and offensive mental graffiti—one dimwitted idea scrawled on top of another—that has accumulated in our heads. With sparkling-clear brains, we'll take the magnets out of our shoes, cancel our alien-abduction insurance, and never again call the Psychic Friends Network. But why are people so anxious to believe such totally daffy ideas in the first place? I think evolution must have encoded credulity into our DNA. Belief must have conferred some survival advantage on our primitive ancestors. Perhaps the Pleistocene forest was just too scary to face without supernatural help. I mean, who's going outside the cave unless they believe the amulet they wear will ward off saber-toothed tigers? So while the scientists are discovering the gene that makes people fat and the gene that makes them gay, maybe they could keep an eye out for the belief gene. It's causing people a lot more trouble than obesity.

—*Robert L. Park*
PROFESSOR OF PHYSICS

238

Late night in New York City, and early mornings as well, as in Cambridge, where I live, and many other American cities, presents a dispiriting display of plastic bags filled with garbage and debris, often broken under the assault of marauding cats, dogs, and rats. When the sanitation department trucks come through, of course they leave a trail of garbage behind them.

The contrast with Paris and with some other European cities is striking. There, uniform garbage containers are distributed to householders and apartment house superintendents; they have secure lids, and even more remarkably, the container mouths fit snugly to special attachments in the pickup vehicle. Garbage moves from sealed container to sealed truck with minimum spillage, and another modest contribution to a more livable city has been made.

If the simple aesthetic advantage of this form of garbage collection is insufficient to sway Americans, consider the health advantages. Sealed containers would help to control the rat population, which lives on the garbage. Their numbers, we are told by the press in New York and Boston, have increased substantially in recent years.

In European cities one also sees trim uniforms for the sanitation department force, as opposed to the motley assortment of clothes worn by the garbage collectors of Cambridge and many other cities, and that, too, contributes to the sense of a city run by professionals, rather than—as the present dress of the collectors suggests—a group of political hacks handing out patronage.

These would admittedly not be costless improvements. One must design the uniform containers to be distributed, pay for or charge for them, design attachments for the sanitation department trucks (or order new trucks), and design and pay for the uniforms, and all this leads one to wonder whether the management capacity of most of our cities is up to the task. But such a transformation in how we collect garbage would certainly add to the attractiveness of American cities. Our new breed of energetic mayors, from Giuliani in New York to Riordan in Los Angeles, should be inspired by the opportunity to catch up, even if decades late, to the better European cities.

—*Nathan Glazer*
PROFESSOR OF SOCIAL RELATIONS

239

ONE GOOD IDEA

Abolish the CIA. That is a worthy act in itself, and it would have good side effects. It would remove a body that is unconstitutional (public money must be accounted for), immoral (subversive acts in over three dozen foreign countries), and destructive (the harm done us has been greater than any done others—the missiles were accepted in Cuba because of CIA plots against Castro).

As for side effects, we would call into question the whole cult of secrecy that hides things from Americans that foreigners know (e.g., Castro knew we were trying to kill him, only we did not). It would make us assess realistically the intelligence activities we do need (now largely done by the NSA). It would stop the buildup of CIA "assets" who are a rogue force for other governments' dirty tricks and for our own (where else would Nixon's men recruit Watergate break-in men but from the ranks of former CIA operatives?).

—*Garry Wills*
PROFESSOR OF HISTORY

240

If America cannot exemplify environmentalism, we will no longer lead the planet.

We need to start thinking in a truly global sense. If what we do is good for our environment, it's good for our planet and, therefore, good for America.

That requires more than just governmental action. One way to make America better is by every citizen making environmental choices in his or her everyday chores and lifestyle.

It's as simple as choosing organic when you're grocery shopping. Putting on a shirt that's made of environmentally aware materials. Skipping the pesticides when you're doing your lawn care. Just making small everyday decisions that do not pollute the earth.

As we continue to see the by-products of our processed culture manifest in health problems, poor drinking water, and other environmental crises, environmentalism will become increasingly important in every nation and to every person.

If we continue to allow the destruction of the planet, the question of how to make America better will seem almost irrelevant. Already, more than 90 percent of the world's species have been lost. And of what remains, nearly the same percentage is unstudied and not understood.

By making these simple, environmental decisions at every opportunity, Americans will make a difference. And America will improve its environment, health, and spirit.

—*Horst Rechelbacher*
BUSINESS EXECUTIVE

241

Get *over* it. You fell in love and she broke your heart? She was probably too cool for you anyway—so find a different woman and make *her* happy. Took lumps from gross negligence or a neighbor's golf ball? You survived, didn't you? The next lumps you get may be malignant and incurable. Those lumps in the potatoes—remember them? Mom always wrecked your dinner and your life. So be a hero, digest your rotten childhood experience, and try making your own damned potatoes. (It's not so easy to eliminate the lumps.) Been in an accident? Injured, maligned, bent, stapled, cashiered, or KO'd? OK, you can sue their pants off, but will *that* be a pretty sight? In Shakespeare's day, combatants often shook hands and said, "I sue for peace." Offenders kneeled and said, "I sue for grace." Not a bad idea.

The true victims—those who make the evening news and those who don't—are not, usually, you and I. Of the world's population, that lucky fifth to which we belong consumes 80 percent of the earth's resources. Meanwhile the poorest fifth gleans 1.4 percent of global income and 90 percent of genuine human misery. As Walt Kelly's Pogo used to say: "We have met the enemy, and he is us."

—*Donald Foster*
PROFESSOR OF ENGLISH LITERATURE

242

The best single idea for making America better is compulsory national service for all eighteen- to twenty-two-year-olds, with a particular emphasis on programs to help younger kids. If large numbers of national service enlistees were assigned to supervise after-school activity, we'd address a huge social problem, enrich two age groups at once, and help pull the country together.

—*Jonathan Alter*
MAGAZINE EDITOR

243

IDEAS FOR MAKING OUR LIVES BETTER
THAT WON'T COST US MUCH

Ban recitation of specials by the waiter. Ever since the last real waiter died (in 1967), waiting tables has been the purview of actors and actresses. That's fine. But why do we have to sacrifice all knowledge of what the restaurant is serving so that they can get monologue practice? No one can really follow, and most are reduced to registering "broiled pompano with a basil sauce and julienne potatoes," "veal in a jejune sauce with okra pomade," and "Linguine pesto with extra pesto" as "fish-meat-pasta."

By the way, when your waiter gives you one of those French looks—if you get my drift—in response to your asking him to repeat one of the specials, ask him what's his best wine, look amused, and say, "Oh, yes, of course I know it; it's a captivating little number—brash, but not insubordinate." I don't know what this means, but it works every time.

And while we're at it . . . let's make handwritten menus illegal. I realize that the writing is very pretty, but you can't read it. I'm tired of eating "the third one down."

Make phones on television have a unique ring. The phone rings. I get up to answer it and find no one on the line. I get back to the TV to find Columbo saying into the phone, "Yes, sir, Captain, it took us the whole two hours to unknot those unbelievably complicated clues, but he's definitely the one who did it. Good-bye, Captain." This couldn't happen if television phones rang with a "teeeeveeee, teeeeveeee, teeeeveeee."

Make each denomination of currency a different color. I suppose they make all denominations the same color—and guarantee that you'll occasionally give away a twenty as a ten—so that we can refer to money as "the green." But is this really sufficient reason to do something so dopey? We could avoid endless confusion and expense by making ones red, fives blue, and so on. And we certainly could come up with another term for money (though I'd advise against "the coloreds"). And while we're at it: *let's dump pennies.* Who needs them? I don't care what it costs us to get rid of them. It's worth it.

Let's finally agree on a word that means "Coffee black, no sugar." Why isn't there a simple word? Those who order coffee black, no sugar, know the extra effort and wrong orders that would be saved here. But what do you expect of a language that hasn't come up with a word for a cow or a bull (the Elsie and Ferdinand kind) that doesn't require you know the sex (as "horse" doesn't require you to know whether it's a stallion or mare).

—*Steven Goldberg*

PROFESSOR OF SOCIOLOGY

244

I think the media has to start treating politics as a noble profession and, most important, give the presidency back its honor. When I was growing up, kids wanted to be president, so they could help and inspire people. Now kids just want to be rich.

I think much of the reason for this change is that the media plays up every tawdry charge thrown at politicians, and in particular at this president, because editors think that's what people want to hear about.

President Clinton will probably go down in history as one of our greatest presidents. But the fact that we have to wait for history to tell us this is ridiculous. If we gave this office the honor it deserves, the president and the men and women around him could do way more.

In the entertainment industry, people used to refer to CBS Television as the Tiffany network because of its great programming and brilliant news department. And that's what people were proud of. Now it's all about being number one, the top grosser, the most economically successful—as opposed to quality and pride. This is the result of the tabloid mentality.

Journalists have to stop writing down to their audience, stop writing only what they think people want to hear, and start writing what they hope will inspire people. I'm convinced that readers will step to the plate, and this would serve as an inspiration for all of us.

—Harvey Weinstein
BUSINESS EXECUTIVE

245

A story is told of a New England farmer asked to attend a forthcoming meeting at the county seat. "Why?" the farmer asked. "What benefit will I get?"

"Well, the meeting will teach you how to be a better farmer!" came the enthusiastic reply.

The farmer was thoughtful for a few moments, then commented, "Why should I learn how to be a better farmer when I'm not being as good a farmer as I know how to be now?"

We are not being as good an America now as we already know how to be. And we don't need more experts telling us what our country needs, because the essentials are clear: that every individual deserves access to good health care, child care, education, and work that is accorded dignity and economic reward; that we desperately need to insist on clean air, water, and food and a safe, livable earth; that women and minorities should be represented, valued, and included in every aspect of language, politics, and culture; that we must pay passionate attention to the voices of those women and men we have learned "don't count"; that family values ought to be our highest priority, meaning that *all* families have value and that we value the many family forms that make up America today; that we cannot afford to ignore even one despairing or angry child who is falling through the cracks in school or at home.

We also know that the earth won't sustain us if we don't rein in our reproductive leanings, and that "we" includes privileged parents whose children use up more than their fair share of the world's resources. We know that a competitive, production-oriented, profit-driven society isn't good for anybody's health. We know the world needs more kindness, honesty, caring, and community. We know how difficult it is to keep our behavior congruent with our stated beliefs. And we know that every item we put on any list is interconnected. As naturalist John Muir put it, "When we try to pick out anything by itself, we find it hitched to everything in the Universe."

So what keeps us from being as good an America as we already know how to be? When anxiety is high and resources appear scarce, people react rather than think. We get polarized, divide into opposing camps, yo-yo back and forth between distance and blame, and lose the capacity for creative problem solving that takes into account the needs of all. As stress mounts, the extraordinary challenge is to move from blaming people toward understanding downward-spiraling patterns and our own part in them.

Mahatma Gandhi said, "Peace between countries must rest on the solid foundation of love between individuals." Although the connections are not always obvious, social and political change are inseparable from personal change. With this in mind, we can each move toward the most difficult people in our lives with loving, creative, and generous hearts. We can be mindful of how we navigate our key relationships because, in every encounter we have, we will either enhance, include, and empower others—or we will do the opposite. If we fail to take solid positions with friends and family members that regard both the self and the other, how can we expect our nation's leaders to meet this same challenge in larger, more complex systems?

We can long for—and work toward—a world where the dignity and integrity of all human beings are honored and respected. More to the point, we can live *today* according to the values we wish would govern the world in the hypothetical future we hope to achieve.

—*Harriet Lerner*

AUTHOR/PSYCHOTHERAPIST

246

Reprinted with special permission from Bil Keane.

—*Bil Keane*

CARTOONIST

247

American educators have to pay attention to the needs of children. We can't educate them if we don't understand them, or if we don't realize that they have their own agenda. Youth culture by nature is rebellious—and some of the things they rebel against are quite legitimate. A young person's perspective is insightful and in many ways a lot smarter than ours. We must give credence to their ideas.

Take the spoken word, for example. If we had a spoken word category in fine arts, it would contribute so much to promoting and sustaining literacy. Young rappers who are halfway educated—or even fully educated—are remarkable poets with a great command of language. They appreciate the fine arts on their own level, in their own terms. It's about time we, as American adults, do too.

—*Russell Simmons*
MUSIC PRODUCER

248

We all know how blessed we are to live in such a free country. Unfortunately, we easily forget about the true meaning of success. In America, we are led to believe that success is measured by how much power we have, how much money we have, or the size of our office. As a result, we spend too much time focusing on ourselves and our own accomplishments. Really, the true meaning of success is how much of a difference we make in other people's lives, especially in the lives of our families. In one hundred years, no one will remember, nor will they care about, our accomplishments, but we will be remembered for the positive difference we make in the lives of those around us. This simple truth is the single greatest lesson I learned during my year as the first disabled Miss America. In the past three years, I have been a board member of the President's Committee on the Employment of People with Disabilities; I was inducted into the American Academy of Achievement; I spoke at the Republican National Convention in San Diego at age twenty-three and won countless awards and honors; but honestly, no one cares about any of that. However, people do remember me for my faith in God and the inspiration I gave them by having the courage to dance ballet in spite of the fact that I am profoundly deaf. I believe it is our duty as Americans to set a positive example for others around the world and to strive to be role models in everything we undertake. America is the global standard bearer for freedom, peace, and security. We alone bear the worthy burden of leadership, and I believe that we must strive to set the standards for the world to follow. Whether we like it or not, we shape the world around us, and I truly believe that America needs to return to the days when we celebrated good character, honesty, integrity, and, most of all, faith in God.

—*Heather Whitestone McCallum*

AUTHOR

249

It's insane for America to keep cutting arts programs in the schools. When I walk into schools these days and nobody's doing plays, nobody's dancing, I wonder how severely this is wounding the next generation in terms of American culture. Being involved in the arts (especially from a young age) generates creativity, ideas, soul, and humanity. It fosters an individualistic voice that is distinctly American.

The United States has always boasted a great culture, a dynamic culture. Without this we're losing the sense of the individual. We're losing the American voice. And in an attempt to resurrect the opinions of the individual, we organize focus groups and polls asking, "What do you think the president should be saying?" and "How do you want this movie to end?"

Some days I want to take a poll to determine whether I should wear a red sweater or meet a friend for supper.

—*Wendy Wasserstein*
PLAYWRIGHT

250

Ours is the best nation in the world. One of the reasons this is true is that we Americans always believe we can make America even better. Today, I believe we can make America better by encouraging our children to dream and dream big.

We don't do that simply by asking them to go to bed earlier.

We do it by making the critical investments in their future—the investments that inspire hope, shake souls, and convince our children that their impossible dreams are indeed possible.

We live in a time of outstanding, sometimes overwhelming, technological advancement. And these advancements have benefited us in ways that are beyond comprehension. But in some ways they have also created a culture where time is compressed. Everything is immediate. The result is often that investments are made only with an eye to short-term gain.

In other words, too often we steal from the future to survive in the present.

If there is one thing I've learned as administrator of the National Aeronautics and Space Administration (NASA), it is that we can't afford to measure investments by the dollars that go in. We must measure the vitality of what we do by the product that comes out. And sometimes that product comes out ten, twenty, thirty years down the line.

That shouldn't deter us. It should motivate us.

If we were concerned only with short-term gain, we would never have gotten off the starting block in the race to the moon. If we worried only about the here and now, the International Space Station would be the stuff of science fiction, not history's largest peacetime scientific endeavor.

But we dreamed. We dreamed of discovering the unknown. And because we did, we expanded the frontiers of space and enhanced life here on Earth.

Tonight, a young boy may dream that he is going to be the doctor who enhances life by curing cancer. His sister may dream that she will expand frontiers by becoming the first astronaut to travel to Mars, perhaps beyond.

He can be that doctor. She can be that astronaut . . . or a scientist . . . or an engineer . . . or president of the United States. The big dreams can come true, but only if we continue to be a nation that presses forward, that takes on bold tasks, that lets our children know we're making the critical long-term and high-risk investments in their future.

Encouraging big dreams, then making them come true: that's how we can make the greatest nation on Earth . . . greater still.

—*Daniel S. Goldin*
NASA ADMINISTRATOR

About the Editor

Carolyn Mackler's articles and essays have appeared in the *Los Angeles Times, Ms., HUES,* and the anthology *Adiós, Barbie: Young Women Write About Body Image and Identity.* A contributing editor to *Ms.,* she has researched a screenplay for Mike Nichols and Elaine May, appeared on *CBS Sunday Morning,* and recently completed her first young-adult novel. She lives in New York City.